Stones of Hope

Stanford Studies in Human Rights

# Stones of Hope

*How African Activists Reclaim Human Rights
to Challenge Global Poverty*

Edited by Lucie E. White and Jeremy Perelman

*With a Foreword by
Jeffrey D. Sachs and Lisa E. Sachs*

Stanford University Press
Stanford, California

Stanford University Press
Stanford, California

Printed in the United States of America on acid-free, archival-quality paper

Library of Congress Cataloging-in-Publication Data

Stones of hope : how African activists reclaim human rights to challenge global poverty
/ edited by Lucie E. White and Jeremy Perelman ; with a foreword by Jeffrey D. Sachs and
Lisa E. Sachs.
    p. cm.--(Stanford studies in human rights)
  Includes bibliographical references and index.
  ISBN 978-0-8047-6919-8 (cloth : alk. paper)--ISBN 978-0-8047-6920-4 (pbk. : alk.
paper)
  1. Human rights advocacy--Africa--Case studies. 2. Social rights--Africa. 3. Human
rights--Africa. I. White, Lucie, 1949- II. Perelman, Jeremy. III. Series: Stanford studies in
human rights.
  JC599.A36S76 2011
  323.0973--dc22                                              2010030289

Typeset by Bruce Lundquist in 10/14 Minion Pro

*We dedicate this book to the courageous people whose stories are chronicled in it.*

*JP: To my grandparents, and to M*

*LW: To Anna, Caroline, and John*

We will be able to hew out of the mountain of despair a stone of hope.

Martin Luther King Jr., Speech at the Lincoln Memorial,
Washington, D.C., August 28, 1963

# Contents

# Foreword

Jeffrey D. Sachs and Lisa E. Sachs

More than sixty years after the worldwide adoption of the Universal Declaration of Human Rights, in 1948, economic and social rights (ESR)—the very foundation of human survival and well-being—still elude billions of people, especially the estimated 1.4 billion people who live in extreme poverty. Making ESR operational is an enormous challenge for human rights activists, development practitioners, lawyers, and citizens. The important new book *Stones of Hope*, edited by Lucie White and Jeremy Perelman, explores this critical topic persuasively and creatively, by delving deeply into several African case studies where ESR has made a real difference in people's rights and well-being. The cases—involving urban evictions, access to AIDS treatment, rural land tenure, and the healthcare rights of indigents—are terrific in their own right, and in combination make the powerful point that ESR can be a driver of deliberative democracy, institutional innovation, and significant betterment of the living conditions of the poor.

For the world's poorest people, daily life is a struggle for survival, with millions of impoverished people each year losing that struggle to famine, disease, environmental catastrophes, and violent conflicts that arise in conditions of extreme deprivation. Similar desperation applies to girls and women in societies where legal, political, and social institutions offer them scant opportunities and little protection from violence, and to ethnic minorities and indigenous populations that are deprived of access to basic social services and protection by the political system. Ironically, in many parts of the world it is often the descendants of the first arrivals—the indigenous communities—who suffer the bitterest combination of poverty and exclusion. Today's dominant groups often wrested their dominance through conquest and exploitation of the indigenous inhabitants and maintain power through violence and extralegal methods.

The pressing challenge of ESR for our generation is not so much in defining their contents—which have been elaborated in the International Bill of Human Rights (the Universal Declaration of Human Rights of 1948, the International Covenant on Civil and Political Rights of 1966, and the International Covenant on Economic, Social and Cultural Rights of 1966) as well as dozens of treaties, global agreements, and national laws over the past half century—but rather in maximizing their usefulness as a means of leverage for spreading human survival, dignity, and hope to those trapped in the bitter clutches of extreme deprivation and exclusion. Both of us face this practical challenge as well. As Special Advisor to UN Secretaries-General Kofi Annan and Ban Ki-Moon on the Millennium Development Goals (MDGs), Jeffrey has looked for ways to promote the MDGs through a "rights-based" approach, that is, promoting the achievement of the MDGs through appeal to the instruments of ESR. Lisa is currently at an academic institution (the Vale Columbia Center on Sustainable Investment at Columbia University) whose aim is to promote sustainable foreign investment. Through the center's work with organizations promoting corporate social responsibility, she has been engaged in translating ESR into norms for corporate responsibility and accountability.

There are many ways to promote the MDGs and corporate social responsibility. Donor nations give development assistance for many reasons, including formal standards like ESR as well as considerations of national security, foreign policy, and national values. Similarly, companies adopt standards of corporate social responsibility, including ESR, for many reasons as well: legal codes, reputation, workplace morale, and customer satisfaction. Economic and social rights is but one of the motivations driving governments and businesses. We strongly endorse the viewpoint of a former UN Rapporteur on the Right to Health, Paul Hunt: "Confronted with such a complex and colossal challenge as global poverty, it is extremely important that development practitioners use all the tools available in their workshop, including the national and international human rights commitments of developing and developed states."[1]

International law is notoriously fragile and hamstrung in protecting and promoting ESR adequately, especially in the poorest countries where the need is greatest, such as those of sub-Saharan Africa. There are, of course, several complex challenges. One basic point, not always remembered, is that impoverished countries lack their own budgetary resources needed to supply vital—indeed life-saving—services such as primary healthcare or support for smallholder farmers. The poor are thereby trapped. The lack of public services leads to hunger, poverty, and disease, while the poverty means that the tax base of government is too small to support public policies to alleviate hunger, poverty, and disease. Foreign assistance is then needed to break the vicious circle. In principle, the International Bill of Human Rights creates a poor country's "right" to receive assistance from the rest of the world. In practice, this "right" (or conversely, the "duty to assist" of high-income countries) is difficult to enforce, to say the least.

Of course, the obligations of developed countries vis-à-vis poor countries are joined by the equally or even more critical obligations of domestic governments to realize basic human rights within their own countries. Poor governance, discrimination, corruption, and warped ideologies are unfortunate realities and deep impediments to the realization of ESR in many countries, developing and developed alike. Even when the ESR challenges are more "domestic," the use of courts, government agencies, and politics to defend ESR, as well as the overall challenge of leveraging rights into results, is extraordinarily difficult, requiring bravery, persistence, and ingenuity. Efforts to improve governance, accountability, equitable distribution, access systems, and social justice are absolutely necessary. Those efforts are the focus of this pathbreaking volume.

Importantly, the case studies in *Stones of Hope* demonstrate that there is no single model for ESR activism, even if there are common strands among successful and meaningful campaigns. The activists in this volume range from national-scale legal organizations to a community-based "Mothers' Club," from constitutional lawyers arguing in the highest courts in South Africa to people on Ghanaian streets signing a petition that powerfully restates their right to health. What is common among these case studies are campaigns of empowerment, community engagement, and inclusiveness, information sharing and pragmatism, and especially resilience, persistence, and creativity. As White and Perelman note, these cases demonstrate the power of the shared language of human rights to bridge social, cultural, and political differences in a common pursuit of dignity, well-being, and survival. That the advocates assert the rights and needs of these communities within the normative context of basic human rights gives crucial legitimacy to their campaigns. Importantly, the advocates use a variety of outreach tools to build the size and cohesion—and therefore power—of their communities and use this power to leverage the institutional and structural changes in the ESR delivery framework that would remedy the relevant injustices. In each case, litigation—a common and expected tool of lawyers and rights-based activists—is but one tool in a strategic and multifaceted approach to promoting ESR, and courts are used, if at all, more often to enhance the visibility, gravity, and effectiveness of the more extensive political and social efforts than to defend ESR through court orders.

Although the editors note historical and political similarities among the countries in which these cases transpired, the differences are also notable. The specific rights at issue, the population (size and makeup) affected, the concentrations of power, the political institutions, and the resources of the activists vary widely from case to case. But the editors skillfully present the array of strategies, tactics, and targets used in the case studies explored in this volume and usefully distill the common challenges, victories, and lessons. In each chapter, the authors explain the importance of institutional change to ensure that "success can be structurally grounded in order to carry some promise of broader, and lasting, transformative change" (Chapter 3). The case studies that White and Perelman have brought together will usefully enable ESR activists (and development practitioners) in Africa and elsewhere to learn from the various political, legal, and social practices the activists in these case studies have used to achieve such lasting reform—some successfully and some less so.

The chapters in this volume also highlight some of the important actors in a successful ESR campaign. First and foremost is the "convening authority," who brings the community together, keeps the discussions and strategies focused, and, importantly, engages the "local power holders and interested groups [in] a deliberative dialogue" (Chapter 6). It is critical that the convening authority earn the trust of the community and interested parties as well as the respect of and access to the "power holders" and local authorities. Additionally, achieving true institutional change often requires the cooperation of institutional "insiders . . . work[ing] to change the agencies from within" (Chapter 6). Working directly with government officials and civil employees on institutional reform can reinforce external pressure on the institution in a positive feedback mechanism, each force giving strength and support to the other. Finally, the editors note the legitimizing power that external groups can give to a domestic campaign by providing not only material resources but also information, skills, and influence.

It should be noted that while White, Perelman, and their cocontributors focus mainly on ESR activism in the national context, they acknowledge the important roles of global actors in assisting, or restricting, the realization of ESR even in "domestic contexts." For instance, the "financial muscle" of international financial institutions (IFIs) such as the World Bank, if improperly used, can "aggravate the poverty of target beneficiaries," as in the case of the

World Bank–funded drainage and sanitation project in Lagos, Nigeria, which resulted in the brutal and unlawful eviction of thousands of indigents and the destruction of their houses (Chapter 1).

In that case, a prominent local human rights organization—the Social and Economic Rights Action Center (SERAC)—used a public advocacy strategy to force the World Bank to address the unlawful evictions in Lagos, to provide SERAC with relevant information, and to engage directly with the affected community. (Incidentally, the authors describe the important political considerations in Nigeria that steered SERAC away from litigation as a primary strategy in halting the forced evictions.) That the more recent projects funded by the World Bank (and other IFIs) in Lagos and elsewhere have taken steps to internalize the importance of community engagement and human rights impact assessments is a testament not only to national advocacy campaigns like SERAC's but also to direct pressure exerted by human rights practitioners worldwide on international financial organizations to internalize processes into standard lending procedures, specifically to ensure that ESR are respected in such IFI-financed projects.

Chapter 2 documents the remarkable ESR campaign led by the Treatment Action Campaign (TAC) for a national treatment plan for all South Africans with HIV/AIDS. One of TAC's important and successful strategies was to use "international networks of human rights organizations to pressure . . . the multinational pharmaceutical companies" (Chapter 2). The obligation of "big pharma" to assist with the realization of the right to health is one of the early and prominent examples of the important responsibilities that the private business sector has in realizing ESR within its spheres of influence. This important role of the private sector has been notably advocated by socially responsible institutional investors, such as the Interfaith Center on Corporate Responsibility (where Lisa worked), who use shareholder advocacy and company engagement to promote industry-wide business practices that not only respect but promote ESR as a matter of good business sense. Efforts to promote corporate social responsibility have been especially active in the pharmaceutical industry, extractive industry, and finance sector, and such advocacy is now extending to many other sectors. Fortunately, by dint of CEO commitment, concern over corporate reputation, employee morale, and the goodwill and patronage of suppliers and customers, an increasing number of major companies are internalizing ESR norms within core company policies. Many other major companies, however, remain to join the cause!

While not featured centrally in this volume, the obligation of developed countries to assist in the realization of ESR in developing countries is also critically important. In Chapter 5, Perelman and White correctly point out that African governments "often lack the funds or governmental capacity to solve such big-ticket problems as healthcare without help from other sources" (Chapter 5). As we mentioned above, adequate financing is needed to alleviate the poverty-related burdens of weak governance, inadequate infrastructure, excessive population growth, poor health, low literacy, and resource depletion, which all contribute to extensive ESR violations. Yet economic development is precluded by precisely these poverty-related burdens, which decrease productivity, earning ability, and economic investments. The implication of poverty traps is that poor countries, on their own, are often unable to honor their basic economic and social rights obligations. Realizing these human rights requires increased public outlays and infrastructure that are beyond the financial means of poor countries. This is not to remove the responsibility of the home governments of low-income countries, but it is to emphasize that ESR is often a partnership affair—achievable through the joint efforts of rich and poor countries alike. That is why, for example, the Millennium Development Goals from the start incorporated global partnership as MDG 8.

Developed countries that are parties to the International Covenant on Economic, Social and Cultural Rights (ICESCR) have a legally binding obligation "to take steps, individually and *through international assistance and co-operation, especially economic and technical,* to the maximum of [their] available resources, with a view to achieving progressively the full realization of the rights recognized in the present Covenant" (ICESCR, article 2[1]; emphasis added). The ICESCR also refers to international assistance and cooperation for the full realization of the rights in the treaty, in articles 1, 11, 15, 22, and 23. General Comment 3 to the covenant, on the nature of states parties' obligations, clarifies that "in accordance with Articles 55 and 56 of the Charter of the United Nations, with well-established principles of international law, and with the provisions of the Covenant itself, international cooperation for development and thus for the realization of economic, social and cultural rights is an obligation of all States. It is particularly incumbent upon those States which are in a position to assist others in this regard."[2]

Several United Nations resolutions and declarations have reaffirmed UN member states' commitment to international assistance. The Millennium Declaration, adopted by the General Assembly in 2000, recognized "a collective responsibility to uphold the principles of human dignity, equality and equity at the global level."[3] Developed countries agreed to undertake concrete actions such as the adoption of fair trade rules, a debt relief program for the heavily indebted poor countries, and increased development assistance to poor countries committed to poverty reduction. It is critically important that developed countries fulfill these commitments to enable poor countries to break free of the poverty trap and to make necessary investments for the basic needs of their low-income populations, needs that include improved health, infrastructure, education, governance, and environmental security.

Even when necessary international transfers are made to under-resourced governments, ESR advocates will be needed to ensure that the domestic institutions create proper management systems to oversee the reliable and accountable distribution of the international resources to the communities in need. As White and Perelman describe, this will require that ESR advocates work within the relevant "national ESR-delivery framework" with the respective agencies, authorities, and institutions, in cooperation with scientists, economists, public-sector managers, and, of course, the communities. In the end, the tools of local ESR advocacy will be essential.

The case studies are interesting stories in their own right, and, importantly, they demonstrate that with creativity, ESR provides important tools for confronting, and resolving, the global injustices of poverty, hunger, and disease—by fighting discrimination, exclusion, exploitation, and neglect. We agree with the authors that crucial advances have been made on the use of ESR to address social challenges facing the poor and dispossessed, and that ESR will play a growing role in confronting these challenges in the coming years. *Stones of Hope* will be an important milestone in this work and should generate further case studies dedicated to additional aspects of the ESR challenge, including international development assistance, foreign investment law and practice, the role of multilateral development agencies, and other international dimensions of our increasingly globalized society. Our generation is the first with the practical possibility of ending extreme poverty. Economic and social rights will be among the critical tools for that historic achievement.

# Contributors

RUTH BUCHANAN is Associate Professor at Osgoode Hall Law School, Toronto. Her research interests span the fields of law and development, international economic law, social and legal theory, and law and film. Her recent publications include "Writing Resistance into International Law," *International Community Law Review* 10 (2008) and "International Institutions and Transnational Advocacy: The Case of the North American Agreement on Labour Cooperation," *UCLA Journal of International Law and Foreign Affairs* 13:1 (2008): 129–60.

WILLIAM FORBATH holds the Lloyd M. Bentsen Chair in Law, is Associate Dean for Research at the School of Law, and is Professor of History at the University of Texas, Austin. He teaches constitutional law and legal and constitutional history. He is the author of *Law and the Shaping of the American Labor Movement* (1991) and about seventy articles on legal and constitutional history and theory. He has two books in progress: *Courting the State: Law and the Making of the Modern American State* and *Social and Economic Rights in the American Grain*. His journalism has appeared in *Politico.com*, *American Prospect*, and the *Nation*.

PETER HOUTZAGER is a Political Scientist and Research Fellow at the Institute of Development Studies (IDS), United Kingdom. He is the coeditor of *Changing Paths: International Development and the Politics of Inclusion* (2003), author of *Os Ultimos Cidadaos: Conflito e modernizacao no Brasil rural (1964–1995)* (2004), and author of a library of scholarly articles in English and Portuguese that examine citizenship practices and empirical forms of civil society, rural social movements, and institutional and legal change in Latin America.

DUNCAN KENNEDY is Carter Professor of General Jurisprudence at Harvard Law School, where he has taught since 1971. He was one of the founding members of the critical legal studies movement. His books include *Legal Reasoning: Collected Essays* (2008), *Legal Education and the Reproduction of Hierarchy* (2007), *A Critique of Adjudication [fin de siècle]* (1998), *Sexy Dressing, etc.* (1995), and *The Rise and Fall of Classical Legal Thought* (1975). He has taught Law and Development and Low Income Housing Law and Policy.

HELEN KIJO-BISIMBA is Executive Director and Secretary to the Board of Directors of the Legal and Human Rights Center (LHRC), an independent legal and human rights Tanzanian nongovernmental organization. She is an active member of the Board of Women in Law and Development in Africa and the Tanzanian Women Lawyers Association, and serves as Chairperson to the Southern African Human Rights NGOs Network (SAHRINGON). She is the coauthor of *Justice and Rule of Law Tanzania: Selected Judgments and Writings of Justice James L. Mwalusanya and Commentaries* (2005) and *Law and Justice in Tanzania: A Quarter Century of the Court of Appeal* (2007), both with C. M. Peter.

FELIX MORKA is founder and Executive Director of the Social and Economic Rights Action Center (SERAC) (http://www.serac.org/), a nongovernmental organization concerned with the promotion and protection of economic, social, and cultural rights in Nigeria. Prior to earning his LL.M. degree from Harvard Law School, Morka served as the Washington, D.C.-based International Human Rights Law Group's Legal Officer for Africa, and was the Legal Director of Nigeria's Civil Liberties Organization (CLO). He has presented testimony before the United States Congress and meets regularly with policy makers to raise human rights concerns.

KERRY RITTICH is Associate Professor at the Faculty of Law, the School of Public Policy and Governance, and the Women and Gender Studies Institute at the University of Toronto. She teaches and writes in the areas of labor law, international law and international institutions, law and development, human rights, and gender and critical theory. She has been a fellow at the European University Institute and a visiting professor at Harvard Law School and the Weatherhead Center for International Affairs, Harvard University, at the Centre for Transnational Legal Studies in London, and at the Watson Institute for International Studies, Brown University.

JEFFREY D. SACHS is the Director of the Earth Institute, Quetelet Professor of Sustainable Development, and Professor of Health Policy and Management at Columbia University. He is also Special Advisor to United Nations Secretary-General Ban Ki-moon on the Millennium Development Goals. He has been a senior advisor to governments in all parts of the world, and has worked with international agencies, businesses, and humanitarian organizations to forge new strategies for sustainable development. He is author of hundreds of scholarly articles and many books, including *Common Wealth* (Penguin, 2008) and *The End of Poverty* (Penguin, 2005). Sachs is a member of the Institute of Medicine and is a Research Associate of the National Bureau of Economic Research. He has twice been named among the one hundred most influential leaders in the world by *Time* magazine.

LISA E. SACHS is the Assistant Director of the Vale Columbia Center on Sustainable International Investment. She received a J.D. and a Master of International Affairs from Columbia University in May 2008, and her B.A. from Harvard University in 2004. Her work focuses on foreign investment, corporate responsibility, human rights, and economic development. She is the author with Jeffrey D. Sachs of "Realizing the Human Right to Health in Low-Income Countries," in B. A. Andreassen, S. P. Marks, and A. K. Sengupta, *Freedom from Poverty as a Human Right: Economic Perspectives* (UNESCO, 2010).

KATHARINE YOUNG is a Research Fellow at the Center for International Governance and Justice at the Regulatory Institutions Network of the Australian National University. She holds a doctoral (S.J.D.) degree from Harvard Law School and has taught courses on human rights and constitutional rights at Harvard Law School, Melbourne Law School, and Boston University School of Law. Her recent publications include "The Minimum Core of Economic and Social Rights: A Concept in Search of Content," *Yale Journal of International Law* 33 (2008): 113; "Freedom, Want and Economic and Social Rights," *Maryland Journal of International Law* 24 (2009): 182; and "Securing Health Through Rights," in *Incentives for Global Public Health: Patent Law and Access to Essential Medicines*, ed. Thomas Pogge, Matthew Rimmer, and Kim Rubenstein (Cambridge University Press, 2010).

LUCIE E. WHITE is the Louis A. Horvitz Professor of Law at Harvard Law School. She specializes in domestic poverty law and international economic and social rights, particularly in Africa. For a decade, she has collaborated with Harvard University students as well as faculty at the University of Ghana on an interdisciplinary right-to-health project that focuses on the human rights dimensions of Ghana's health finance system. Since 2005 she has been a working group coordinator for the Harvard University Africa Initiative. White has also been a Fulbright Senior Africa Scholar and received a Fulbright grant to encourage teaching innovation. She has been a Carnegie Scholar on Teaching and Learning, a scholar in residence at the Harvard Divinity School, and a Bunting Scholar at Radcliffe College. In 2006, with support from the Rockefeller Foundation's Bellagio Center, she initiated Stones of Hope, a collaboration among African human rights activists and distinguished human rights scholars to examine innovations in economic and social rights advocacy. This collaboration culminated in the present volume.

JEREMY PERELMAN is Lecturer in Law and Visiting Scholar and Fellow in Residence at Columbia Law School, and a doctoral candidate at Harvard Law School. In the spring of 2011 he will be a visiting professor at the University of Connecticut School of Law. He researches and teaches in the fields of international human rights and development, and his current research explores the intersection between post–Washington Consensus human rights approaches to economic development and social change advocacy in the global South. His publications include "The Way Ahead? Access to Justice, Public Interest Lawyering and the Right to Legal Aid in South Africa: The *Nkuzi* case," *Stanford Journal of International Law* 41 (2005): 357; and "Beyond Common Knowledge," book review, *Harvard International Law Journal* 47 (2006): 531.

## Assisting Contributors

ZACKIE ACHMAT is a founder of the Treatment Action Campaign (TAC) and from 2000 to 2008 served as its National Chairperson; TAC is the leading HIV/AIDS activist organization in South Africa. He holds a B.A. Hons (cum laude) from the University of Western Cape and an M.Phil in Law at the University of Cape Town, and was awarded the first Desmond Tutu Fellowship in October 2001, an Honorary Master's Degree at the University of Cape Town in 2002, and an Honorary Doctorate in Law from the University of Natal in 2003. Achmat was also awarded the Jonathan Mann Award for Global Health and Human Rights

(2003), the Nelson Mandela Award for Health and Human Rights (2003), and was elected *Time* Europe's Hero of the Year in 2003. He was nominated in 2004 for the Nobel Peace Prize by the American Friends Service Committee (AFSC).

MAHAMA AYARIGA is the Deputy Minister of Trade and Industry, and the former spokesperson for John Atta-Mills, the President of the Republic of Ghana. He is also a founding member and former Executive Director of the Ghana Legal Resources Center (LRC), Ghana's leading human rights organization. Ayariga holds an LL.M. degree from Harvard Law School and served in Ghana's Parliament from 2004 to 2008.

GEOFF BUDLENDER is an advocate (barrister) practicing in Cape Town, South Africa. He was previously the National Director of the Legal Resources Centre, South Africa's leading public interest law center. He was the attorney for the Treatment Action Campaign in its litigation on the duty of the government to provide free antiretroviral medicine to prevent mother-to-child transmission of HIV.

MARK HEYWOOD is the Director of South Africa's AIDS Law Project and is a founder and executive member of the Treatment Action Campaign.

# Acknowledgments

We would like to express our gratitude to the Harvard Committee on African Studies' Africa Initiative for sponsoring Stones of Hope workshops and meetings in Berlin (2007), Ghana (2008), Cambridge, Massachusetts (2008), and Brighton, United Kingdom (2009). We are also grateful to the Rockefeller Foundation for launching this project by hosting the Stones of Hope team members for a two-week residency in its Bellagio Center in December 2006. We also received financial support from the European Law Research Center at Harvard Law School; Harvard Law School, particularly its Faculty Summer Research Fund and Cravath Summer Research Fellowship Program; and the Institute of Development Studies at the University of Sussex, United Kingdom.

Our deepest gratitude goes to members of the Stones of Hope project, including, in addition to the contributors to this volume, Raymond Atuguba, Jacqueline Bhabha, Mara Bustelo, Caroline Elkins, Eitan Felner, Colin Gonsalves, Lisa Joy, and Mwambi Mwasaru.

Special thanks to Peter Uvin and Rick Abel for supporting this project from the outset, to John Nockleby for invaluable comments on its many iterations, as well as to Peter Rosenblum for many inspiring discussions.

This project could not have been completed without the energy and commitment of Moira Harding, who was with us from the outset, in Italy as well as Boston. Ellen Keng gave her expert attention to the book's production. Also in our thoughts are the students who participated in Harvard Law School's Legal Resources Center Ghana project from 1999 to 2009.

Finally, we would like to acknowledge Mark Goodale, Kate Wahl, Joa Suorez, and Mariana Raykov from Stanford University Press for enthusiastically guiding the book through the editorial process.

Lucie White gained inspiration from her daughters, Anna and Caroline, who were with us in spirit from the project's inception.

Jeremy Perelman is most grateful to Lucie White for inviting him on this unique journey, and for being the outstanding mentor and teacher that she is. He would like to thank his wonderful parents and brother, as well as his late Holocaust-surviving grandparents, for inspiring him to do this work. Finally, he thanks Miranda, whose patience, love, and unwavering courage kept his spirits high through the flows and rhythms of a very special period.

# List of Acronyms

| | |
|---|---|
| ANC | African National Congress |
| ARV | antiretroviral |
| ARVT | antiretroviral treatment |
| CAPCOM | community action program committee |
| CLO | Civil Liberties Organization (Nigeria) |
| ESR | economic and social rights |
| GDP | gross domestic product |
| HIV | human immunodeficiency virus |
| IFI | international financial institution |
| LDSP | Lagos Drainage and Sanitation Project |
| LHRC | Legal and Human Rights Centre (Tanzania) |
| LRC | Legal Resources Center (Ghana) |
| LMDGP | Lagos Metropolitan Development and Governance Project (Nigeria) |
| MCC | Medicines Control Council (South Africa) |
| MSF | Médecins Sans Frontières (Doctors Without Borders) |
| NGO | nongovernmental organization |
| PMTCT | preventing mother-to-child transmission (of HIV) |
| PRSP | Poverty Reduction Strategy Papers |
| SERAC | Social and Economic Rights Action Center (Nigeria) |
| TAC | Treatment Action Campaign (South Africa) |
| TLC | Treatment Literacy Campaign (South Africa) |
| UNDP | United Nations Development Programme |
| WHO | World Health Organization |
| WTO | World Trade Organization |

Stones of Hope

# Introduction

Jeremy Perelman and Lucie E. White

## Foundations

### Structural Injustice

My name is Abdullah Abdul Muman. I am thirty-five years old. I live in Nima, in house number E 501/15. My house is right next to the big gutter. I have lived there for almost eleven years. It is very unhealthy next to the big gutter—there is always disease. My three children (aged fourteen, seven, and three) play around the gutter, which brings them sickness and disease. They get rashes, fever, and colds from the gutter. They also get cut by broken bottles in the gutter. It worries me to live where I do. It affects my mood every day—day and night. . . . I can go into my room, but the wind brings it all in—the diseases and the smell that is so bad that I can't breathe. There are also a lot of flies that come when we eat. . . . The gutter is especially dangerous during the rainy season. This past rainy season has damaged the bridge and made it difficult to cross the gutter. There is also a problem with erosion; houses fall into the gutter when it rains. I think my house is in danger, and I worry about my family. I worry that my house will collapse, and I fear for my children.[1]

This book is about the violence of radical poverty.[2] It is about overt physical violence—the sickness, the stench, the rashes, fevers, and colds, the cuts from broken bottles, the flies, the houses that fall in the gutter when it rains, the worry, the fear.

It is about the murder of people for "trespassing" on a wild animal reserve, once their home, to "poach" for food. It is about the bulldozing of entire communities to make way for "higher" uses of their land. It is about a government's calculated denial of the viral cause of AIDS, a denial that deprives too many

1

people of life-saving treatment. It is about state policies that fund healthcare by detaining discharged patients on hospital grounds until their families come up with the cash to pay their bills. This book is about the patterns of structural injustice[3] that are woven into the supposed "misfortune"[4] of global poverty and are wrongly considered an *inevitable* cost of development.[5] At the same time, this book is about a few African lawyers and activists who have used economic and social rights—the values, the doctrine, the language, and the tactics—to challenge such wrongs.[6]

## *Human Rights in Practice: Current Questions and Beyond*

Several scholarly discussions have recently developed around the question of human rights practice.[7] Two of these discussions are especially relevant to this volume.

The first of these discussions focuses on two themes. Scholars like Makau Mutua have persuasively critiqued the Western origins and colonial heritage of human rights practice. A central argument in this critique claims that Western human rights lawyers who practice in the Third World think of themselves as "saviors," who must rescue their "victims" from the "savages" who inflict human rights abuses on them.[8] A second critique, advanced by David Kennedy and others, examines the formalist limitations of the human rights paradigm. They cite a long tradition of skepticism toward the rights paradigm in liberal legal theory.[9] This critique, which is widely accepted among contemporary critical legal scholars, argues that rights discourse disrupts political solidarity and undermines social movement. The human rights skeptics then note that in the end "you can't eat rights," and that the effective delivery of social goods requires not fancy legal maneuvers but hard-nosed massive resource shifting and fine-tuned system reform.[10]

A second field of discussion, opened up by recent ethnographic work by Sally Merry and others,[11] explores the nuances of local human rights practice on the ground. That work uses a "translation" lens to show how grassroots human rights workers in Third World settings shuttle back and forth between indigenous moral rituals, formal juridical games, and transnational human rights discourse.[12]

*Stones of Hope* does not directly enter either discussion. Rather, building upon them, it responds to the recent call for scholars to theorize human rights *practices*, as those practices are enacted by lawyers and others on the ground.[13]

Our work has centered on four case studies, in East, West, and Southern Africa, in which activist lawyers worked with organizers and others to challenge structural injustice on the ground. The Stones of Hope project has brought the lawyers and organizers who spearheaded these projects together with economic and social rights scholars to think about the common patterns, missed opportunities, and promising features of the advocates' practices.

The project brought these particular activists together because they are doing profoundly challenging—and creative—economic and social rights (ESR) advocacy. They are among a new generation of social justice activists who have seized upon human rights values, language, and tactics to challenge the realities of extreme poverty. All in this new generation share a striking similarity in how they do their work. Although embracing human rights values, they reject traditional notions of human rights practice as a top-down, lawyer-driven, professional "game." Each of these advocates has understood human rights activism as a political practice. Without any a priori idea of what might replace the taken-for-granted moves of traditional practice, each has found his or her own way of working. Though each of these activists' innovations is unique, when we mapped them all out, we saw striking common trends.

These distinctive features of their practice converge in the ESR campaigns that these advocates launch to combat the life-defeating poverty they encounter every day. As the book shows, such campaigns can sometimes produce moments of psychological, political, and ideological movement, hewing "stones of hope" out of injustice so thick that it seems like a "mountain of despair."[14] Such moments of hope can sometimes gain sustained force through the ways they are named, remembered, and repeated, so as to inspire future struggles. Such work is hard, slow, and uncertain. But, as the book suggests, a network of iconoclastic African ESR activists, most of them also lawyers, is taking it on. Their work is but one example of a trend in which, as a prominent African writer recently described, African peoples "have learned to ignore the shrill screams coming from the peddlers of hopelessness. We motor on faith and enterprise, with small steps. On hope without hysteria."[15]

## Why Africa?

The new style of human rights activism that we analyze is emerging all over the world, yet the activists on the Stones of Hope team come from East, West, or Southern Africa. Three reasons account for our decision to feature African advocates in the book.

The first reason lies in the Stones of Hope project's method and objectives. The method, which we describe below, calls for engaging the scholars and activists in intense conversation, with the goal of opening reflection *among* the activists. In order for such conversation to take place and ground our theoretical inquiry, all of the activists had to have significant but not overwhelming cultural and political commonalities. We resolved this tension by joining with activists from a region united in its broad political culture and history, but at the same time rich with regional diversity.[16]

The second reason for our African focus was to make use of preexisting relational networks as we assembled the Stones of Hope team.[17] Networks had already formed among some of these scholars and activists. One node from which those networks were building was Harvard Law School. This node is not random: it evinces a trend that postcolonial theorists have mapped out in the present era. This trend refers to the ways in which global flows of dominant knowledge, practices, and legitimacy—for example, university degrees—tend to move from North to South, where they are seized on, adapted, or resisted.[18]

Third, African human rights activists, particularly those working in the ESR field, face a web of challenges. Three of these challenges—radical poverty, the legacy of indirect rule, and postcolonial turmoil—are particularly daunting.[19] Therefore, successful African human rights activists must combine strategies in complex ways. We chose to feature the work of the lawyers and organizers in the Stones of Hope project because of the creative ways in which these activists have responded to these challenges.

## Our Method: Framing, Conversation, and Reflection

We pursued our investigation through intense conversation, which was shaped to spark mutual reflection on the practice of the Stones of Hope lawyer-activists. Our meetings spanned across five venues.[20] Our method was based on interpretive or hermeneutic approaches to qualitative research, approaches that involve active engagement by the interpreter with the subject of interpretation.[21] Through this guided process of reflective dialogue, the group of scholars and activists brought together for the Stones of Hope project probed the activists' *consciousness* about their tactics, calculations, expectations, theories of change, and motivating values. How did they shape their campaigns, and what were their reasons? What contextual factors seemed, in hindsight, to drive their choices? How did they define success and failure in their efforts to make change? Which of those changes, in their view, might be sustained? By surfacing and documenting these implicit choices, we wanted to enable other activists to learn from their practice. At the same time, we wanted to create rich texts from which we, and this book's readers, could theorize more deeply about ESR practice.

We then considered what we learned in these conversations in light of five theoretical vantage points related to the study of human rights practice: critical/transformative legal liberalism, distributive legal analysis, legal experimentalism, subaltern cosmopolitanism, and historical institutionalism.[22] The first of these lenses, *critical/transformative legal liberalism*, refers to an engaged but critical stance toward liberal values and a corresponding set of recognizably legal, but also explicitly political, advocacy strategies. *Distributive legal analysis* refers to a normatively informed analytical approach that searches for nonobvious, distributional effects of legal rules and policy frameworks. *Legal experimentalism* refers to a current school of socio-legal thought that notably explores the way legal strategies may generate innovative modes of democratic, decentralized governance in public bureaucracies. *Subaltern cosmopolitanism* highlights "subaltern" local and transnational activism that undercuts the official legal institutions of neoliberal globalization. In contrast, this perspective endorses alternative "legal orders"[23] to sustain social movement and political mobilization. We elaborate on *historical institutionalism* further below.

We used these approaches to frame further reflective conversations with activists about their practice. These discussions proved an exercise in critiquing the theory itself as well as theorizing the practice. Finally, through those iterative discussions we identified several common features in the advocates' practices, which we explore in Chapter 5.

We observed that in some of the cases these practices opened up *generative spaces*,[24] or social sites for intensive political contestation and institutional experimentation. This ferment could spark episodes of political agency, power mobilization, resource redistribution, and institutional redesign that could enable the *enhanced delivery* of the social goods guaranteed by ESR instruments and norms. Finally, in some cases we saw how this process of episodic change extended into *sustained structural transformation* in specific social welfare sectors, like healthcare, in the short to medium term.

Before we describe the chapters, we will say a few words about one of the theoretical vantage points—historical institutionalism—which we found particularly relevant in framing our analysis.

**Historical Institutionalism**    This theoretical approach is shaped by the work of political scientists who have focused on the spatial, political, and historical patterns behind pathways of institutional practices and design.[25] Some of these scholars focus particularly on how these institutional practices affect disenfranchised people in ways that entrench structural violence over time. At the same time, these scholars examine how these entrenched patterns might be changed.

For instance, Peter Houtzager, one of our team's scholars, has examined the recent shift towards "pro-poor" economic policies in low-income countries through the theoretical lenses of historical institutionalism and network analysis.[26] Houtzager concludes that the withdrawal of the state from the sphere of social provision, which both neoliberalism and poststructural localism imply, is likely to block both rich-to-poor redistribution and the sorts of institutional innovation that would benefit the poor. Houtzager's institutionalist approach advises us to look at entire polities or regimes as complex but *structured* historical formations. His approach offers an analytic tool for mapping what he calls "an emerging politics of inclusion." By this he means contestation among state and nonstate actors to promote more inclusionary practices in government agencies, such as ministries of health. Importantly, Houtzager's approach has a historical dimension, in that it shows how the targeted agency's history limits the range of changes that are possible politically at a particular moment in time.

While the institutionalist lens is generally applied to national states, it can also be applied to governance bodies in the international and local arenas. This lens also draws several *tactical questions* into focus at once, such as (1) what are the present and potential distributions of resources and power, and how can they be leveraged in the interest of change? (2) how can ESR norms, local values, potential allies' organizational rhetoric, and the lawyer-activists' own discursive framings[27] be more closely aligned? (3) how can the geographical reach and governing force of the national state best be reckoned with in the context of ESR advocacy: endorsed, resisted, worked around? (4) how can episodic opportunities for advocacy, such as *pressure points*, *entry points*, and *opportunities for cross-sector negotiation*, be identified and seized on?[28] The challenge for ESR lawyer-advocates is to synchronize such factors so as to make the best possible strategic judgments at each moment in time.

Yet even when advocates are savvy in the moment, the institutionalist lens throws into question the scope of systemic change they might leverage, even through their deftest moves. For institutionalism posits a landscape of regimes that are shaped by their interlocking institutions and thus trace more or less bounded pathways of change over time. This historical vision raises a set of questions that go beyond the strategic calculations outlined above. The questions include how activists can sustain local innovations across entire populations and how they can seize moments of crisis to alter institutional practices that are weighted toward continuity rather than radical change. In short, the historical institutionalist lens exposes terrains of strategic opportunity and systemic constraint. It enabled us to draw lessons from what the advocates in our project did and did *not* consider, and what in the end they achieved.

**Theorizing Economic and Social Rights Practice**    The combination of reflective dialogue and layered theoretical inquiry, grounded in historical institutionalism, enabled us to analyze the dynamics of multidimensional economic and social rights (ESR) campaigns. At the same time, it enabled us to critique and sharpen our theoretical perspectives. As a result, we began to see the contours of a specific, richly textured practice emerge.

The most salient lesson from this theory-and-practice project is that ESR activism, deployed in certain contexts and designed in certain ways, can sometimes open pathways leading to positive changes; this was observed in three domains. First, ESR activism can shift the distribution of socioeconomic goods from rich to poor. Second, it can promote the innovative redesign of social welfare institutions to make those institutions more effective. And, in some cases, creative activism can build the political power of economically vulnerable groups and thus enhance their capacities for active citizenship.

The exercise gave us a sense of what set of practices can spark these effects. In settings where we saw innovative practices spark systemic change, we asked three questions:

1. What do the creative ESR practices look like?
2. How do those practices "clear the ground" for change, disrupting entrenched institutional inequities and unfair patterns of development? What changes do the practices then engender?
3. How do those practices strengthen the capacities of citizens to claim their economic and social rights?

In Chapter 5 we discuss the findings that these questions generated. We map out three common features of the lawyer-advocates' innovative practices[29]: their iconoclastic *strategies of engagement*, their distinctive *normative* orientation, and their capacity to *prefigure*, through the process of their work in the present, the creative innovations that they envision for the future. We also discuss how each advocate's work comprises individual advocacy tactics, creative in their own right, which are artfully and pragmatically combined in ESR *campaigns*. These campaigns can have powerful effects that resound in the social and economic spheres, effects that are not typically characteristic of the more conventional deployment of advocacy tactics[30] in isolated, scattershot ways. Even as these campaigns thus affect many dimensions of the socioeconomic landscape, a striking feature is their overarching *political* character and the close connection between the campaigns and social movements.

While some of the chapters focus primarily on redistributive politics, others show another dimension of the political power of innovative human rights advocacy: it can both promote and prefigure creative responses to structural arrangements that block the delivery of the material goods motivating human rights claims. Taken together, the activists featured in the chapters, all of whom start from the experiences of people like Abdullah Muman and his children, have to find new ways of working. They *have* to break the rules of traditional human rights practice. They *have* to reclaim human rights' political power. They *have* to improvise in order to do justice both to the people they represent and to themselves.

In the following section, we summarize each chapter, showing how our understanding of each is enhanced by the analytical method we have described above.

## The Chapters

The chapters move from several accounts of pragmatic advocacy to counter ESR deprivations; to explicit engagement with national political contests and institutional innovations; to a meditation on the multiple dimensions on which human rights can inspire hope among impoverished people. The book concludes with a theoretical account of how pragmatic and critical ESR advocacy can disrupt structural injustice and promote deep institutional change.

The first chapter describes an anti-eviction campaign by the Nigerian Social and Economic Rights Action Center (SERAC) in the Lagos communities of Ijora-Badia. The SERAC advocates used multiple tactics to build the community's power. These included legal, educational, and organizing efforts that targeted multiple actors—private corporations and public powers, state officials, federal institutions, and World Bank review panels. Though the campaign targeted the nation-state in numerous ways, it also directed tactics at powers beyond, and below, the domestic governmental structure. This array of targets and tactics formed a matrix that helps to account for the campaign's force.

The chapter shows how the World Bank eventually invited stakeholders, including Ijora-Badia leaders, to help plan how a massive urban development loan would be disbursed. It raises the question of how chapter author Morka and community leaders would respond to this double-edged offer—double-edged because on the one hand it could be used to raise living standards in Ijora-Badia, but on the other, such improvements could make the land even more financially out of reach for the lowest-income residents.

The chapter also shows how the group used economic and social rights as a galvanizing social justice language through which to spark social movement and incite resistance. In doing so, it points to the *transformative potential* of liberal values in SERAC's work. At the same time, it highlights the limits of that approach—both as a theoretical perspective and as an activist's strategic orientation. Indeed, the chapter shows that the Ijora-Badia campaign was guided by astute advocates who understood how rights protect the rich more readily than they promote redistribution to the poor.

The chapter draws on what we call *distributive analysis* to highlight several features of the Ijora-Badia struggle. As we have noted, distributive analysis refers to a way of interpreting advocacy campaigns so as to expose underlying patterns of resource distribution that may not be obvious on a first reading. For instance, this chapter focuses on the fact that the struggle takes place in a site where the tenants' legal rights with respect to the land were not clear. In this circumstance, the government's failure to regulate the occupants' interests in the land was a failure that had affirmative distributive consequences. Indeed, the government's failure was a de facto decision to privilege the private actors who sought to evict Ijora-Badia residents.[31] Yet this distribution was neither static nor all in one direction: the community's resistance heightened the legal consciousness and political confidence of the residents and thus redistributed power from elite actors back to community members in subtle and surprising ways.

Second, the chapter applies distributive analysis to the question of whether SERAC's decision to accept a World Bank loan might play out against the interests of the poor, no matter how much SERAC sought to prevent this from happening. Indeed, the chapter highlights how the World Bank's upgrading urban project would price the most deprived of the poor out of the Ijora-Badia housing market, and analyzes more broadly the distributional consequences of housing rights regimes in Third World urban settings. In doing so, the chapter hints toward innovative land and housing rights regimes that could move the claims of anti-eviction activists beyond narrow self-interest.

Finally, the chapter illustrates the historically embedded contexts—and constraints—in which the activists act politically to seek institutional change. Within the limits posed by that "regime,"[32] the Ijora-Badia actors could alter the trajectory of Nigeria's neoliberal politics only so much, no matter how creative their moves: the path in which the action was embedded could only be shifted so far. But that did not mean that their moves were entirely dependent on that path; rather, the questions presented were how the tactics could expand the "stretch" of that semibounded path and how the shift could be sustained.[33] Can the massive mobilization among Ijora-Badia's residents give them more clout in negotiating the terms of the World Bank loan to reduce the risk of displacement? If so, how can these favorable loan terms be enacted as intended, over time? And can SERAC's work to shift the state's policies toward informal-sector dwellers spread its effects to the state's other social welfare sectors, such as health or education? Stated differently, can the Ijora-Badia community's victory prefigure wider change?

The second chapter traces the South African Treatment Action Campaign's (TAC's) collaboration with litigators to compel a recalcitrant South African government to provide drug treatment to prevent the transmission of the human immunodeficiency virus (HIV) from infected pregnant women to their newborn infants during labor and birth. The chapter sets forth a "politics-centered" approach to ESR advocacy. This vision is instantiated through a close collaboration between lawyers and social movement organizers to shape a complex political campaign, which mobilizes thousands of South Africans around the right to health as a political aspiration. At the same time, the campaign produces substantial redistribution and democratic innovation in the health delivery system.

The chapter emphasizes that activists must focus their attention on national, as well as local and international, actors in order to leverage structural change. It provides a dense historical narrative of TAC's campaign around mother-to-child transmission of HIV. In addition to offering an insider's account of the lawsuit, the chapter describes an innovative effort by TAC to transform primary care clinics into sites where people who are HIV-positive can empower themselves to demand and then administer complex dosage regimes of antiretroviral medication. This Treatment Literacy Campaign mobilized volunteer activists to make these changes happen. The activists found that as clinic staff, local activists, and patients democratized the operating routines at the clinics, they expanded their capacity to treat not just HIV infection but also a broader range of other complex health conditions. A hope emerged from the Treatment

Literacy Campaign: that its organizing methods would transform these clinics, and indeed the entire primary care system, into a more inclusive, democratic, and effective network of health delivery sites. The chapter thus shows how TAC's treatment literacy project politicized HIV-positive people, provided quite effective healthcare, and prefigured a strongly democratic network of primary healthcare institutions, on the ground.

Finally, the chapter suggests how creating networks of such local innovations is a way to sustain a campaign's impact on social welfare delivery over the long term. The chapter brings several important questions into focus. How did the social movement help the litigators bring the government to its knees in the mother-to-child transmission lawsuit? How did the Treatment Literacy Campaign take hold in impoverished rural areas? Why did the activists pressure the South African government to bring them *inside* the state's own HIV/AIDS policy hierarchy, and how did they succeed? What led the state to introduce TAC's treatment literacy innovations into its formal primary health system? Finally, how can activists ensure that law-centered tactics complement, rather than overshadow, social movement?

The third chapter tells the story of a lawyer working through a newly constituted national human rights commission to challenge mass evictions of pastoralists from Tanzania's savanna in order to clear the land for tourist development on an animal reserve. Even after the evictions, the pastoralists and gatherers who had previously used the land continued to use it, or "poach," in the language of the Tanzanian government and international donors promoting tourism as an economic development scheme. The Nyamuma people's effort to use ESR law to recover their land triggered violence from these elites and then tragically failed. The chapter describes that failure and asks why. As such, it shows that moments of political disruption and mobilization do not necessarily engender political empowerment or structural change.

Through the careful retrospective analysis of the eviction case, the authors trace the multilevel politics at play in the story. Specifically, the chapter shows how the human rights commission did not stand behind the evicted people. Rather, it further strengthened local and international elites, some of whom had funded it. Nonetheless, at the end of the chapter the lawyer suggests how the experience at Nyamuma helped to raise the awareness of other groups at risk of eviction or other forms of land loss. The advocate senses that the Nyamuma struggle had an empowering effect on these people, encouraging them to confront rather than submit to government officials, and to report their grievances to the larger world. Thus, the narrative turns back in the end toward the theme of hope that figures throughout this book.

The Nyamuma lawyers are distinctive in the volume for their acute awareness of the *pluralist*[34] challenges that their work raises. More was at stake in the Nyamuma case than a few hectares of savanna. It was also a conflict over the government's development priorities and people's access to the power to take part in development choices. It was a conflict over basic values and over different ways of life. Through a wide-ranging conversation that drew on a critical, explicitly anticolonial analysis of plural values, the chapter shows how inventive legal schemas for land use might shift legitimacy toward the so-called trespassers, thus defusing the apparently zero-sum conflict between two different takes on the scope of the property right.

Chapter 4 tells the story of Mohammed Zakari. Mr. Zakari was an elderly Ghanaian man who found himself involuntarily detained in a public hospital compound after being medically discharged, because he could not pay his bill. This practice of postdischarge detention is regularly used in Ghana and other countries as a means of shaming impoverished patients' families into raising funds through extended family networks to pay what are often illegal charges. In the Zakari case, the activists filed a legal claim of habeas corpus, alleging the unlawful detainment of Mr. Zakari by the Ghanaian state. The activists then linked this violation of Zakari's formal "negative" liberal right to freedom from unlawful detainment to a more controversial claim for his right to health, around which they mobilized an entire community to spark political momentum for structural change.

The chapter uses a metaphor of "rights as footprints" to explore the significance of rights-claiming to the social movement to which the Zakari case gave rise. In doing so, it brings together several themes of the book, which are elaborated in Chapter 5. First, the wide-ranging, multilevel tactics used by Mohammed Zakari's advocates illustrate the *pragmatic* approach to human rights activism. Second, the chapter shows how each of these tactics flipped embedded power in a different way. It shows how those disruptions of power came together in a powerful and myth-making *performative* moment, guided by a clear normative compass, in which Mr. Zakari spoke confidently at a press conference about his story. Third, the chapter also illustrates some of the *pluralist* challenges faced by the advocates and the community, such as a dilemma about whether to embark on an unlicensed march or to comply with formal human rights processes. It demonstrates the use of an experimentalist litigation remedy to provide a framework for the ongoing negotiation and renegotiation of the applicable regulatory scheme. Finally, this framework *prefigures* an approach to regulation that might constitute a more democratic system of health finance and delivery.

Overall, the Zakari chapter most fully illustrates the interplay of rule-breaking advocacy, transformative human rights values, momentary shifts of power, shocks to institutional practice, the power of memory, and the challenge of sustaining change. It weaves these themes together, posing, in the end, the question of how people fighting against almost insurmountable odds can sustain hope, and with it, the political engagement and institutional vision that hope can engender.

We conclude the book with two forward-looking theoretical essays, which arise from the case studies.

In Chapter 5, we highlight three features of the lawyer-advocates' practices that emerged from our investigation: their iconoclastic *strategies of engagement*, their distinctive *normative* orientation, and their capacity, through the process of their work in the present, to *prefigure* the creative innovations that they envision for the future.

Building on the Introduction, Chapter 5, and case studies in this volume, the sixth and final chapter looks at the advocates who are featured in each chapter and the hard work they faced in helping to make real, sustainable change. The authors examine more closely the link between the innovative advocacy practices described in these chapters and subsequent changes in the design and delivery of social and other public goods. In short, the chapter examines *how* innovative advocacy links up to institutional change. The chapter shows how the most savvy advocacy and social justice mobilization will not have an impact on structural injustice unless those practices promote change in the institutions that provide food, shelter, healthcare, housing, jobs, and the like to impoverished people, on the ground. The authors outline an "arc" that traces how creative ESR advocacy moves across a set of four interconnected temporal fields, which span from local "generative spaces" toward the spread of innovation on the ground.

By "generative political space" we mean a political field in which experimentation and contestation over the production and delivery of a core social good can take place, often for the first time. We speculate that in the best cases such *contestation* and *experimentation* can shift social welfare regimes toward more equitable distribution, greater client-citizen empowerment, and more effective institutional design, all measured against so-called rights-based, or social democratic, evaluative criteria. The dynamic among these three regime-wide trajectories—greater redistribution, invigorated client-citizen empowerment, and smarter institutional design—can then enhance the delivery of core social goods, at least over the medium term.

Some of the chapters in this book suggest that retrograde ideological forces can repeatedly co-opt the savviest strategy, to turn signals of hope into circuits of despair. For as the Nyamuma eviction story in Tanzania powerfully shows, neoliberal programs are sticky, or "path dependent." Thus, without ongoing mobilization, human rights campaigns that push toward more equitable microinstitutions—of primary healthcare delivery, for instance—tend to lose their momentum. Other chapters, such as that on the South African Treatment Action Campaign, emphasize the potential of linking rule-breaking advocacy tactics together with social movement to shake up inequitable social welfare schemes.

Perhaps the book's most important lesson is that the significance of these rule-breaking practices, when woven together into human rights campaigns, is greater than the sum of their parts. The power of these campaigns comes through the disruption of entrenched power relationships—and the resulting space for renaming—that the campaigns open up. Because of the force of these power formations, such disruptions are usually momentary rather than sustained. Yet the disruptions will be remembered and replayed in ways that *can* open more sustained space for ideological challenge and institutional innovation. It is this hope that the book's chapters explore and affirm, each in its own way.

# PART I

# Case Studies

## Chapter 1

# A Place to Live

## Resisting Evictions in Ijora-Badia, Nigeria

Felix Morka

This chapter is the result of a dialogue between Felix Morka and Duncan Kennedy that took place at a Stones of Hope meeting in May 2008. It explores the threat of forced evictions faced by the residents of the Ijora-Badia community in Lagos, Nigeria, and the way their resistance created challenges, and also opportunities, for the community's development.

With a total area of about 160 hectares and a population of over 600,000 people, the community of Ijora-Badia[1] is currently ranked higher than over one hundred other informal settlements as the most blighted community in Lagos. It provides a compelling example of a community's long struggle for a place to live against persistent efforts of government and city managers to forcibly evict them. The Badia story illustrates how an unbridled use of the combined political power of the state and the financial muscle of the World Bank can aggravate the poverty of target beneficiaries. While highlighting the repressive force of these actors, the chapter also examines the community's creative use of human rights to transform their consciousness and bolster their capacity to resist power asymmetries at the root of their deprivation and marginalization. The chapter also demonstrates that by challenging eviction, communities like Ijora-Badia can amass significant power and resources, which can potentially enable them to remap their development over the long term.

In 1973, three years after the end of the country's civil war, the federal military government of Nigeria acquired a large tract of land comprising a sprawling old settlement known as Oluwole Village in Iganmu (central Lagos) for the purpose of building Nigeria's National Arts Theatre. The theater was to be a key edifice gracing the African Festival of Arts and Culture, which Nigeria was to host in 1977. The festival was one of several sociocultural events convened to showcase a unified and resurgent Nigeria poised to tackle the challenges of reconstruction and development after a three-year civil war that claimed the lives of over one million people.

The grandiosity of the theater only masked the brutality and injustice meted out to the local landowners. In a sequence of events that is becoming increasingly familiar throughout the developing world, the federal military government, without adequate notice or consultation, forcibly evicted the Oluwole villagers from their ancestral homes. Following largely uncoordinated protests by the residents, the federal authorities retroactively paid paltry sums to some of the evictees as compensation for their demolished homes. Other evictees, who insisted on resettlement, were allocated vacant plots of land, measuring on average 9 meters by 15 meters (30 ft. by 50 ft.) in Badia, a community located less than one kilometer away. A final group of evictees was abandoned to find their own means to build new houses for their families. Many built sheds made mostly of stilts and corrugated iron sheets of various shapes and sizes, as each family could afford.

Prior to the displaced persons' arrival, Badia was already inhabited by the ancestral land-owning Ojora chieftaincy family, their assignees, and tenants. From the 1960s through the late 1970s, Badia had also become home to other populations displaced by development activities, such as major road and bridge construction and industrial layouts.

The federal military government failed to address the host community's (Badia's) preexisting severe lack of basic social and economic infrastructure, such as water, roads, drainage facilities, a solid waste disposal system, health-care facilities, and schools. The unplanned relocation of the Oluwole evictees to Badia only worsened an already dire situation. These exacerbated social, economic, and environmental deprivations have come to characterize and continue to frame the heightened blight levels in Badia.

The urgency to rebuild Nigeria's infrastructure, which was devastated because of the country's civil war, an unprecedented oil boom in the 1970s, and the international development agenda, drove massive infrastructural investments. These investments were neither carefully planned nor carefully implemented, however. These forces, as well as groups of elites capturing rents corresponding to increasing values of urban real estate, all came together to promote a high tolerance for forced evictions as being necessary for building a solid infrastructural base that would support rapid economic growth and development. At the same time, observes Professor Kennedy in the commentary that follows this case study, in some circumstances resisting forced evictions can enable threatened communities themselves to capture these rents and use them to choose development strategies for themselves. Nowhere were these risks and potentials more evident than in Lagos, which until 1991 was the capital city of the Federal Republic of Nigeria.

## Lagos, a City in Crisis

Although Lagos is one of the largest cities in the world, it is unquestionably one of the least planned, studied, and understood. With an estimated population of fourteen million in 2010, Lagos is also one of the world's fastest-growing cities: with only 252,000 people in 1952, Lagos is projected by the United Nations to have a population exceeding seventeen million by 2015.[2] The rise of Lagos as a major economic and political center, its sprawling seaports, and its offer of an alluring (but elusive) promise of the "good life" to all manner of migrants have contributed to the city's population pull.

Arguably, the most important factor in Nigeria's rural-urban population surge is the reckless destruction of the agricultural sector[3] (both as a major provider of sustenance and as the largest employer of labor), owing to the discovery of crude oil in 1956 and the country's near total dependence on its export earnings. The dramatic wealth from crude oil created a perverse set of incentives that discouraged investment in non-oil sectors of the economy, especially agriculture.[4] Lacking critical essential inputs such as seeds, fertilizers, pesticides, irrigation facilities, tractors, and other modern tools and machinery, many people who were once gainfully employed in the agricultural sector abandoned their occupations. The international dip in prices of commodities during the 1970s further discouraged growth in that sector. The emergence of a new class of upwardly mobile oil merchants, speculators, and skilled and unskilled workers in the oil industry further escalated the momentous drift to the cities, worsening the upward trend in real estate values. As land values inflated at extraordinary rates, these forces came together to lock impoverished people and elites in a struggle over the soaring rents this inflation generated, particularly in Lagos.

To say that Lagos is a city in crisis is to understate the severity and enormity of the challenges that confront its residents. Lagos remains the epicenter of Nigeria's high urbanization rate of 5.5 percent. This rapid population growth has not been matched by the provision of social and economic infrastructure, such as adequate housing, healthcare facilities, schools, roads, transportation, water, solid waste disposal, and drainage facilities. Over the years, successive state and federal governments have approached the inadequacy of the city's infrastructure with astonishing levity. Where infrastructure development initiatives have been launched, they have generally been haphazardly planned or implemented.

For example, the Lagos Master Plan (1980–2000), which was developed in 1979 with the support of the United Nations Development Programme (UNDP), laid out a framework for addressing various challenges, including the provision of housing, creation and expansion of economic activity centers (to disperse pressure and population concentration on existing city centers), and the identification and upgrading of major informal settlements. In a recent report, the Presidential Task Force on the Lagos Mega City concluded that the Lagos Master Plan "was not implemented." Instead, the experience had been one of "significant distortions in many parts of the plan" with impacts that have been "far reaching, resulting in lopsided population distribution, high cost of infrastructure development, drainage obstructions, environmental and sanitation challenges, traffic congestion and numerous other problems."[5] Perhaps unrealistically given the lack of political will, the Lagos Master Plan mandated that "between 1980 and 2000, 1.4 million additional housing units should be constructed, out of which a million should be deliberately earmarked for low income households." Commenting on the failure to implement this plan, Francisco Bolaji Abosede, the Lagos State commissioner for physical planning and urban development, stated that although the plan "accurately analyzed the housing needs of Lagos [ . . . ] by the year 2000 when the plan expired, not more than ten percent of the housing needs were satisfied."[6] The state's failure to implement the master plan entrenched a regulatory framework that left poor people without basic services and thus vulnerable to housing instability.

Indeed, one major consequence of the population explosion in Lagos is an acute housing shortage. Less than 20 percent of the city's residents own their homes. Furthermore, over two-thirds of the population of Lagos live in the informal settlements that are scattered around the city.[7] The 1980–2000 Lagos Master Plan had identified and classified forty-two slums or informal settlements in the city. There are now over one hundred such communities in Lagos. Many poor and low-income families excluded from access to land and housing in the formal sector find refuge in these informal settlements, where housing can be built according to means and capacity. Although they generally lack security of tenure (by virtue of not having the requisite certificate of occupancy), many residents of these informal settlements hold bona fide legal rights and interests in the land on which they live, having validly acquired land from legitimate landholding families, communities, or authorities.[8]

The informal settlements at issue in this section are often called slums. An expert group of the United Nations Human Settlements Programme (UN-Habitat) defines a slum as a contiguous settlement where the inhabitants are characterized as having inadequate housing and basic services. It is often not recognized and addressed by public authorities as an integral or equal part of the city. The expert group identifies insecure residential status, inadequate access to safe water, inadequate access to sanitation and other infrastructure, poor structural quality of housing, and overcrowding as eminently characteristic of slums. Nearly one billion people now live in such settlements around the world. In policy and planning circles, these informal settlements are perceived and treated as anomalies rather than as integral and equally important parts of the city. Officials also tend to be in denial of the fact that the residents of these communities are human beings.

While there are several explanations for the proliferation of informal settlements and the acute shortage of formal housing in Lagos, three are highlighted here: (1) use of forced evictions as an urban planning tool, (2) restrictive and discriminatory land use policy, and (3) executive focus on direct government provision of housing stock. All three can be sources of opportunities as well as risks for urban communities like Ijora-Badia, seeking to stabilize themselves and ensure their residents' basic social and economic protections.

### Use of Forced Eviction as an Urban Planning and Development Control Tool

In its quest to eliminate or drastically curb the spread of informal settlements, the government has used forced eviction as a preferred tool of urban engineering, with counterproductive outcomes. Since 1990, over 700,000 people have been forcibly evicted from their homes or businesses in Lagos without adequate notice, compensation, or resettlement. Across the country, nearly three million people have been forcibly evicted since May 1999, when the present elected civilian government was inaugurated. In all more people have been forcibly evicted from their homes and businesses than the government has been able to provide housing for since the country's independence.

In addition to the broad range of social, economic, psychological, cultural, and physical havoc inflicted on the victims, forced evictions also fuel the growth of new slums and the expansion of existing ones. These communities are routinely denied funds needed for the provision of basic services, such as community health centers or potable water.

In a downward spiral, these new communities' poverty and lack of basic services are cited as justification for their demolition. The government typically rationalizes the mass evictions in paternalistic terms. For example, when the military government of Lagos State demolished the homes of over 300,000 residents of the Maroko community in July 1990, it claimed that the community was prone to flooding and unfit for human habitation. When the democratically elected government of Rivers State forcibly evicted over one million Rainbow Town residents in 2001, it claimed that the community harbored too many criminals. When the government of Lagos State forcibly evicted and burned the homes of over three thousand Makoko residents in April 2005, it claimed that it was helping some private citizens flush out miscreants and undesirable squatters. Further, the ongoing indiscriminate forced eviction of hundreds of thousands of residents in Abuja by the Federal Capital City Development Authority has been presented as an effort to correct distortions to the city's 1979 master plan. In addition, the Lagos State government's persistent efforts to forcibly evict the Badia community have been explained by the need to rid the community of filth, flooding, and prostitution. As these examples show, however, the *threat* of a forced eviction can offer skillful activist-lawyers a foundation for rallying community members around economic and social rights campaigns and thus greatly enhance their power.

### Restrictive and Discriminatory Land Use Policy

Among the many reasons for which the dwellers of informal settlements have little access to formal sector land is the misapplication of the Land Use Act of 1978. Enacted to harmonize preexisting customary land tenure systems and free up land for new development, the act constitutes the most aggressive and far-reaching declaration of the power of eminent domain over urban and rural lands in Nigeria. It provides that "all land comprised in the territory of each State in the Federation are hereby vested in the Governor of that State and such land shall be held in trust and administered for the use and common benefit of all Nigerians in accordance with the provisions of this Act."[9] The act makes certain that "all land in the urban areas shall be under the control and management of the Governor of each State."[10] Similarly, "all other land shall [ . . . ] be under the control and management of the Local Government within the area of jurisdiction of which the land is situated."[11] The act invests immense powers in the state governor and the local government to determine, regulate, and manage land use, including the power to grant statutory and customary rights of occupancy.

Although the Land Use Act preserves the entitlement of the holder of a right of occupancy to the sole and absolute possession of all improvements on the land,[12] it provides that such improvements may be transferred, assigned, or mortgaged only subject to the prior consent of the governor.[13] Furthermore, the act makes it unlawful "for the holder of a statutory right of occupancy granted by the Government to alienate his right of occupancy or any part thereof by assignment, mortgage, transfer possession, sublease or otherwise however without the consent of the Governor first had and obtained."[14] The most significant and controversial power vested in the governor by the act is the power to revoke a right of occupancy or to compulsorily acquire land for "overriding public interest" subject, in some cases, to compensation.

The Land Use Act, as currently applied, is fundamentally flawed and unsustainable for three main reasons.

First, the act has been used to expropriate land that was owned and controlled by individuals, families, and communities under the customary land tenure system. Under the act, as technical ownership of land became centralized in the office of the governor, most undeveloped urban lands were expropriated by the governor for sundry purposes, leaving little land in the hands of families and communities. Consequently, many poor and low-income citizens (who by virtue of their membership would normally gain access to family or community land for housing development) are stripped of access and entitlement. This dispossession is often aggravated by a poor compensation regime that is calculated on the basis of an arbitrary valuation of structural or economic crop improvements on the land. Land taken in this manner is sold by the government at near prime market value to land speculators and affluent developers, putting land and housing further out of reach of the poor.

Second, the mandatory requirement of the governor's consent to land transactions such as sales, assignments, transfers, or mortgages of land in urban areas constrains housing development and optimal social use of land resources. The consent process is fraught with great difficulties: it is costly (with fees assessed at upwards of 35 percent of the market value of the underlying land), laced with bureaucratic delays, and exploitative, so that only a very small percentage of landowners ever bother to apply for consent. Absent the governor's consent, the landowner remains without a valid title to the land (evidenced by a certificate of occupancy) and as such has no security of tenure, thus making herself and her family vulnerable to forced evictions.

Finally, the government has further excluded the poor from access to land by a discriminatory application of the act's provisions, so as to afford preferential treatment to the government and affluent private developers. For example, in Lagos, as in the rest of Nigeria, only expansive and expensive plots are officially demarcated for allocation and titling. On average, a plot of land demarcated for residential purposes must be 680 square meters (60 ft. by 120 ft.) or more. Such a plot would typically cost anywhere between three million naira (about US$24,000) to over ten million naira (US$80,000) depending on its location. The federal monthly minimum wage in Nigeria is 7,500 naira (about $60). Mortgage credit facilities are generally unavailable; thus, such plots are beyond the reach of the poor.

### Excessive Focus on Direct Government Provision of Housing Stock

Since national independence in 1960, the efforts of successive governments to address Nigeria's housing deficit have centered on direct government provision of formal housing for low-income groups. This strategy gained preeminence during the period of the Third National Development Plan (1975–80) when it was decided that the provision of housing should not be left to the private sector alone. Of the 202,000 new housing units projected to be constructed during the period, less than 15 percent were actually built.[15] The record was not too different for the Fourth National Development Plan (1980–85). Only 600 million naira were expended out of the 19 billion naira budgeted for the National Low-Cost Housing Program. In the small wake of this poor investment, the National Housing Policy of 2002 declared rather soberly that "the impact of the programme on the overall housing market was negligible."[16] The program had been an easy target for overpricing, nepotism, patronage, and the bureaucratic secrecy that often shrouds the allocation process.

In its obsessive focus on the low-cost housing approach, the government has not explored other viable options for expanding the housing stock and improving the quality of housing, such as expanding the productive capacity of the building materials sector; enhancing affordability of input materials; promoting access to mortgage credit; ensuring equitable access to land; expanding the capacity of planning authorities to anticipate and plan effectively for the housing needs of the growing population; and creating a regime of incentives (policy, institutional, fiscal, and budgetary) designed to encourage the poor to undertake self-help housing cooperatives or building societies. In many megacities around the world, slum dwellers and other low-income groups are taking the initiative to design and implement strategies such as community organizing, land banking, savings schemes, job creation, and other microenterprise activities that increase their economic capacity and political leverage to provide housing and other amenities for themselves and their communities.[17] By creating an enabling policy, legal, economic, and social environment, the government can empower and stimulate the poor to explore feasible, innovative, and sustainable means for expanding housing production and improvement.

All of these problems with the Land Use Act are rooted not in the letter of the law, however, but rather in the law as the government has applied it. The act could just as well be used to create urban communities in which the social value of land, government-owned land trusts, and limits on occupants' equity appreciation could stabilize communities over the long term.

## The Plan to Destroy Badia

When they were relocated in 1973, the Oluwole evictees were never informed about the rationale behind the choice of Badia as a resettlement location. Except for the allocation papers issued to some of them by the federal government, there was nothing to evidence their title to the Badia lands. Thus, they were vulnerable to persistent eviction threats and to attacks by the Lagos State government. There was also palpable tension between the new settlers in Badia and the Ojora chieftaincy family that had occupied the land when the Oluwole were resettled there, a tension that has continued to this day. Lacking security of tenure in Badia, many evictees were discouraged from undertaking any real investment in their living environment and had little choice but to choose to build temporary shacks to meet their immediate shelter needs.

By the early 1990s, Badia, like many other informal settlements, had become a choice place to live for many who could not afford the cost of living in the formal residential districts of the city. The community's location less than one mile from the major seaport town of Apapa, and its proximity to a major oil depot also made it a prime and strategic place to live. The existence of the

Apapa railway line traversing the community to other parts of Lagos and beyond provided further incentive for population concentration.

Meanwhile, Apapa's rather small land area had become stretched to the breaking point, and pressure was on to expand the borders of the town to accommodate the needs and interests of big corporations. Badia had become a highly attractive frontier marked for demolition and eventual upscale development for the benefit of affluent individuals and big corporations. In the state's estimation, Badia's poor were expendable and undeserving of the land. In the estimation of many of Badia's residents, however, they deserved the land on which they were residing.

On July 15, 1996, residents of fifteen Lagos slum communities learned of plans by the Lagos State government to forcibly evict them from their homes and businesses as part of the $85-million World Bank–funded Lagos Drainage and Sanitation Project (LDSP).[18] The project was designed to build drainage systems to deflood parts of Lagos.[19] Then Lagos State commissioner for environment and physical planning, Oladipo Ashafa, explained that in order to accommodate the drainage systems and renew the blighted areas, it was necessary to demolish parts, if not most, of the targeted communities.[20] Commissioner Ashafa further stated that the Lagos State government had no intention or plan to compensate or resettle persons whose homes might be affected by the project, adding that such losses should be taken as the victims' contribution to the development of Lagos State. The targeted settlements had a total population of over 1.2 million people. Except for media reports of the threat to destroy the communities, the affected populations were not notified, consulted, or even contacted by the state government or the World Bank regarding the project itself or its forced-eviction component.

The community's first direct contact with the LDSP came in 1997 when bulldozers and eviction officials, backed by heavily armed police and military personnel, invaded the community and demolished the homes of over two thousand people. While bulldozers flattened houses and property, armed security men harassed, brutalized, and arrested residents who attempted to salvage personal effects from their homes. These officials instantly extorted monies from residents desperate to secure their freedom or pick up their possessions. The terror unleashed on these residents was made more despicable by the suddenness of the attack, which found mostly women, children, and old people at home to bear the brunt.

Prior to the July 1996 eviction announcement and the partial demolition, activist-lawyers based at the Social and Economic Rights Action Center (SERAC)[21] were already working with elites and opinion leaders in the Badia community, such as chiefs, religious leaders, and those with wealth, professional status, high levels of formal education, and the like. SERAC was providing basic human rights education and helping the community to strengthen its capacity to engage various institutions of the government on critical issues. As a part of its intervention, SERAC launched an investigation into the LDSP to learn more about its objectives, key actors, and plans for its Badia project. Initially, both the Lagos State government and the World Bank stonewalled SERAC's inquiries. Claiming that information on the LDSP was "classified," they withheld information about the eviction plan and the mandatory environmental and social impact assessments. However, after SERAC obtained vital project information from other sources and began using specific information in its public advocacy, the bank made an abrupt change to its information disclosure policy and furnished the organization with a copy of the project's Staff Appraisal Report dated May 10, 1993.

In response to SERAC's inquiry, the World Bank's country director for Nigeria, Yaw Ansu, a Ghanaian national, confirmed that the bank was funding LDSP but suggested that the threatened evictions may have been unilaterally planned by the Lagos State government. He added that the bank was "aware that several administrations in Lagos have resorted to large scale demolitions."[22] Admitting that 286 residents had lost their homes, Ansu claimed that these people had been "well taken care of," without providing any evidence as to the people's identities or what type of remedy had been provided. He stated further that the bank could not countenance the eviction of the marked slums "without compelling justification, extensive planning and the identification of huge resources." The bank's broad-stroke denial of responsibility for the evictions revealed to the community that the bank was in the ambiguous role of friend and enemy. Meanwhile, the Lagos State government's intransigence in the matter only elevated the community's resolve to halt further evictions under the LDSP.

Unquestionably, the government's threat to demolish Badia was a concern that was shared by all of the residents, regardless of their legal claims to the land. For some it had to do with the potential loss of a home, a place of business, a school, recreation, community, or the loss of means of livelihood. For others it signified the destruction of their very existence. Decades of living on the edge of repeated forced evictions had created a strong sense of victimization. But shared outrage failed to overcome the fear, suspicion, cynicism, and apathy that pervaded the community, and it proved insufficient to galvanize residents to protect their homes.

Some of Badia's residents also felt a sense of apathy because they lacked control over the decisions of Nigeria's federal government. This lack of control was partly attributable to the flaws inherent in any government; however, in the mid-1990s the military dictatorship in Nigeria had gained global notoriety for its brutal suppression of human rights and democratic freedoms. After nearly three decades of political repression by successive military regimes, people had learned to cope with silence, fear, and apathy. Opposition and dissent were severely penalized. The police, state security service, and the military were virtually licensed to arrest, torture, detain, disappear, or kill without remedy. The lawlessness of the military dictatorship helped to reinforce an already strong perception that the government, its decisions, and its actions were beyond moral or legal reproach.

The situation was compounded by the illiteracy and poverty of Badia's majority.[23] Like other impoverished areas, the community was preoccupied with the challenge of daily survival in the informal economy. Like most people in Nigeria, Badia's residents had become highly disillusioned by the unresponsiveness of government, both as a provider and as a regulator. The idea of the state as a social contractor seemed meaningless. Outside of the threatened demolition, the people of Badia did not feel the presence of government, and many did not care about it either. Government was virtually irrelevant to their well-being—their health, education, security, environment, food, housing, water, employment, and their overall well-being. On a day-to-day basis, they had no reason to look to the state for their material needs. With no access to official or alternative sources of information, people were unaware of the social and economic forces propelling the government to destroy the community; the extent of the threat; or the competing interests at play. And many could not fathom why the remote and amorphous World Bank would invest in their displacement and dispossession.

Given these forces of repression and poverty it is not surprising that the threat of eviction failed to trigger a spontaneous or coordinated resistance. Was the failure of many community members to think, strategize, and act together merely a function of lack of power due to their impoverishment? Was it their fear of an overbearing Weberian sovereign power?[24] Was it the lack of any compelling justification or incentives to resist? Was it for want of a viable organizing philosophy, model, or framework? Or was it their failure to develop a shared identity and understanding of the problems that would, in Arendt's[25] analysis of discursive communities, enable or empower "its constituent individuals to act in the name of, or on behalf of, the community as a whole"?[26] Among many of the community members with whom the activist-lawyers worked, the notion of citizenship signifying a continuum of relations and engagement with the state was tenuous at best, and absent at worst. Participatory theory suggests several incentives for individuals or groups to get involved in the affairs that affect them, including the personal benefit incentive, the social responsibility incentive, the psychological incentive, the pressure-induced incentive, and the cooptation incentive. In the case of Badia, none of these triggered participation. Enabling groups of Badia residents to work together to interrogate adverse official policies and actions was central to any effort to address the challenges. It was also crucial to address the power asymmetries at the roots of the community's marginalization.

When SERAC decided to work with the Badia community, its strategies were informed by the prior experience of its leaders with an earlier forced eviction in the Maroko community. In the case of Maroko, the Civil Liberties Organization (CLO)[27] decided to respond to the eviction through litigation; thus, in 1990 it filed a lawsuit on behalf of the community seeking an injunction to restrain the Lagos State government from demolishing it. The court refused to consider the case despite persistent requests by CLO. Following this refusal, a long line of bulldozers backed by heavily armed soldiers, police, and security forces invaded and unleashed mayhem on Maroko. Homes, schools, community clinics, churches, mosques, and businesses were flattened. Residents who attempted to salvage their personal possessions were brutally beaten by security agents. In the ensuing confusion, many women were repeatedly raped and assaulted by security and eviction officials. In the wake of the eviction, over 300,000 people were forced into the streets of Lagos. The state made no provision whatsoever for alternative accommodation for the evictees.[28] When CLO returned to court to express outrage, the judge responded that he could not entertain any discussion about the case of a community that no longer existed.[29] Nearly eighteen years later, the original lawsuit remains pending in court.[30]

The lessons of Maroko are unmistakable, profound, and unforgettable.[31] The case vividly illustrates the inadequacy of litigation in such circumstances, especially in societies with repressive political systems. The CLO's decision to pursue litigation was dictated by the circumstances of the case. At the same time, it was a tacit choice by the organization to stay within its comfort zone of legal advocacy. Like most traditional human rights organizations, litigation was central to the CLO's methodology. It had used litigation to uphold a wide range of civil and political rights, particularly arbitrary arrests and detention without trial. However, the nature, complexity, and magnitude of the Maroko case highlighted the limits of using litigation as an exclusive strategy. CLO did not consider additional strategies, such as engaging the community through popular education, community organizing, mobilization, or other collective action strategies.

In effect, community members had no opportunity to discuss alternatives to litigation or the best ways to address the social, economic, political, psychological, cultural, and human rights implications of forcibly evicting over 300,000 people. As there were no backup plans, once litigation was sabotaged people were left weakened and unprotected against the erratic actions of the state. It was as a result of the lessons from the Maroko case that a different organizational model—SERAC—was imagined and launched.

## Resisting Forced Eviction: The Badia Experience

As one of SERAC's earliest community partners, Badia presented a litmus test to the young organization and significantly helped shape its thinking and planning and how it would respond to multifaceted cases that affect a large number of people. In the beginning of its work, SERAC encountered a mixture of curiosity, cynicism, and resignation.[32] While some residents were forthcoming in their interaction with the organization, many were suspicious of the visitors who asked often intrusive questions about their private and communal affairs.

SERAC's first hurdle then was to gain the trust of the people. It needed to reassure residents that it had no hidden agenda and was independent of the state. Through sustained presence, individual and group discussions, dramas, community meetings, solidarity visits, and targeted advocacy, clusters of Badia residents gradually started to work together with SERAC to address issues of common concern. A community action program committee (CAPCOM) was established by SERAC to secure community participation in all of its activities. SERAC created CAPCOMs in many of the communities with which it worked; the CAPCOMS provided platforms for residents to share information, voice their concerns, and keep SERAC rapidly informed of developments within their communities. SERAC's CAPCOMs are usually composed of community volunteers. These individuals receive training on leadership, organizing techniques, and information gathering, compilation, utilization, dissemination, and management. Selected representatives also receive training on advocacy and public-speaking techniques. With time, Badia's CAPCOM evolved into a self-sustaining, integrated, and trusted community circuit. It proved to be a critical element in the interventions to halt demolition of the community.

At the same time, SERAC sought to frame a strategy that would pull wide-ranging individual perspectives into a comprehensive account of the challenges facing the community. Furthermore, it needed a conceptual, analytic, and programmatic framework that would give meaning to the community's lived experiences, promote common understanding of underlying problems, and unite all residents—landlords and tenants alike—in the search for solutions.[33] SERAC decided that human rights conceptions and values would serve these purposes, as they were relevant to and might provide a useful lens for examining the threat to destroy Badia. The organization was also interested in exploring how human rights might be used to support a collective vision of change in Badia, and to energize residents' struggle for a place to live. It was less concerned about the risk that a human rights framework might undermine communal solidarity.

## Educating for Change

As we have seen, most residents of Badia saw themselves as victims of the government's callousness. SERAC was resolved to help Badia residents think differently of themselves in relation to the state. But how do you overcome a perception of powerlessness that has deep historical, social, cultural, economic, and political dimensions and that is reinforced by daily experiences? How can an individual or community that has been consistently alienated, oppressed, or victimized regain a perception of themselves as dignified persons with an inherent power of action? How can they rise from apathy to active consciousness on behalf of their community's survival? How can they resist the arbitrary and pervasive power of the state to prevail over their will and preferences?

One initial strategy that SERAC used to respond to these questions was popular education. A starting point in this method was for community members to identify from their own perspective the issues they were facing. Residents were encouraged to express their views on a wide range of social, political, legal, economic, ethnic, leadership, land, environmental, and cultural factors that were leading to the community's marginalization. They also identified persons, institutions, and authorities that either were responsible for creating the problems or had responsibility to address them. They took stock of previous efforts to solve the problems, analyzed steps and processes followed, evaluated the outcomes, and tried to ascertain why the problems had persisted.

Out of these conversations a consensus on what the problems were, their causes, and the interventions that might positively affect the community's situation began to emerge. For example, lack of security of tenure, poor housing, poverty, lack of access to information, weak community structures, political repression, lack of access to basic social amenities, poor participation, and exclusion of women emerged as recurrent themes. As expected, most residents blamed the government for its failure to provide basic amenities in the community. Although stopping the planned demolition was an urgent priority, residents were well aware that it was important to deal with these other challenges in order to reinvent the community as a sustainable one.

In these reflections the residents were often self-critical of their roles and responsibility in exacerbating the situation. They were also open about the community's inability to initiate self-help efforts to address problems such as solid waste disposal, which made their environment unsightly and unhealthy. Residents also held difficult discussions about the challenges posed by the community's ethnic and religious diversity, and by gender roles. They reflected on tensions between the Community Development Association, a quasi-official association, and other legitimate communal structures. In particular, they considered the often divisive role of traditional chiefs. Tension between the Ojora chieftaincy family and leaders of the former Oluwole evictee-settlers has been and remains a source of disharmony in the community.[34]

As the process of self-reflection unfolded, SERAC began to introduce an aggressive program of human rights education,[35] in which the nonprovision of essential social services was a particular focus. The threat of eviction was cited as a violation of a range of human rights, including the right to adequate housing, the right to family life, and the right to human dignity.[36] This approach sought to transform the way basic social and economic goods and services, including healthcare facilities, housing, education, and water are understood. In this view, the provision by the state of these goods and services is seen at best as a matter of political responsibility, administrative expediency, or moral imperative. At worst, it is seen as a matter of official charity or discretion. In this tradition, the denial of access to these basic services is viewed as nothing more than an administrative lapse or as political inefficiency to be corrected through the political process. In this liberal, pluralistic view it is the duty of individuals to use their capacities to secure their own needs, irrespective of structural obstacles that may limit them.

In statist economies like Nigeria, the provision of basic services is undertaken by state ministries, parastatal agencies, and quasi-government entities that are often liable to political control and manipulation. It is common practice for services to be extended or denied for reasons of political patronage or reprisal, thereby increasing the vulnerability of poor communities like Badia. By framing these basic goods and services as objects of human rights, residents felt entitled to have the state provide them. They also felt entitled to challenge the state when it refused to do so.

Notions of human dignity, fairness, autonomy, justice, equality, and nondiscrimination were not entirely strange, as many residents eagerly shared their various understandings of the meaning and essence of these ideas. However, many were surprised to learn that these values constituted the bedrock of a legally instrumented human rights corpus. Information about specific rights, including life, dignity, private and family life, adequate housing, health, freedom of association, education, and work resonated widely within the community. By framing the threat of forced eviction in human rights and justice terms, the community set itself up to demand an effective remedy from identifiable duty-bearers in an exercise of their own social power.

Human rights language offered the Badia residents a nuanced philosophy for reflexive thought and collective action. The freedom to think, learn, agitate, share, participate, act, own, and contemplate new ideas became contagious within the community. It gave a new world of meaning to their lived experiences and offered visions of new possibilities. By naming themselves as critical change agents, they were able gradually to bolster their confidence to interrogate adverse policies, programs, and actions of the government and other entities, and to propose alternatives.

Energized by this outlook, community leaders increased their public engagement through regular visits to relevant official agencies, convening large rallies and protest marches, and engaging in extensive media activities designed to draw public attention to their predicament. The fear of attacks by security agencies, which previously inhibited community members from publicly organizing against the government, was gradually dissipated by people's growing empowerment.

Another important element of the human rights education strategy was a focus on key public actors and institutions that were relevant to the community's struggle. Information on human rights standards as well as best practices relating to urban planning and governance, access to land, and housing upgrading were disseminated to officials who were then invited to meetings with the community. The officials initially resisted; however, they gradually realized the enormous potential these meetings presented to them. At these gatherings, officials were able to explain the government's plans and policy objectives, as well as to judge levels of acceptance of or opposition to them. Thus, the importance of consulting residents in the planning, implementation, and evaluation of programs often became the subject of heated debate.

### Challenging the "Power" Behind the Planned Demolition

Through the human rights education project some members of the community became determined to resist the World Bank's plan for demolishing their community under the LDSP.[37] Averting this plan was their most urgent challenge. Through community workshops, seminars, focus groups, town hall meetings, and legal clinics, SERAC led exploratory discussions about various legal and nonlegal options that might stop the plan. In these interactions, community members explored the option of litigation, which promised many benefits. Given the seriousness and urgency of the situation, filing a lawsuit seemed likely to be effective. A successful lawsuit against Lagos State could have yielded an injunction prohibiting the demolition. A lawsuit could also have provided the community a forum to articulate its grievances in a way that would lead to judicial validation. Further, litigation might have helped to compel the Lagos State government to disclose valuable information about the LDSP and other plans that might damage the community in the future. Further, litigation could have bolstered the courage of community leaders and offered some protection to them. Finally, through its investigations, SERAC's CAPCOM learned that the World Bank and the state government had certain enforceable legal obligations to community members, whether or not they had valid legal title to their lands.

CAPCOM was able to clarify that the World Bank and the Lagos State government were under a duty to consult community representatives and ensure the community's full participation in the project's design and implementation. The legal obligations also required the World Bank and the state government to provide adequate notice, compensation, resettlement, and rehabilitation to the residents of endangered communities should forced eviction become inevitable in order to accomplish the project's purposes. Enforcing these various legal obligations under the LDSP represented another potential argument for using the litigation route. In spite of these many advantages, however, CAPCOM's leaders ultimately rejected litigation as the prime strategy for resisting demolition.

A major reason for dropping litigation was that the political circumstances made it unfeasible. Between 1996 and 1998, at the height of the threat to demolish Badia, Nigeria was ruled by a brutal military dictatorship, which had replaced the bill of rights and other important constitutional provisions with draconian military decrees. Under the decrees the authority of the courts to intervene in human rights or political cases was drastically limited. Thus, the prospect of judicial intervention was dim, and the military junta would have probably ignored any judicial order. Furthermore, although a successful legal action against Lagos State would have blocked the implementation of the forced eviction component of the LDSP, SERAC grappled with the difficult jurisdictional question of whether the World Bank could become the subject of judicial review in Nigeria's municipal courts. For these reasons, SERAC along with community leaders decided not to rely on litigation as their primary tactic.

The possibility of using international and regional human rights mechanisms was also considered. In 1996, in collaboration with the Center for Economic and Social Rights, SERAC filed a communication with the Banjul-based African Commission on Human and Peoples' Rights regarding massive violations of the economic, social, and cultural rights of the Ogoni community in the oil-rich Niger Delta region. That communication was pending during the critical period prior to the Badia planned evictions. However, the commission's highly politicized history, and its well-known delay in processing cases, did not inspire any confidence in its capacity to issue an unbiased and timely judgment. In any event, the commission's lack of compulsory jurisdiction and capacity to enforce its decisions also made that prospect unappealing.

In the end SERAC and community leaders decided to explore using the World Bank's own accountability mechanism to challenge the LDSP. In the political circumstances of Nigeria, it was correctly assumed that the bank would be more amenable to persuasion, or susceptible to pressure, than the military junta. If the bank was pressured to reconsider its funding of the project, then quite obviously the military junta would lose its capacity to carry out the demolition and takeover of the community as planned.

On June 16, 1998, SERAC filed a request for inspection before the World Bank Inspection Panel,[38] stating the community's opposition to the government's intentions under the LDSP, and alleging that the project was being implemented in flagrant violation of the bank's own policies and operational directives. Furthermore, the request alleged that the LDSP agreement, which stipulated standards and guidelines to be followed in the implementation of bank-funded projects having an involuntary resettlement component, was not being complied with. The request further alleged that the project was being implemented in violation of constitutional and international human rights standards. Specifically, it alleged that the forced eviction of two thousand Badia residents and the threat of demolition of the entire community violated their human rights to adequate housing, life, private and family life, dignity, and security.[39]

On September 9, 1998, the World Bank Inspection Panel visited Nigeria and carried out an on-site preliminary inspection of Badia. A single inspector, Professor Edward Ayensu, a Ghanaian national, conducted the mission, contrary to the panel's established practice of assigning at least two inspectors for missions of this kind. At his first meeting with SERAC staff at the Lagos Sheraton Hotel, the inspector expressed his desire to resolve the matter "the African way." The inspector rescheduled his visit to the community without notice, so that many witnesses never had the opportunity to share their experiences. Except for his initial visits to the community in the company of SERAC staff and government officials, Ayensu conducted the greater part of his inspection in the company of state government and security officials, who intimidated and harassed witnesses presenting critical evidence. On many occasions he showed outright hostility to witnesses who dared to challenge officials' accounts of events under investigation and failed to reprimand or exclude erring officials. With the community, he was more preoccupied with convincing residents of the World Bank's positive intentions than with gathering and analyzing the abundant evidence of the LDSP's breaches of bank policies and human rights standards. In addition, he repeatedly stressed that many of the affected residents did not possess formal title to their land, and he sought, unsuccessfully, to polarize the ranks between "legal house owners" and squatters, often blaming so-called squatters for provoking the eviction of "legal owners." The request for inspection's framing of issues around "housing" rather than "land" rights and the community's concerted focus on the housing dimension of the eviction helped community members resist his divisive efforts.

As SERAC expected, the inspection panel returned a report that was incoherent in significant respects.[40] For example, the panel report identified only eight structures in Ijora-Badia.[41] The report continued that "from the composite aerial maps there seem to have been no dwellings in the drainage site area at the time of the signing of the Credit Agreement."[42] The panel concluded that the owners of the officially recognized existing structures should be offered compensation in accordance with the World Bank's policies.

Badia's population density and patterns of settlement made it unthinkable that in fact a large area of land was uninhabited and undeveloped, and ready for the commencement of the LDSP. That the composite maps did not show existing houses in the project site did not mean that no one lived there. In SERAC's view, the maps, which were drafted by the government and the bank, depicted only images that suited their predetermined objectives. Developing maps and gathering other project data were clearly not matters within the control of the affected communities. Following the panel's findings, the bank and Lagos State paid out sums ranging between $58 and $165 as full and final compensation to residents whose homes the bank identified as having been destroyed. Many who declined to accept these paltry payments remain, to date, without compensation for their losses.

Although the request for inspection did not deliver the justice that was hoped for, it nonetheless provided a platform for global scrutiny of the LDSP and raised the profile of the community's struggle. The process garnered media attention that exerted pressure on the World Bank to halt further support for the project. The most significant outcome of the inspection request process, however, was the focus, energy, and solidarity it galvanized. Community members found a collective voice to launch opposition to powerful government and international financial actors who threatened to destroy their homes. The panel acknowledged "the concerns and efforts of SERAC for exhibiting such courage in defending the rights of the affected people during the past regime in Nigeria."

### Bulldozers, Resistance, and Human Rights Advocacy

The relative calm that prevailed in the community following the successful challenge of the LDSP was disrupted in July 2003 when the democratically elected government of Lagos State launched fresh efforts to forcibly evict the Badia community. On July 24 the governor of Lagos State, Bola Ahmed Tinubu, paid an unscheduled visit to Badia during which he issued an ultimatum to the residents to vacate their homes within forty-eight hours or be forcibly evicted. On July 29 a demolition squad from the Lagos State Environmental and Special Offences Enforcement Unit, escorted by heavily armed policemen, destroyed a strip of the Oke-Eri settlement in Badia. They pulled back momentarily after meeting vehement physical resistance from the youth and women of the community.

On the assumption that a democratically elected government, in contrast to a military junta, would be amenable to the rule of law and the authority of the courts, SERAC filed a lawsuit, *Adewale v. The Governor of Lagos State*, on August 1 on behalf of Badia residents.[43] The lawsuit sought to enforce the residents' fundamental rights and to secure an injunction restraining the authorities from continuing with evictions pending the resolution of the lawsuit. On August 19 the judge granted leave to the applicants to seek enforcement of their fundamental rights. The order of leave was then served on the respondents, which included the Ministry of Justice.

In outright disregard of this order of leave, the Lagos State government mobilized its demolition machine on October 19 and, without warning, attacked Badia. A lineup of bulldozers backed by heavily armed policemen destroyed houses and other structures, leaving over three thousand people, mostly women and children, homeless. But the state had grossly underestimated community members' resolve to keep their homes.

At this point in the campaign SERAC launched a major international advocacy initiative to halt further evictions in Badia. When it seemed clear that the state government was determined to follow through with its threat to demolish the entire community, SERAC called for a protest march to send a strong signal of the community's will to resist further evictions. On December 3, the Commonwealth Summit of Heads of States and Governments opened in Abuja, Nigeria's federal capital. On the same day in Lagos, SERAC led a peaceful protest march of the Badia residents comprising men and women, the aged, youth, and children. Thousands of residents from ten other slum communities joined the protest in solidarity with Badia, all carrying placards and chanting songs demanding justice for the poor. Over twenty-five civil society organizations also participated in the march. At about 7:30 A.M. the protesters besieged the road and gates leading to the offices of the state governor. More than ten thousand people assembled to demand that the eviction of Badia be halted. Overwhelmed by the number and vehemence of the protesters, the state governor immediately announced a moratorium on further evictions pending the outcome of a dialogue, which was launched at a meeting held that day between heads of various state government ministries, community representatives, and SERAC officials.

## In Search of Sustainable Solutions

In a rather dramatic turn of events, SERAC's research revealed that a significant portion of the Badia lands, including the areas frequently targeted for eviction, was not owned by the Lagos State government; rather, it had been acquired by Nigeria's federal government for the use and benefit of the Nigeria Railway Corporation as far back as 1929. The fact that federal authorities were well aware, in 1973, of their ownership of a large portion of Badia lands helps explain their decision to relocate the Oluwole evictees to Badia that year. The finding that the state government did not own Badia lands profoundly altered the subsequent course of events.

In a SERAC-backed petition to the federal minister of housing and urban development, Badia residents narrated the story of their suffering at the hands of the Lagos State government for more than three decades. They blamed the federal government for forcibly evicting them from their original villages in 1973 and relocating them to Badia without legal protection, security of tenure, or decent and habitable homes and environment. They demanded immediate action by the federal government to remedy this enduring violation of their human rights. In particular, the residents demanded the minister's intervention to have the Lagos State government desist from harassment and threats of demolition of their homes. They also demanded that the state government clarify titles to Badia's land in order to forestall future threats of evictions. In an uncharacteristically swift reaction, the federal minister of housing notified the state government of the ministry's longstanding legal ownership of the Badia land and directed it to keep away from Badia.

The federal minister also accepted responsibility to upgrade and redevelop the community for the benefit of its residents. In furtherance of this commitment, the federal government appointed urban planning and development consultants to undertake feasibility studies and prepare technical plans for Badia's redevelopment. Under the community's close scrutiny and hands-on engagement, the consultants instituted an inclusive and participatory technical committee comprising all stakeholders, including representatives of the various sections of the community as well as SERAC. Regular town-hall meetings were held to provide residents an opportunity to ask questions, request information, or contribute to the debates and discussions of the proposed plans.

Meanwhile, in 2006, the Lagos State government embarked on a $200-million urban upgrading project, the Lagos Metropolitan Development and Governance Project (LMDGP), funded by the World Bank.[44] The project was designed to increase sustainable access to basic urban services through investments in critical infrastructure such as solid waste management, drainage construction, and rehabilitation in nine target slum communities, including Badia. So far, the project's planning process and governance framework appear to have drawn useful lessons from the failures of its predecessor, LDSP.

Community members remain cautiously optimistic that the LMDGP will succeed and that the new infrastructural facilities envisaged under it will be responsibly delivered. However, they have left nothing to chance, as they have established local monitoring and response systems designed to collect, analyze, and use information that can safeguard the community's interests. They are also collaborating with other LMDGP target communities to ensure that the project is carried out in accordance with its founding objectives and the World Bank's operating policies and guidelines, as well as their basic human rights. Badia is a founding member of the Lagos Marginalized Communities Forum (LAMCOFOR), an umbrella body that aims to unite and advance the welfare of its members through policy dialogue, program monitoring, solidarity activities, and collective self-help. Established in 2007 under SERAC's auspices, LAMCOFOR now has over thirty-five Lagos informal settlements as members. It is currently seeking affiliation with major international federations of slum-dwellers to further expand its network and political clout.

In its continuing search for sustainable solutions, the community is working with SERAC and several local and international development partners to explore the feasibility of undertaking a social housing program alongside the proposed redevelopment of the community. Proposed as an innovative and integrated program, it comprises four interrelated components: economic development, including job creation, skills acquisition, microcredit, and savings; housing, including the renovation and construction of new durable and affordable homes; social development and cohesion; and health and the environment.

A social housing program in Badia will help community members identify pragmatic approaches to challenges posed by housing shortages and the urban environment. It will make concrete the idea of housing as a human right, by helping community members secure government investment, private sector partnerships, and market opportunities to build their community. It will also foster a shared sense of community among landlords, tenants, and squatters alike through joint participation in housing and savings cooperatives.

Most importantly, a social housing program could help provide a framework for addressing the critical issue of access to land in the community. Such a program may mitigate the fierce competition for land by focusing on a social creation and distribution of housing stock based on clearly defined and agreed-on criteria. For example, within the context of the proposed redevelopment of the community, rather than parcel out portions of land to individuals, large sectors might be vested to groups of residents in innovative forms of housing ownership such as housing cooperatives, which residents can hold, develop, and manage in their common interests. Other models of housing development and management, which disrupt existing formalistic and individualized modes of land use, ownership, and titling, may also be explored in order to secure the right of marginalized people like the residents of Badia to a home.

When Felix Morka presented this contribution at the Stones of Hope meeting in May 2008, Duncan Kennedy raised several questions and set forth several possibilities for the Ijora-Badia community. What follows is based on his questions and comments at that meeting and on further exchanges between the two authors.

## Commentary on Anti-eviction and Development in the Global South

Duncan Kennedy

Land occupied by low-income people in the cities of the global South is sometimes potentially valuable for strong economic actors, who could make large profits if they could demolish the existing housing and appropriate the land for another use, typically middle- or upper-income housing, commercial development, or expansion of industrial or port facilities. Since this is not an intuitively obvious fact, it seems worthwhile to dwell for a moment on the reasons for it.[45]

Residential segregation by income class is characteristic of much, although not all, urban housing all over the world, so the relevant units for understanding land values are usually neighborhoods.[46] A city that decades or just years ago was relatively small and compact likely had some low-income neighborhoods in close proximity to middle-income and/or upper-income neighborhoods, to the original commercial center, and to whatever industrial sites existed. Low-income neighborhoods were often located on terrain that was undesirable because it was swampy or hilly, or close to polluting uses, or subject to flooding, and therefore more expensive to develop for middle- or upper-income uses than other land, often nearby. In port cities, low-income neighborhoods were often close to the water, not far from port facilities.

Because cities in the global South have been growing rapidly for decades, land use patterns often look very different today than they did at earlier points in the city's development. Land that was once obviously undesirable because of peripheral location or topography may become eminently developable once it has been surrounded by higher-value commercial, residential, or industrial uses.[47] A second important aspect of the situation is that a poor neighborhood in a once undesirable but now desirable location, even with woefully inadequate infrastructure, is likely to be attractive to low-income in-migrants looking for cheap housing close to jobs and to informal commercial opportunities in the developing center. (A third factor is that sometimes poor neighborhoods turn out to be located on top of mineral or other extractable resources.[48])

One way to look at this kind of situation is in terms of occupancy rights: will the poor residents be evicted from their poor housing and unserviced neighborhoods or not? But it may be useful to ask a related yet distinct question: who will appropriate the potential surplus, or economic rent, that derives from the current locational desirability of the land in the poor neighborhood?

Again, the potential surplus derives from the difference between what the land would be worth redeveloped and what it is worth in its current slum use. (It should be kept in mind that the current slum value has typically been enhanced by the willingness of poor in-migrants to pay for a central location.) If the poor residents are evicted without compensation by the developer (public or private) and, for example, the developer can sell high-end residential housing there for a price that is double (because of location) what it costs to construct the housing, then the developer makes a one hundred percent profit on his investment.

If the developer has to pay compensation based on the value of the land in its old use, then he will make less profit, and those to whom the compensation is paid get a share. If the developer has to compensate on the basis of the value of the land in its new use, then he will make a profit only on the difference between his cost of construction and the value added to the land by that construction (in other words, only a "normal" entrepreneurial profit).

Who among the occupants of the neighborhood get a share of the surplus depends only partly on the formal legal compensation regime, which could favor, for example, original chiefly titleholders, holders of informal title able to extract payment from the chiefs or the developer, or both. But tenants without legal entitlements, if they are politically organized and able to resist physically so as to make it sensible for the developer to pay them off, may also end up with a share, in the form of relocation allowances.

At the same time, government officials with power to condemn the land, or with control over police or army units that will do the evicting (whether legally or illegally), are in a position to demand a share of the surplus in the form of bribes. A government oriented to development might exact a large part of the surplus from the developer as a tax, and then allocate it to projects that would benefit some and injure others in the population at large. In other words, the distribution of the surplus is only influenced, not determined, by whatever legal regime of formal property rights combined with "takings" law is nominally in force.

Although it is common for economists to see the surplus as a return to landownership, in fact all that is required in order to obtain a share is the *practical power to prevent* the new use of the land. An anti-eviction movement that can organize a community to prevent demolition of a slum neighborhood to make way for high-end residential or commercial development may therefore be in a position to bargain over the surplus as well as occupancy.

To take a simple example, if the movement could negotiate the reallocation of half the land to the new high-value use, it might be able to extract from the developer a share of the surplus that would amply compensate or rehouse the displaced residents while funding significant improvement of conditions in the remaining low-income area.

Of course, the minute a popular movement moves from the straightforward rhetoric of anti-eviction, and contemplates bargaining with the developing forces, a host of complex choices and accompanying problems come to the fore. In the Ijora-Badia case, Felix Morka tells us very little about how the movement conceptualized its demands beyond the demand not to be displaced. SERAC clearly had in the background the idea that the state and federal governments should invest in infrastructure to improve the neighborhoods, and that there should be "social housing."

The approach I describe below might be helpful in connecting the concrete accomplishments of anti-eviction campaigns worldwide (combining community mobilization and international human rights advocacy) with a set of forward-looking proposals about housing and infrastructure. My assumption is that the anti-eviction campaign has been successful enough in blocking displacement so that the private developers, governments, and international institutions involved have decided to negotiate, directly or indirectly.

I emphasize that the ideas that follow are tentative and impressionistic, suggestions for future discussion and nothing more. As well as assuming that the development forces will make concessions, I am going to assume that the community has a representative, along the lines of SERAC and the other organizations described in chapters of this book, that has real autonomy from the developer's side, some claim to popular legitimacy, and significant "capacity" in the sense of legal and technical resources. Legitimacy means that the organization can negotiate stable agreements among the different segments of the community regarding the costs and benefits of bargaining with the development force. Where this is not the case, none of these ideas have much relevance.

One question that could be asked of Morka's account is how SERAC established itself as a legitimate representative of the community. In our discussions of his account, Morka elaborated as follows:

> Regarding the question of how to bring people out of a mode of alienation, distance, to become political agents, to take action to alter their circumstances even if those are created by forces beyond their understanding, and engage with the political process [ . . . ], we saw human rights as a powerful empowerment tool and as a framework for action. At every stage, the process of decision making about tactics and strategies was collective and very inclusive. [ . . . ] But at the essential core of why the Badia people ended up rising up together in a sustainable way to ask for change and win success [ . . . ] is a clear consciousness, progressively building, that you can't be pushed around by the state or even by the World Bank—you just can't be pushed around—you can't take us out of here, because this is our land. Whether or not I have a formal title, I live here; I know that my father and his father lived here. So I'm not going anywhere. And for those who had already been resettled in Badia, the idea was that since you have already moved us here, we're not going anywhere further—what would be the justice of that? Notions of how community residents were treated unfairly became part of the common consciousness, and allowed [them] to start breaching the various divides among the community—ethnic, religious, and socioeconomic.

What I find missing here, and in many similar descriptions, is a concrete description of "the ethnic, religious, and socioeconomic" "divides," and of legitimate and nonlegitimate authority in the community. *Someone* at SERAC must have figured out what the "divides" were, and what moves and gestures would conceivably persuade people to do something together.

Felix highlights the crucial role of human rights as an "empowerment tool and framework for action." But human rights do not define themselves and do not empower of their own accord. Someone has to decide which rights to focus on, what they mean as applied, and how to deal with conflicts and ambiguities of rights within particular contexts.

Whoever makes those decisions surely acts on the basis of complex, explicit or implicit, understandings of local divisions and of preexisting structures of hierarchy, prestige, and domination. Rights rhetoric, moreover, empowers specific actors (lawyers? the more schooled members of the community?) at the expense of others. The universalism of rights rhetoric—its undifferentiated character—may be key to understanding its effectiveness in the face of social divisions, but it has also been in a sense an obstacle to the analysis of the concrete processes by which it operates.

Because I have been associated with the "critique of rights,"[49] I'd like to emphasize that I am not critical of the use of rights rhetoric in contexts like these. I think it is the general structure *of world discursive power* that makes human rights discourse a potentially important mobilizing tool.[50] I don't think it is the validity or intrinsic truth of the discourse that makes it valuable, and for myself, given a choice, I would prefer the rhetoric of socialism (without claiming that it is any more internally coherent). Nonetheless, as time passes, different discursive modes gain and lose hegemonic power. And it would be wrong to say that because one prefers, for instance, socialism as a slogan, one should not use human rights opportunistically. Precisely because it is internally flexible and ambiguous, human rights discourse can serve as the vehicle for projects that might be better described as socialist.

That said, the choice of rights discourse for pursuit of a left project does lead to some quite specific rhetorical dilemmas, as will become apparent as we move from its role as "empowerment" to its role as a "framework for action."

It is basic that the community is bargaining: giving up territory for development in exchange for money and nonmonetary benefits. Many intricate alternative bargaining strategies are likely, ranging, just for example, from selling off a significant border strip adjacent to the higher-value land, to promoting "in-fill" style development designed to spread effects across the whole area without full displacement from any discrete area. Leaving bargaining strategies aside, not because it is not important but because it seems hard to generalize, I will focus on the form of the surplus payment.

At one extreme, the "pure individual property rights" solution would be to have the developer compensate according to the existing takings law of the jurisdiction, presumably paying formal titleholders according to a lost market value formula. A less legalistic but still "rightsy" solution would require the developer to make lump sum compensation to everyone who has suffered a loss through development, whether or not the loss would be cognizable under takings law. A further step along the spectrum would be to measure the compensation not by loss to residents but as a share of the benefits of development, that is, of the surplus. Why settle for mere compensation of losses when the community's organized resistance has put it in the position of a stakeholder? Then it will be necessary to decide how to parcel out the surplus, beyond the compensation of downside losses.

While these solutions are intuitively obvious possibilities, others are regularly proposed in analogous situations. These are more or less "collective" solutions, because they use the money (beyond what is allocated to directly compensating losses) to create a "social housing sector." First, they involve setting up a new institutional actor with strong powers: a community land trust, a community development corporation,[51] a housing authority, or an empowered local government.[52]

Second, these solutions distribute the surplus extracted from the development forces to residents in the form of "limited equity" residential tenure, with restrictions on alienability (the right to transfer ownership) that empower the collective to benefit from increases in housing values while maintaining the affordability of the community as a whole. Social housing means housing that gives residents something less than fee simple (absolute formal title), but something more than the status of mere tenant that they would have under a private landlord or a conventional public housing authority.[53]

Here is where the ambiguity of rights discourse comes in. Suppose that we understand social and economic rights to include property rights, and then conceptualize property rights, as does neoliberal development theory, in terms of secure formal tenure for an individual absolute owner. In this case, rights rhetoric seems to push against bargaining toward what I have called collective solutions. It seems to favor a demand that the state recognize community residents as formal titleholders and then compensate them for lost market value when they give up land for development.[54]

In this perspective it is interesting to note that the Nigerian Land Use Act of 1978 decrees that "all land comprised in the territory of each state shall be held in trust and administered for the use and common benefit of all Nigerians in accordance with the provisions of this Act." The act empowers the state and federal governments to regulate and manage land, by "granting statutory and customary rights of occupancy," and also, more radically, requires government approval for all transfers of rights. From Morka's description it is easy to see how one might mount a neoliberal argument that the act denies the right of property and is a major obstacle to development.

Against this way of looking at it,[55] I would prefer to see the Land Use Act as a mechanism for setting up institutions that recognize that property is "just a bundle of rights," a collection of diverse entitlements and exposures that can be adjusted to whatever the goals of the community might be. This is the dominant Western legal theoretical view sometimes summarized as "the disintegration of property."[56] In addition, it would seem plausible that in constructing these bundles, those who bargain on behalf of the community should take into account how African property arrangements have traditionally recognized "nonabsolute" solutions, such as according household members wide rights to veto transfers by the head of the household that disadvantage them, and giving local chiefs an important role, sometimes analogized to trusteeship, in land allocation.[57]

The strategy of creating a powerful community institution (development corporation, land trust) administering a social housing sector based on limited equity and some restrictions on alienability looks, in this perspective, like a quite conventional way to design property as an institution in the service of community ends. In short, a rhetoric of property rights as social, and not only as economic, rights is available to support more collective or socialist projects for administering whatever surplus the community can extract from the development forces.[58] The Nigerian Land Use Act could be conceived as an aid rather than an obstacle to this kind of strategy, supposing that the community could draw the various governments into the bargaining, and then bind them to whatever reconfiguration of rights emerges.

Now suppose that through some combination of popular mobilization, international human rights advocacy, and savvy negotiation the community has secured access to part of the revenues generated by this specific development. And assume, for the future, that the new organization has used the surplus to build a social housing sector based on limited equity and restraints on alienation. Finally, assume, perhaps most heroically, that the organization, deploying its equity in the social housing, its control of access through restraints on alienation, and whatever regulatory powers it can leverage from the government, maneuvers skillfully to access whatever flow of rents becomes available be-cause of the increased desirability of the location, for both high-value and low-income uses. The question remains how the entity should deploy the funds, beyond the initial creation of social housing.[59]

Here the spectrum of possibilities includes, at one end, monitoring the new housing to ensure good living conditions and avoid either gentrification or a downward spiral, and expanding the social sector when possible. In the middle, the organization could undertake, as a joint venture or by itself, the kind of in-frastructure improvement (water, sanitation, roads, and so on) that central gov-ernments have grievously neglected.

At the extreme, the community could conceive itself as a "mini-develop-mental-state-within-the-state," looking for ways to insert itself into global or local value chains.[60] Here I am influenced by Alice Amsden's description of the way in which a government with some financial leverage can influence eco-nomic activity by offering various kinds of subsidies combined with enforce-able conditionalities (training, local content, and the like).[61]

As an example (and no more than that!), rather than simply contracting for infrastructure on the basis of cost and value, the organization could treat the building of latrines as a development project in its own right, requir-ing the use of local labor and materials along with training and technology transfer to a "local champion," which would receive a subsidy conditioned on its ability to do infrastructure work outside the neighborhood. According to Saskia Sassen, global city development creates new needs for unskilled or semi-skilled labor and small-scale entrepreneurship.[62] Perhaps the organiza-tion could exploit the cost advantage provided by central location and social housing to train and then provide labor and enterprise to meet these needs.

Of course, there are many objections to any such scheme, some of which are highly persuasive. Indeed, there are even objections to the first step of trying to formally empower a local community to control its housing patterns. That the approach is usually utopian, however, doesn't mean that it is always utopian; where it could work, it seems to me, there is a lot to gain from experiment, given the alternatives.

To conclude this comment, I will respond, tentatively, to one very plausible objection: to the extent a community succeeded in using extracted surpluses to improve local housing, it would attract in-migrants who would dissipate the gains through overcrowding and social dislocation. The only reasonable re-sponse seems to be to erect a barrier to in-migration, thereby risking turning the experiment into yet another means to exacerbate the social and economic inequalities that groups like SERAC set out to remedy in the first place.[63]

To put it bluntly, I am in favor of the community adopting policies that will seriously limit, without eliminating, the in-migration of groups whose numbers and poverty would threaten the whole enterprise. The means to this kind of limited exclusion is the vigorous enforcement of zoning, housing codes, and occupancy limits, in other words the means that local elites all over the global South already use to retain the elite character of their neighborhoods.[64] These policies have a violent aspect, since their enforcement against squatters inevitably requires the plausible threat of police force.

The boundary involved need not be impermeable. If the strategy works, community development will generate jobs and also construction of new housing deliberately allocated to low-income in-migrants, perhaps targeted to potential small entrepreneurs subsidized by surplus extraction and supported by the relatively high value of low-income housing near the center. A slow-moving upward spiral, without gentrification or displacement of existing residents, should generate opportunities for in-migrants without the danger of a downward spiral that would be posed by uncontrolled open access to the area.

But more generally I would respond to this argument by refusing, at least provisionally, to adopt the perspective of the whole. Radical poverty is a world problem, and even more striking, it is a world *system* problem, meaning that it is generated through the interrelation of the parts of the transnational, global economic system, by relations between as well as within nations.[65] The only way to respond to the problem from the point of view of the whole is through institutional reform at both the national and the transnational levels, as for example through international labor standards.

I don't think, however, that we should just accept either the view that nothing can be done short of national or transnational institutional reform, or the view that the only kinds of programs that are morally acceptable are those without barriers that exclude outsiders. Under those constraints, my sense is that there is very, very little that the slum dwellers of the global South could do to improve their situation.

Fluidity between the subnational, national, and international orders is a deep problem with regard to all development strategies. What I am proposing is to structure access to an asset that derives from popular resistance to eviction in a way that gives nonabsolute residential rights in social housing, but also the potential of strong executive direction, to a local definition of "the community." For example, Badia would make the decision to sell a strip at the border between itself and a richer neighborhood, and use the money for some combination of social housing and latrines for the neighborhood, designing the whole as a development strategy as well as a housing strategy.

Regulating the community so that the wealth that has been created won't be dissipated seems to me acceptable, even if not desirable in the abstract. The ultimate objective is to build virtuous circles that expand the local pie in dynamic and elastic ways. Refusing to defend the accomplishments of creative reform through some kind of formal or symbolic boundary is likely to lead to the opposite—a downward spiral. I do not believe you can have any form of development if you start out with the premise that nothing can be done unless it is universally accessible.

## Chapter 2

# Cultural Transformation, Deep Institutional Reform, and ESR Practice

## South Africa's Treatment Action Campaign

William Forbath, with assistance from
Zackie Achmat, Geoff Budlender, and Mark Heywood

Shortly after ratifying their nation's first democratic constitution in 1996, South Africans began fighting the HIV/AIDS pandemic—and fighting about it. Many called the pandemic the "new Apartheid," bringing forth another great collective struggle and a divisive contest deeply shaped by the past. Today the pandemic afflicts millions of South Africans. About five million are infected with HIV[1]; roughly 600,000 now suffer from AIDS. And each day, hundreds die from AIDS-related illnesses. Because of HIV/AIDS the life expectancy of today's South Africans is fifty-one, thirteen years less than in 1990. These numbers would not be so vast had Western pharmaceutical companies and South Africa's new democratic government acted responsibly in the 1990s and early 2000s. But the numbers would be worse today, and the future bleaker, had the corporations and government not been challenged and their policies transformed by a remarkable social rights struggle led by the Treatment Action Campaign.

The Treatment Action Campaign (TAC) was founded in Cape Town on Human Rights Day 1998 by a handful of gay rights activists, most of them, like the group's leader, Zackie Achmat, also veterans of the anti-apartheid movement. Growing into a social movement and NGO that melded grassroots organizing with mass protests and media, lobbying, and litigation campaigns at the national and international levels, TAC captured the imaginations of human rights and AIDS activists around the world with its inspired battle against international pharmaceutical companies to bring down drug prices and allow the importing of cheap generics to treat HIV/AIDS patients in South Africa. TAC has drawn its rank and file mainly from urban black South Africans, most of them HIV-positive young women and men, mostly poor and unemployed though with secondary schooling. But TAC's organization and networks of support cut broadly across racial and ethnic, class, and occupational lines, drawing in great numbers of healthcare professionals, university students, and journalists. During the first decade of the new democratic South Africa, TAC, most observers agree, became the African National Congress (ANC)[2] leadership's most vexatious, astute, and visible loyal (though militant) opposition. Since South Africa's first democratic elections in 1994, the ANC has commanded a supermajority of votes. No effective opposition party has emerged. Instead, social movements, civil society organizations, the judiciary, and the press have been the key sites of opposition politics; and TAC has bridged them.

In the process, TAC has learned some lessons about creative social rights advocacy. In this chapter we focus on two undertakings. The first concerns the 2002 Constitutional Court decision, *Minister of Health v. Treatment Action Campaign* and its aftermath. The decision ordered the government to provide antiretroviral treatment (ARVT) in the public healthcare system to prevent mother-to-child transmission of HIV. The aftermath concerned the struggle for a national treatment plan for all South Africans with HIV/AIDS. We use the litigation and aftermath to explore the challenges of linking rights advocacy inside the courts to advocacy in myriad other arenas and of using judicial recognition to help bring social rights to earth in the form of actual social provision. TAC has used litigation sparingly in the service of many-sided strategies to prod government to change state policies, to open up policy-making processes, and to fashion and implement robust and democratic programs of social provision. Court victories are not the object of movement campaigns but one of several sources of political leverage and moral authority to promote pro-poor policy changes and institutional reforms.

To help draw out the distinctive features of this politics-centered approach to ESR advocacy, we contrast it with two other, stylized models or ideal types of advocacy: (1) a court-centered model, in which judicial victories are the main objective and determine the other elements of movement strategy, and (2) a decentralized, grassroots empowerment model that links the "local" and the "global" planes of antipoverty and social rights advocacy while avoiding serious, sustained engagement with national policy making, state institutions, or national political organizations. Both grassroots empowerment and international collaborations have proved essential to TAC, as this chapter will make clear. But hewing only to local and international action seems chronically insufficient. Shunning national political action and large-scale national institutions in favor of "glocalization," we think, risks making social rights advocacy a kind and gentle reflection of the neoliberal outlook and policies that social rights advocates oppose.

"Glocalization," in South Africa and elsewhere, comes in both soft neoliberal and ultra-left varieties. The first spurns "politics" and alliances with state officialdom and large-scale national organizations aiming to influence state policy, because it regards the state and political institutions as hopelessly inefficient and corrupt. The second spurns them as "instruments of capitalist domination." The latter view finds many proponents among leaders of South Africa's landless people, shack dwellers, and anti-eviction and antiprivatization movements and organizations. For them, TAC's critical engagements—sometimes assailing but sometimes cooperating—with the ANC government are a betrayal of social-movement radicalism.

Our second case study looks at TAC's Treatment Literacy Campaign. Treatment literacy programs aim to empower people with HIV/AIDS by teaching them about the biomedical workings of HIV and AIDS, of antiretroviral (ARV) medicines and their side effects, and about opportunistic infections and the illnesses accompanying AIDS. Such programs can supply a common ground between public health administrators and policy makers, on the one hand, who need ways to get HIV/AIDS patients to take responsibility for their own care, and civic associations of people living with HIV/AIDS, on the other, who need an ongoing institutional basis for promoting individual and collective dignity and empowerment. TAC's Treatment Literacy Campaign has wedded scientific and medical literacy with lessons about safe sex and women's rights, about the social rights provisions in the South African Constitution and the meaning of rights to healthcare, dignity, and equality in the context of the HIV/AIDS pandemic. The campaign has empowered poor and physically and spiritually debilitated South Africans with HIV/AIDS to participate in and make demands for their own treatment and care—and to remake themselves into rights-bearing members of local communities, activist organizations, and larger publics with a stake in the future of South Africa's healthcare and social policies. By holding countless treatment literacy workshops, not only in hospitals and clinics but in schools, churches, union halls, and workplaces, TAC also succeeded in providing tens of thousands of South Africans with a new and richly informed public vocabulary for understanding and reckoning with the pandemic.

Treatment literacy was a double necessity in South Africa. With a minister of health espousing poverty reduction and garlic-and-beetroots soup as a sufficient national response to HIV/AIDS, and a president loudly doubting the disease's sexual transmission and the efficacy of antiretroviral medicines, it became imperative to supply South Africans of all races and classes with knowledge to make their own personal and political choices. At the same time, finding a way to administer an arduous lifelong treatment regimen of ARV medicines for hundreds of thousands of poor South Africans through a rickety, understaffed public health system's far-flung clinics demanded novel ways to make patients active, knowledgeable participants in their own healthcare.

We recount the Treatment Literacy Campaign here because we think it holds out promise as a model for methods of education, outreach, and institutional reform that will help equip and enable the "clients" of social programs to participate in reforming and reshaping local state institutions and wider systems of social provision. The campaign provides a study in institutionalizing social rights while maintaining political vigor, via movement-based and movement-linked agents and practices in institutional design.

Finally, the Treatment Literacy Campaign's trajectory also illustrates our argument about the limits of "glocalization." We will see that TAC fashioned its first treatment literacy groups in collaboration with the international NGO Médecins Sans Frontières (MSF) (Doctors Without Borders). MSF wanted to show what AIDS experts doubted: that a rickety public health system in sub-Saharan Africa could support—and that poor African patients could adhere to—an ARV regime. MSF supplied a handful of doctors and funds to outfit one urban and a few rural clinics. TAC provided local knowledge, organizational savvy, and volunteers to lead treatment literacy and support groups. Here was "glocalization" in action, asking and getting nothing from the national public health system but permission to launch the modest experiment at MSF's expense.

Four years out, the MSF/TAC experiment was working. Calls for "scaling up" the MSF/TAC model began to ring out, and MSF closed up shop; it was not in the "scaling up" business. Government, however, remained obdurately opposed to any public provision of ARVs, and TAC continued to campaign against that opposition.

Vouchsafing the basic right to HIV/AIDS treatment to the hundreds of thousands who needed it required several more years of action and engagement at the national level, which the decentralized model of antipoverty and social rights advocacy studiously avoids. Painstaking and pragmatic national action ultimately enabled TAC to put community- and clinic-based ARVT at the heart of South Africa's HIV/AIDS program, treatment literacy groups being a key element. The lesson is simple and pointed. Grassroots empowerment and mobilization was essential; so was international support. But sustained action on all three levels—the local and the global, but also the national—was necessary to begin bringing this particular bundle of social rights to earth.

## Minister of Health v. Treatment Action Campaign: A Pragmatic, Politics-Centered Approach to Social Rights Advocacy and Litigation

Social rights are the stepchildren of the rights family. Many thoughtful advocates and scholars believe that precious little can be gained by bringing them to court. Seeking judicial vindication of social rights claims, they insist, diverts thought and energy from more fruitful ways of attacking denials of social needs and aspirations. Winning judicial vindication brings little change in actual social provision and tends to legitimate ongoing deprivations. We don't belittle these arguments and experiences, but we think there are often ways to use litigation to help bring about substantial change by putting litigation into the service of political and social movement strategies outside the courts.

Let's call this a politics-centered approach to rights advocacy and contrast it with a court-centered model. A classic example of the latter comes from outside the social rights arena, in the NAACP battle to win judicial condemnation of the United States' segregated public schools. The NAACP did not ignore other battlegrounds. But harsh political constraints combined with outlook and ideology led the organization to put judicial victories at the center of its strategy, ahead of politics or movement-building, which were subordinate to getting the nation's high court to declare segregation unconstitutional. The Supreme Court's 1954 decision in *Brown v. Board of Education* did so and directed lower courts to follow suit. But remedies famously fell short; most often, nothing changed. Or rather, nothing changed until a decade after *Brown*, when massive and violent resistance to desegregation in the U.S. South combined with a burgeoning grassroots civil rights movement (which courted and bore the brunt of that violence), compelling the nation's lawmakers into action against the segregated schools and social institutions of the South. Even then, however, the NAACP's court-based strategy of orchestrating desegregation of U.S. schools fell tragically short of providing equal education.

South Africa's anti-apartheid legal advocates found inspiration and guidance from the NAACP on the craft of framing "test cases." Even so, during the

1980s anti-apartheid campaigns, anti-apartheid attorneys like Geoff Budlender departed from the classic NAACP approach insofar as they often put litigation at the service of political mobilization strategies. Working with Budlender, TAC has carried forward the craft lessons of the classic civil rights organization; but in many ways, TAC's approach to rights advocacy in South Africa in the 2000s has been the opposite of the NAACP's in the 1950s and 1960s. Thus, TAC's chief sphere for rights claims has been the polity. Movement- and coalition-building, policy proposals and political initiatives, publicity and lobbying campaigns: all these have been forged ahead of litigation strategy, and the latter has been subordinate to them. "Rights talk," however, has been no less central to TAC than it was to the NAACP; TAC has cast its case for the right to healthcare for people with HIV/AIDS in broad social-democratic and participatory- and deliberative-democratic constitutional terms—combining a bold politico-constitutional case with a narrowly crafted legal-constitutional strategy.

In large measure, this difference is a product of circumstances. The South African Constitution forthrightly sets out a host of social rights, including the right to healthcare; it declares that the rights entail affirmative governmental duties, and it makes them justiciable. What is more, South Africa's ANC government has acknowledged, in principle, its obligations to undertake broad provision of social goods. Social rights advocates in the "new South Africa" are also situated differently from the NAACP in the 1950s and 1960s; unlike the NAACP, they don't speak for a disenfranchised racial minority. Poor, overwhelmingly nonwhite South Africans without access to adequate social provision are an enfranchised but dispossessed majority, bearing the brunt of the government's efforts to abide by the strictures of corporate elites and global financial institutions. Hewing to neoliberal economic policies, hoping for "redistribution through growth," the ANC-led government has felt compelled to shortchange many of its founding commitments to the most vulnerable. In this context the need is not for bold, new constitutional principles like the one announced in *Brown v. Board of Education*; it is for large, bold changes on the ground and for judicial interventions that help stir and catalyze them. TAC, as we are about to see in more detail, has chosen to use litigation in the service of many-sided strategies rather than as the object of movement campaigns. It has chosen to use court victories as but one important source of political leverage and moral authority to promote pro-poor policy changes and institutional reform.

In the mid-1990s, just before TAC's founding, came important breakthroughs in HIV/AIDS medicine, allowing simple, effective treatment for preventing mother-to-child transmission (PMTCT). At its founding, in 1998, TAC announced its first programmatic objective: demand for a government program for PMTCT. In an initial show of cooperation that year, TAC and the government issued a joint statement naming drug prices as a major barrier. Thus, lobbying, litigation, and publicity aimed against the manufacturers of antiretroviral (ARV) medications promised to be the heart of TAC's PMTCT campaign and of the broader battle for ARV treatment for South Africans with HIV/AIDS. Drawing on the precedent of divestment campaigns during the anti-apartheid struggle, TAC used international networks of human rights organizations to pressure corporations; only now the targets were the multinational pharmaceutical companies, or "big pharma." Some of these human rights organizations, such as Oxfam, were familiar players during the anti-apartheid era.

Also on hand from the anti-apartheid era was a grammar of symbolic action via civil disobedience. The defiance campaigns of the 1960s and 1980s provided a resonant script for TAC leader Zackie Achmat's public defiance of the national and international legal bars to importing generic drugs. In this highly visible fashion, TAC tried, unsuccessfully, to press the government to invoke the emergency provisions that would trigger exemptions from the World Trade Organization's Trade-Related Aspects of Intellectual Property Rights agreement, or TRIPS, which would have allowed the government to license production of generic ARV medicines. Pfizer, as the manufacturer of the wildly expensive, life-saving medicine whose generic counterpart Achmat illegally brought into the country, became the subject of an international public outcry, while South African pharmaceutical associations became the targets of international mobilization, national protest, and litigation.[3]

In late 1999 a second front opened, this one against the government.[4] The emergence of a denialist outlook in government circles led to resistance and delay on the government's part, even as TAC's efforts against big pharma met with some significant success, and HIV/AIDS drugs became more affordable and accessible. Denialism wove together many strands of culture and ideology. One was "dissident" science originating in the United States and Canada, holding that the evidence linking HIV to AIDS, which the overwhelming majority of the scientific and medical community found compelling, was bogus and unpersuasive; that the AIDS epidemic in Africa was more likely a constellation of many illnesses and the result of many causal factors, including malnutrition and poverty; and that scarce medical resources were ill spent on antiretroviral drugs, which were called dangerous, even toxic.

Another strand was African nationalist and anti-imperialist, postcolonial thinking, which heard in mainstream medical and public health approaches to the HIV/AIDS epidemic in Africa echoes of colonial and apartheid rule: racist stereotypes and stigmas about "savage" and "promiscuous" "African sexuality"; a yoking together of "black Africans" with homosexuals, drug users, and sex workers—a universe of despised and deviant "others"; and finally, brutal memories of experimentation with dangerously toxic drugs on African subjects. Against this backdrop, it was easy to see the promotion of ARV medications as profiting Western drug manufacturers and injuring Africans, while ignoring the sociohistorical roots of the epidemic in apartheid's generations of poverty and neglect.

Perhaps it should be no surprise, then, that this outlook took hold among a significant portion of the ANC leadership. Although it flouts overwhelming evidence that HIV and AIDS are causally linked and that antiretroviral drugs save lives, it gathers support from the bitter historical experiences of racist medical "science" and brutal treatment of black South Africans at the hands of white public health officialdom. It also resonates with popular unease and resistance toward the sexual and gender issues raised by HIV/AIDS, and with well-earned popular mistrust of "Western medicine," "white doctors," and big pharma, as well as with the durable faith of many South Africans in traditional healers, who are free of these distressing associations. Denialism from above has tapped into and bolstered popular forms of AIDS denial from below, those fueled by stigma and shame—driving AIDS sufferers out of families and communities—and by popular "white conspiracy" theories.

Nelson Mandela shunned the topic of denialism during his presidency. The Mbeki-ites, however, vocally embraced it. Peter Mokaba, an Mbeki lieutenant and ANC leader, wrote, a few months before dying of AIDS himself, "The story that HIV causes AIDS is being promoted through lies, pseudo-science, violence. . . . We refuse to be agents for using our people as guinea pigs and have a responsibility to defeat the intended genocide and dehumanization of the African family and society." Lashing out at the bigotry that equates blacks with promiscuity and portrays Africans as diseased, poor, and begging the West for aid, Mokaba's long manifesto concluded:

> Yes, we are sex crazy! Yes, we are diseased! Yes, we spread the deadly HIV through uncontrolled heterosexual sex! In this regard, yes, we are different from

the US and Europe! Yes, we the men, abuse women and the girl-child with gay abandon! Yes, we do believe that sleeping with young virgins will cure us of AIDS! Yes, as a result of all this, we are threatened with destruction by the HIV/AIDS pandemic! Yes, what we need, and cannot afford because we are poor, are condoms and anti-retroviral drugs! Help![5]

Mbeki was more controlled and eloquent making the same point in a 2001 lecture at Fort Hare University, South Africa's leading historically black university:

And thus it happens that others who consider themselves to be our leaders [Achmat and TAC] take to the streets carrying their placards . . . convinced that we are but natural born, promiscuous carriers of germs, unique in the world, they proclaim that our continent is doomed to an inevitable mortal end because of our unconquerable devotion to the sin of lust.[6]

For Mbeki, then, "dissident" HIV/AIDS science resonated with Africanist pride and rage and with revulsion at racism garbed as medical science, and it buoyed resistance to the vast fiscal burdens of taking on broad ARVT for millions of South Africans. Hundreds of millions of rands for ARV drugs were hundreds of millions less for other social programs in a context of neoliberal fiscal constraint, in which Mbeki was constantly fending off demands for more spending. Thus, Mbeki's finance minister, Trevor Manuel, condemned what he called "the medicalisation of poverty": "The rhetoric about the effectiveness of antiretrovirals is a lot of voodoo, and buying them would be a waste of limited resources." Better to spend on fighting the poverty that makes South Africans vulnerable, the Mbeki-ites believed. *Better to spend on the healthy than on the sick and dying* was the not-so-hidden subtext of many of their AIDS pronouncements. And so, steely economic "realism" melded with bitter historical memories and racial and sexual rage to produce wildly dysfunctional, deadly policies.

Mingled with the Mbeki-ites' lunatic dissident science and the denialist current in official circles were genuine cautions about costs, risks, safety, and capacity to implement ARVTs, and even the simple form of PMTCT. Thus, in late 1999 and early 2000 TAC waited with some patience for the outcome of a local South African trial of the simplest Nevirapine regime for PMTCT.[7] The local trial's preliminary results were heartening. At the same time, by virtue of persistent mobilizations and pressure from TAC and its international allies, the manufacturer of Nevirapine, Boehringer Ingelheim, offered to supply the drug at no cost to the South African public health system for five years.[8] Still the government resisted rolling out a PMTCT treatment program, invoking arguments of complexity and institutional capacity (ironically echoing Western "experts" who long doubted the capacity of "third-world and developing" nations to responsibly administer and use ARVT for HIV/AIDS). Here the government's position—lamenting the high cost of ARV drugs, making Nevirapine available in a handful of pilot sites, but deferring full-scale rollout of a PMTCT program while it gathered "more information" about matters like "resistance" (drug-resistant strains bred by inconstant drug regimens) and needed infrastructure—was not obviously unreasonable. On its face, this was the kind of complex policy judgment that courts are loathe to overturn. Thus, TAC pursued a painstakingly patient path to court, tenaciously accumulating and disseminating medical and scientific evidence, repeatedly calling on government to hasten—and make transparent—its decision-making processes, while persistently dramatizing the human toll of procrastination. This patient and multifaceted approach may have been essential in generating broad agreement among many of South Africa's elites (business, professional, trade union, academic, and media) outside the ANC hierarchy that the government's PMTCT policies were in fact morally and medically indefensible. This tack surely was important for the courts' readiness to rule against the government and order the rollout.

Although it resumed preparations for litigation against the government in July 2000, once more TAC paused on the path to court, this time to await registration of Nevirapine by South Africa's Medicines Control Council (MCC) to avoid the issue of "off-label" use of the drug for PMTCT and to avoid framing litigation around demand for AZT, which was registered but entailed a more complex course of treatment.[9] Meanwhile, TAC renewed and intensified its campaign for a nationwide PMTCT program in the media and in civil society via public discourse, debate, demonstrations, and protests, keeping in the public eye the results of manifold tests and pilot programs of Nevirapine for PMTCT and the intransigence and resistance-to-reason of government decision makers.[10]

After the MCC registration process was completed, the protests, framed around denial of constitutional rights to life and health, grew increasingly militant. TAC activists occupied government offices. Achmat confronted the minister of health face-to-face in a tense televised public meeting. The government, TAC charged, was bringing about needless deaths—hundreds each month—

killing the children of the poor; the government had no more justification for denying the right to treatment.[11] A poster appeared on township and city walls, juxtaposing the iconic photograph of a teenage boy carrying a younger brother, who had been killed by the security forces during the 1976 Soweto uprising, with a photo of another teenager carrying a younger sibling, felled by AIDS. Achmat and TAC were rekindling charged and bitter memories of apartheid, adapting the cultural forms and practices—the songs, chants, funeral marches, defiance campaigns, and mass demonstrations—that were wielded against the white apartheid government in the freedom struggle, and wielding them against the ANC. According to Achmat,

> We could not have mounted TAC a generation later [. . . .] Everyone would have forgotten the steps. Everyone remembered the songs; the women [HIV-positive, urban, black Africans living in townships] remembered the demonstrations for our rights [. . . .] The human rights networks in England and the U.S. we relied on for support were still alive. And the strong links to COSATU [the trade union federation].[12]

Mbeki and ANC spokespeople and ministers assailed TAC as extremist and irresponsible, a tool of big pharma and "Western capitalists." There was much popular anger and mistrust among ANC rank and file against TAC. It was seen as disrespectful of ANC leaders and a troublemaker. But TAC's mobilizations from below—built on the growing base of TAC-run treatment literacy groups and on TAC's coalition-building and education campaigns with COSATU and the churches, bringing union and church activists into the public fray on TAC's side—meant that the government's claims were met by the voices of articulate and outraged poor and working-class black South Africans, largely unemployed women, suffering from HIV/AIDS and demanding ARVT for themselves, their family members, and their children, as well as others who'd lost family and church and union brothers and sisters to the pandemic, and each day watched more wasting away without treatment. Despite Mbeki and the party leadership's suppressing dissent and debate in the ministries and Parliament, here was dramatic evidence that it was not only the "white medical establishment" and "white liberals" who demurred from the popularly elected government's ambivalent, procrastinating HIV/AIDS policies. The mobilizations showed that the policies had generated anger and opposition among the nation's black poor and working classes, whose interests the government claimed to represent and defend in its clashes with TAC.

❖

Culminating months of mobilization, TAC staged rallies and marches around the country and an all-night vigil outside the Pretoria courthouse on November 26, 2001, as hearings opened in the High Court on TAC's suit. The suit challenged the government's policy limiting provision of the ARV drug Nevirapine, for the purpose of preventing mother-to-child transmission of HIV, to a handful of "pilot sites." TAC rank and file in their familiar "HIV Positive" T-shirts, scores of doctors and nurses, and dozens of journalists packed the courtroom for the two days of hearings. Outside the few pilot sites, TAC showed, government was refusing to allow public health service doctors to provide the life-saving drug, even though it had been made available for free and had been found by South Africa's MCC to be safe and effective, and even though a large portion of the clinics and hospitals in the public health system had the capacity to provide HIV testing and counseling.

Three weeks later, the High Court ruled in TAC's favor, finding that this refusal violated the affected mothers' and babies' constitutional social right to basic healthcare. The Court ordered the government to remove the restrictions on Nevirapine, and to develop and implement a comprehensive, nationwide program for PMTCT, including Nevirapine, voluntary testing and counseling, and formula milk (to prevent HIV transmission through breast-feeding). The court, in an exercise of "supervisory jurisdiction," also ordered the government to bring the program back to court for scrutiny by March 31, 2002.

The narrow demand in court, focused on Nevirapine for PMTCT, contrasted with the broader demand for ARVT rollout for all HIV/AIDS sufferers, which TAC was pressing with equal vigor in public political arenas and petitions, protests, proposals, and reports to government. The Nevirapine-for-PMTCT claim was one that enabled the High Court (and later the Constitutional Court) to find a constitutional ESR violation and order a remedy, without "intruding" on more complex policy judgments about resource allocation, basic treatment options, or the public health system's readiness for broader programmatic initiatives. Nevirapine was in use for PMTCT throughout the private sector and at pilot sites; it was available to government at no cost, and the heart of TAC's claim rested on the unreasonableness of the government's prohibiting doctors throughout the public health system from prescribing, in the Constitutional Court's words, a "potentially life-saving" "single dose of Nevirapine at the time of the birth of the child," when the drug is freely "on offer" from its manufacturer.

The High Court's decision was terse in its reasoning. With almost no discussion of constitutional doctrine, the decision is chiefly given over to distilling the many affidavits on both sides. Revealingly, however, the High Court took advantage of the way TAC had crafted its claim to characterize the constitutional violation at hand in terms of a "negative" right: "I am of the view that the policy [of] [ ... ] prohibiting the use of Nevirapine outside the pilot sites in the public health sector is a breach of [government's] negative obligation (see Grootboom's case *supra* at para 34) to desist from impairing the right to health care."

In this one sentence, TAC's painstaking path to court paid off handsomely. Courts and jurists shaped by classical liberal legal traditions are more comfortable with the judicial role of vindicating "negative" rights and liberties over against "positive" ones. Economic and social rights are seen as quintessentially "positive" rights, imposing "affirmative" duties on government, and ill suited for a host of familiar reasons to judicial elaboration and enforcement. Thus, the groundwork TAC and its allies had laid in arenas and settings outside the court—pressing big pharma to a point where the drug was on offer without cost; pressing the health ministry to the point where relevant public facilities were equipped to administer the single-dose regimen; and encouraging the system's physicians to make known they were keen to prescribe it but thwarted by the state from doing so—enabled the High Court to recognize and enforce the "positive" right to basic healthcare while casting the core claim for relief in "negative" terms: government must desist from its wrongful, because "unreasonable," restrictions on healthcare provision that would otherwise be "already there." Of course, this is word play, and patently not true of the aspects of the order that compelled a PMTCT program, with timetables, across the country. But the reassuringly "negative right"—government's duty to desist—rested on the spare way TAC had crafted its core claim. And that, in turn, hinged on the partial victories TAC and its allies (in and out of government) already had won. Far from litigation leading social movement strategy, the political approach TAC adopted involved the two shaping each other, as TAC engaged the institutions and officialdom of the nation-state in persistent and pragmatic ways, finding footholds and allies on a terrain whose complexity the "glocalists" tend to ignore.

Some of this complexity—of opposing interests, ideologies, and political impulses within the state—revealed itself in the government's response to the High Court decision. On one hand, the High Court ruling prompted President Mbeki to declare in a television interview that the provinces should be able to provide PMTCT programs according to their capacities, and those "with the resources to extend the program should not be delayed."[13] Mbeki's declaration was read by many senior ANC politicians as a go-ahead to providing Nevirapine wherever capacity existed or could be created. Thus, the ANC premier of Gauteng, Mbhazima Shilowa, announced a bold rollout of the province's PMTCT program: "[D]uring the next financial year," he said, "all public hospitals and our large community health centres will provide Nevirapine." Nine hospitals would commence the program within the next hundred days.

But for her part, the minister of health was taking a hard line against the High Court's "interference" with executive authority. She assailed the Court for breaching "the principle of separation of powers [ . . . ] [and] interfering in health policy [by] ordering the government to supply a specific medicine." Government would not comply with the court's order but instead would seek leave to appeal directly to the Constitutional Court to save "executive policy-making" from "disarray." While subordinates in her own department had indicated that the Gauteng rollout was authorized, the minister publicly rebuked Premier Shilowa and ordered him to retract his announcement. Shilowa gave the appearance of doing so. Still the Gauteng rollout continued and was widely reported. Much the same occurred in KwaZulu-Natal.

Health Minister Tshabalala-Msimang's rebukes and the government's various appeals from the High Court's orders were lambasted by political cartoonists and editorial writers. TAC mobilized for the case in Constitutional Court, rallying "stand up for your rights" demonstrations in Johannesburg and elsewhere. Then, on April 17, 2002, two weeks before the main hearing in Constitutional Court, the cabinet took South Africa by surprise—and revealed something of the divisions that had begun to open within the high reaches of Mbeki's government—by releasing a statement on HIV/AIDS policy that promised "a universal rollout plan" of ARV treatment for "people living with AIDS [ . . . ] in accordance with international standards" "to be completed as soon as possible."

Against this backdrop, over five thousand TAC supporters marched to the Constitutional Court on May 2, as hearings began. The government vigorously assailed the High Court's order. Three months later, when the Constitutional Court handed down its judgment upholding TAC's claim and issued a bold but different order of its own, the Court had much more to say than the High Court about constitutional economic and social rights and the role of courts, government, and civil society in what the South African Constitution calls the "progressive realization" of those rights. Its unanimous decision rebuffed the government's arguments; it also disappointed many South African human rights advocates who had hoped for broad judicial declarations of the "core" substance and programmatic contours of social rights like the right to health. The Court, we will see, favored a more polity-based, less juristocratic or court-centered conception of the realization of economic and social rights. In this, it seemed to reflect and draw on TAC.

The Constitutional Court's opinion thus offered a vision of judicial collaboration with civil society organizations, on one hand, and government, on the other. Its narrative of the events surrounding the litigation evoked the interplay of politico-constitutional rights claims and legal-constitutional interventions: the first a matter of organizations like TAC backing up their protests and claims of right with the exchange of views, information, and expert opinions between civil society and the state via petitions, proposals, reports, conferences, joint commissions, hearings, and negotiations; the second a matter of the courts keeping the civil society–state exchanges and negotiations open and vital, and prodding and compelling the state when it falls short of its procedural or substantive constitutional duties and commitments. The Court holds out the judiciary as a space for the poor—and the civil society associations representing them—to hold government to account and to rectify government inaction and failure with respect to fashioning adequate ESR programs or translating general ESR legislation, policies, and programmatic commitments into actions and institutions on the ground.

The Court also responded directly to government's arguments that the judiciary violates the separation of powers if it goes beyond finding constitutional fault with government social programs and seeks to enforce such findings by ordering government to take action. Any such court orders, the government argued, would intrude on the policy-making and budget-setting prerogatives of the political branches. The Court spurned this. The ESR provisions of the constitution, it declared, are obligations that "[c]ourts can, and [ . . . ] must enforce." "Particularly in a country where so few have the means to enforce their rights through the courts, it is essential" that rights be "effectively vindicated." Constitutional remedies, including mandatory and structural decrees as well as supervisory jurisdiction, to enforce and monitor the realization of ESR are not "breaches of the separation of powers" but essential tools, notwithstanding that such exertions of judicial power "affect policy as well as legislation" and may have deep "budgetary implications."

These are bold-sounding affirmations, but the Court was equally at pains to stress their limitations, which for the Court go to the ways ESR are defined and the ways they are enforced, and which emphatically put the main burden of change on ESR advocacy *outside* the courts. The South African Constitution states that "everyone has" ESR, and alongside this provides that the "state must take reasonable legislative and other measures, within its available resources, to achieve the progressive realisation of each of these rights." This raises a dilemma. Shouldn't the Constitutional Court, as it decides cases, offer government and civil society at least an outline of the minimum content and meaning of ESR? After all, how do we know whether the government is making adequate progress toward realizing South Africans' ESR without clear constitutional standards that set out what the government must achieve? Surely, the dispossessed and impoverished citizenry are entitled to have the minimum content of their ESR articulated, so that they and their political and legal advocates may more readily hold the government to account. This argument was made by amici—not TAC—in the *TAC* case. The notion of a "minimum core" definition of ESR has been embraced by the UN Committee on Economic, Social and Cultural Rights. The Constitutional Court had rejected this path before, and it does so again in *TAC*. For many human rights advocates in South Africa, the "minimum core" idea embodied the hope that the Court would begin decreeing the substance and programmatic content of ESR.

But instead, the Court in *TAC* reiterated its view that the text of the South African Constitution's social rights provisions will not support the elaboration of a freestanding set of social rights with a core substantive content. Rather, the meaning of the constitution's social rights provisions can't be defined and specified independently of the adjacent language that qualifies those rights, declaring that the state must take reasonable steps to realize those rights "progressively" and "within available resources." The constitutional right, in other words, is access to what the state reasonably can do within its present resources. Even so, the Court could outline the core content of the various social rights, while taking account of resource constraints and the necessary temporality of institution-building. Thus, the Court could supply the polity and government with a blueprint of what the constitution minimally demands, and the blueprint could inform and empower advocacy.

But the Court has embraced a different role. Rather than a set of ESR blueprints, it has chosen to offer only case-by-case, contextualized assessments of the "reasonableness" of challenged ESR policies and programs. Many South

African critics complain that the "reasonableness review" approach, which the Court reaffirms in *TAC*, is a cop-out, a purely procedural or at best highly deferential standard of judicial review that won't seriously question the substantive adequacy of government policies and programs. On this view, the Court simply shied away from the inevitable confrontations with ANC leaders and the risk of backlash that a bolder blueprint-drawing approach would have engendered.

There is surely an element of institutional self-preservation in the way the Court has begun to carve out the judiciary's role in ESR cases. But plainly the Court also thinks—and we agree—that there are sharp limitations to court-driven social transformation. The resources, policies, social alliances, and political will for constructing decent and democratic institutions of social provision must be generated elsewhere; courts can be invaluable partners and catalysts in the process. The *TAC* opinion evokes a very broad conception of the full constitutional reach of ESR and substantive equality guarantees, while at the same time assigning most of the tasks of demanding, charting, and implementing those guarantees to civil society and the public sphere—the Legislature and the Executive.

Constitutional Court justices often repeat the warning sounded by Justice Mokgoro shortly after the *TAC* decision: litigation "tends to be the privilege of the economically empowered"; therefore, a "vigilant civil society" must "agitate for change and monitor implementation" via "more accessible and direct strategies."[14] There is peril in burdening the associations of the poor with tasks that are themselves costly and complex and, like litigation, require tools "of the economically empowered." But this has been TAC's mode: agitation and disobedience, politicking, policy making, and monitoring, while (as we'll see) seeking to empower poor South Africans by democratizing the resources and expertise some of these tasks require—and using litigation in an essential but back-up role.

Still, by the Constitutional Court's own account, there remains the "justiciable" right and the promise that social rights will be "effectively vindicated." Is "reasonableness" review a cop-out? In *TAC*, at least, the Court's reasonableness review of government policy making is neither purely procedural nor deferential; indeed, it is searching and substantive[15]: the Court narrates TAC's efforts outside the courts to press government to fashion and implement a program for PMTCT; the Court highlights the government's own decisions (at TAC's and its allies' prodding) to adopt Nevirapine plus testing, counseling, and other measures for PMTCT; then the Court walks through the reasons government offers for limiting Nevirapine's availability to the pilot sites. The Court is stern and thorough, and finds the reasons wanting. Its assessment of government's biomedical cost-benefit analysis plunges into the biomedical expert debate, and it is withering. True, even a single dose of Nevirapine might induce "resistant strains of HIV," but "this mutation is likely to be transient." Besides, the weight of this possibility "is small in comparison with the potential benefit." "The prospects of the child surviving" absent the treatment "are so slim and the nature of the suffering so grave that the risk [ . . . ] is well worth running."

The Court concluded by ordering the government forthwith to permit doctors throughout the public health system to prescribe Nevirapine for PMTCT treatment for HIV, and to implement a comprehensive PMTCT program throughout the system. Taking note of the government's legitimate concerns that the Nevirapine regimen presented risks and might not be the best alternative, the Court provided that the government could substitute any policy or program that met its social rights obligations to women and infants at risk of HIV transmission.

The Constitutional Court stepped away, however, from the High Court's order that government report back within three months with a PMTCT program, whose adequacy the Court would assess and whose implementation it might preserve jurisdiction to supervise. Noting that the government's PMTCT policies had not stood still during the course of the *TAC* litigation but had grown more responsive and responsible, the Court accepted the bona fides of the government's commitments to implement a PMTCT program throughout the public health system. The Court indicated confidence that TAC would monitor vigilantly the progress of PMTCT treatment implementation across the country; but in retrospect, supervisory jurisdiction would have put greater pressure on the government to comply—and on TAC to maintain a sharp focus on PMTCT implementation, while its energies and resources poured into securing ARVT for all HIV/AIDS patients in the public health system.

The period following the Constitutional Court decision saw uneven and gradual implementation of PMTCT programs throughout the country but also renewed government denialism, rage, and resistance. The *TAC* ruling would prove a crucial resource over the next several years of bitter conflict and halting accomplishments. It dramatized that one branch of the national government decisively rejected the ambivalent, denialist-tinged outlook of Mbeki, the minister of health, and their lieutenants, emboldening reformers within government to reach out to TAC. The decision provided an important incentive for building up a similar public record of nonjudicial efforts to persuade government to institute ARVT for all HIV/AIDS patients in the public health system, on which new litigation could rest. The decision also supplied a credible threat of "going back to court" as well as legal authority in actual litigation, both used to great effect at many stages of the contest for a national treatment program. Finally, much like *Brown v. Board of Education* half a century earlier, the Constitutional Court's judgment in *TAC* provided TAC with what Achmat has called a "legal and moral anchor." "No matter what dark moment we had, we had two major things on our side: one is our constitutional rights which we could always assert, and the other one was that we actually had a judgment [. . . . ] We always could say that we won in the courts."[16] One hears an echo of Martin Luther King Jr., who often declared during dark moments of the civil rights struggle of the early 1960s, "If we are wrong, the Constitution of the United States is wrong. If we are wrong, God Almighty is wrong [. . . . ] If we are wrong, justice is a lie." As we'll see, when TAC returned to the courts along the way—demanding in 2004, for example, that government make public its targets and timetables for implementing the national treatment plan it adopted in late 2003—the judiciary would uphold TAC's demands, reaffirming the moral and strategic support promised in the 2002 decision.

Losing in court on PMTCT seemed to steel Mbeki and his obdurate minister of health's determination during 2002 and most of 2003 to thwart efforts by TAC and the medical and public health professions to bring the health ministry into the essential work of drawing up national HIV/AIDS prevention and treatment plans for the public sector. But TAC forged ahead with widely publicized professional gatherings, reports, and proposals. Thus, after many preliminary workshops with health economists and academic experts and medical practitioners in the HIV/AIDS field, TAC and a host of professional associations organized a large gathering of clinicians from the public and private sectors, and from rural and urban treatment programs run by NGOs, along with medical and public health school academics specializing in HIV/AIDS treatment, to fashion a set of national guidelines on ARV use. TAC and the other hosts invited senior officials from the Ministry of Health, but true to form, they declined. This conference—held in the poor black township of Bredell outside Johannesburg—produced the *Bredell Consensus Statement on the Imperative to Expand Access to Anti-Retroviral Treatment for Adults and Children with HIV/AIDS in South Africa.*[17]

Meanwhile, TAC's allies in the trade union leadership lit on the idea of circumventing the baleful minister of health by drawing important labor department officials into high-level planning for a national HIV/AIDS treatment program. For the first time government dispatched a negotiating team to work with TAC; together with national business and labor leaders, they produced a draft national plan, with agreed-on "targets, timetables, and resources for treatment." As with the Constitutional Court decision, here again a critical line was crossed. Negotiations between TAC and government over the terms of a national treatment plan changed the terrain on which the president, the minister of health, and other die-hard ANC denialists had to do battle.[18]

Now even the ANC denialists' efforts to stymie the process sometimes produced unintended consequences that strengthened TAC's hand. Thus, confronted with the labor department's deliberations with TAC and business and labor leaders, the health minister insisted on a health and treasury joint task team to research "the cost implications" of making ARVs broadly available in the public health system. Waiting for the task team's report served to justify a three-month delay in any cabinet discussion on the use of ARVs. But the tactic backfired, for the task team's report ended up endorsing a broad national rollout of ARVT. Leaked to TAC, the report to the cabinet provided a detailed confirmation by high government officials that a national treatment plan was affordable and necessary. And TAC would soon publicize the report—and the cabinet's efforts to bury it—to support a new round of civil disobedience and to signal the government that it would encounter the task team's report in court, if the government persisted in refusing to adopt a treatment plan.[19]

Collaboration with high state officials was accompanied by grassroots work. TAC participants in the negotiations, like Mark Heywood, kept local branches abreast of the negotiations. Rank-and-file members followed the process carefully, organizing letter-writing campaigns in support of the process and developing what Heywood has called "a sense of ownership in one of South Africa's new democratic institutions."[20]

Out of the negotiations emerged a draft framework for a national plan, its terms agreed on by all sides to the negotiations but still unsigned by the government. As HIV/AIDS denialists and reformers in the government deadlocked on the question, TAC returned to the streets, staging a mass march on the day of President Mbeki's 2003 State of the Nation address. Confrontation seemed essential "because of the growing urgency for access to treatment" as mounting numbers of TAC volunteers along with thousands of others were "becoming sick with HIV-related illnesses."[21] Confrontation also seemed more promising "because TAC was now armed" with the judgment of the Constitutional Court, the draft agreement on a national treatment plan, and the official joint task team report on the affordability of a national rollout of ARVT. A new mood of defiance found expression in a poster framed around a photograph of Mandela wearing an "HIV-Positive" T-shirt and bearing the slogan "Stand Up for Our Lives." A "Treatment Train" brought six hundred activists living with AIDS from Johannesburg to join the fifteen thousand who marched to the gates of Parliament, led by people with HIV/AIDS, religious and trade union leaders, doctors, and healthcare workers. This largest mass mobilization for the right to treatment was met by representatives of Mbeki, the ANC, and Parliament's health and finance committees. The chair of the latter declared that "a march of this size could not be ignored by the ANC."[22]

But it was. Months passed. Deputy President Jacob Zuma met with TAC and hammered out a public statement affirming government's commitment to continue working with TAC on a national treatment plan along the lines agreed to in negotiations. But these talks broke down. Growing numbers of TAC volunteers, including several who had led the march, were dying; their numbers tracked the national toll, which had reached six hundred people dying from AIDS each day. TAC decided, by an overwhelming national convention vote, to turn again to nonviolent civil disobedience, demanding that the government make good on the right to treatment and halt the vast toll of suffering and dying which ARVT would have prevented.[23]

TAC launched the disobedience campaign on March 20, 2003, a day before Sharpeville Day, which commemorates the storied 1961 massacre. Six hundred TAC volunteers, symbolizing the six hundred dying daily, marched to police stations in Sharpeville, Cape Town, and Durban to lay charges of homicide against the ANC ministers of health and trade and industry for failing to prevent the deaths of friends and family members felled by AIDS. At each station, volunteers staged sit-ins and were arrested. Over the next month, TAC staged protests and sit-ins at the Human Rights Commission, the Commission on Gender Equality, and the Departments of Health and of Trade and Industry. TAC demonstrators rallied, and were arrested, at a cocktail party hosted by the minister of health for the CEO of the Global Fund to Fight AIDS, TB and Malaria. Also, for the first time, TAC called for international demonstrations against the South African government. Demonstrators across Europe, the United States, and Asia held protests outside South African embassies, depositing symbols commemorating the deaths of people with HIV/AIDS: empty shoes at the Washington embassy; paper cranes in Tokyo. For the first time, the ANC government found itself the object of public moral censure in the world's capitals.[24]

The homicide charges at the city stations were accompanied by a widely publicized "criminal docket"—a private criminal complaint akin to private prosecution practiced in the United States in the nineteenth century—alleging that "in their capacity as Ministers—both accused [the ministers of health and trade and industry] had the legal duties and powers to prevent 70% of AIDS related deaths during this period through developing a treatment and prevention plan, providing medicines and using their legal powers to reduce the price of essential medicines."

The docket recounted TAC's efforts over the previous years to persuade the government to carry out the "positive duties" imposed by the constitution and affirmed by the Constitutional Court in *TAC*, which if fulfilled would have saved the lives of thousands. Throughout the civil disobedience campaign, TAC plastered the streets and carried on placards and picket signs a volatile poster bearing photos of the two ministers and a large, bold text that read **WANTED—for failing to stop 600 deaths a day**.[25]

While the disobedience campaign involved no more than a few thousand volunteers, its impact was great, producing a political crisis and a plea from Zuma on the government's behalf that TAC suspend the campaign in return for further meetings and a promised consideration by the cabinet's HIV/AIDS advisory panel of TAC's call for a national treatment plan. Achmat and other TAC leaders pushed the decision to suspend the campaign upon a reluctant rank and file, which responded: "You can suspend the campaign, but you cannot suspend our pain!" Rank-and-file delegates ultimately acquiesced on the condition that the suspension be short, and followed by renewed civil disobedience as well as litigation if a national plan was not soon forthcoming.[26]

At this juncture TAC leaked to the South African press the joint task team report to Mbeki's cabinet, which detailed the affordability and necessity of a national treatment plan. This, combined with the threat of litigation and renewed civil disobedience, propelled the government finally to form a task team with the urgent mandate to develop an implementation plan. TAC welcomed the announcement despite the government's exclusion of TAC and its allies in the scientific, clinical, and research communities from the team. With these allies, TAC set about fashioning a "shadow" plan for submission to the government team, highlighting what they feared the government would leave out, namely the centrality of community- and clinic-based ARVT and treatment literacy programs, as these had worked with such remarkable success in the NGO-based clinics, including the MSF/TAC clinics we will explore shortly.[27]

The government's plan materialized a few months later, in November 2003; and it did omit these features. Ironically enough, the plan mimicked the Western HIV/AIDS establishment's emphasis on capital-intensive, hospital-based, specialist-run ARVT centers, leaving most of the nation's far-flung public health system's clinics out of the picture, and with them the hope of bringing ARVT to where poor people lived. Nevertheless, the government's plan set out a reasonably ambitious target of providing ARV therapy to fifty-three thousand people by March 2004 and creating at least one treatment site in every district within the year, and one in every local municipality within five years.[28]

This new phase in South Africa's response to the pandemic brought no respite for TAC but only continuing conflict with the health ministry and treasury over the procrastinating, uneven, ill-led implementation of the new national plan. Implementation became a new theater for the president and minister of health and their followers in government to continue dramatizing the clash between antipoverty programs plus (crackpot) "Africanist" AIDS remedies on one hand, versus "expensive," "racist," "toxic," "Western capitalist" ARVs on the other. Once more, the pandemic proved a tragic stage for government to act out this ambivalent, postcolonial psychodrama.

During 2004, TAC's efforts to prod government to implement the new plan occasioned two more instances of using litigation, or the threat of litigation, as part of broader political strategies. The emergence of a national ARVT plan, however, changed and widened the strategic landscape. For the first time, TAC's attention was riveted on the nitty-gritty details of drug procurement and distribution, and on staffing, salaries, and working conditions of healthcare personnel in the hard-strapped public health system, as it slowly took on the vast new task of treating thousands of South Africans living with AIDS. At the same time, TAC began to address in a more systematic fashion the broader political economy of healthcare, the gross inequalities of resources between the private and public sectors, and the range of institutional reforms needed to make HIV/AIDS treatment effective. Simply put, the new strategic challenge lay in wedding the immediate task of pushing for implementation of the operational plan the government had adopted with the longer-term goal of promoting the broader distributive and democratic reforms in the healthcare system, which seemed essential to TAC. The rollout of a national treatment program, however flawed, created new opportunities to deepen the involvement of TAC volunteers, activists, and treatment literacy practitioners in the public health system, prefiguring the programmatic and institutional reforms TAC envisioned.

In its 2002 decision, the Constitutional Court had been inspired by TAC to evoke and endorse an open and participatory vision of the implementation of HIV/AIDS treatment involving collaboration between government officials and civil society organizations like TAC. In particular, the Court promised that the judiciary would ensure that government conducted its HIV/AIDS programs in a transparent and responsive fashion. Now, in 2004, TAC seized on this promise and launched its "Right to Know" Campaign. Emblazoned across TAC posters and pamphlets were the words "MY RIGHT TO KNOW, MY RIGHT TO LIVE!" and below them the "words of the Constitutional Court in the Minister of Health v. TAC judgment": "A public health program must be made known effectively to all concerned, down to the District Nurse and patients."

The 2004 "Right to Know" Campaign enacted TAC's—and the Court's—vision of bottom-up planning and implementation of HIV/AIDS treatment programs. It aimed, with modest success, to combine governmental transparency with TAC's organizational capacities and grassroots energy and activism, and embed them into the national, provincial, and local rollouts of ARVT. But going to court remained as before: a lever for broader strategies and a nucleus for public education and media campaigns, high visibility protests, and large-scale mobilizations of TAC's rank and file.

Within months of the November 2003 promulgation of the national plan, a few provincial public health departments seized on opportunities the new plan created to gear up swiftly for ARVT in all the facilities that the plan allowed. TAC offered technical and personnel assistance wherever it could and collaborated closely with provincial public health officials. But only relatively well-heeled provinces could follow this path without national support and leadership, and not all followed the lead of Gauteng and the Western Cape in doing so. At the national level, the process of procuring ARV medicines for the public health system proved needlessly drawn-out and distracted, and it lumbered along for months with little progress. The minister of health excused the unconscionable delays as the result of complex legal requirements and legal snares. While the minister stymied provincial officials' efforts to purchase ARVs on an interim basis, she also used her office to launch a publicity campaign on behalf of a German vitamin manufacturer, touting his "African" herbal "cure" for HIV/AIDS and his wildly inaccurate "warnings" about the toxicity of ARVs.

TAC staged demonstrations against the deceptions and delays, publicizing the readily available legal avenues for interim purchases and laying the needless deaths and suffering once more at the minister's door. In March 2004 TAC began preparing papers for litigation to compel the minister to use interim measures herself to procure ARVs while the longer-term (and long-delayed) procurement process unfolded. Responding to the threatened litigation, the minister agreed to allow what she had been thwarting: the use of interim purchasing by the provincial governments. Then, in February 2005, the first annual procurement process was finally concluded, and the Ministry of Health awarded tenders for ARVs worth three billion rands.[29]

Meanwhile, across the nation during 2004, wherever the rollout was lagging, local and provincial TAC branches wrote open letters and staged open meetings with provincial health ministers and officials, attended by hundreds and sometimes thousands of TAC rank and file and people living with HIV/AIDS, to hear monitoring reports on the rollout, protest the slow and uncertain progress, and demand information about dates and targets. "We want to assist government by helping to provide treatment literacy at clinics where ARV treatment is and will be available," explained TAC's March 2004 newsletter. "We need to know the dates that sites will begin ARV treatment and the targets that have been set such as the number of people to be put on ARV treatment. This is important because it helps us monitor the success of the Operational Plan and hold government accountable to meeting its own targets." By way of illustration, the newsletter reported that Obuku Rural Home-Based Care, a local TAC branch, "have requested HIV/AIDS statistics from the Uthungulu district health clinic and Ntambanani local clinic so they can plan for the numbers of HIV/AIDS patients they can anticipate caring for in their area."[30]

Throughout 2004, TAC also repeatedly sent letters to its old adversary, the national minister of health, "asking for important documents [ . . . ] that contain business and treatment plans for implementing the Operational Plan." Thus, the November 2003 plan had referred to an "Annexure A" containing the plan's detailed targets, but the Ministry of Health repeatedly refused to make the latter public; in the fall of 2004, TAC announced that it "reluctantly has applied to court to get access to Annexure A." On the date of the hearing, TAC held demonstrations around the country "pleading for the right to know—because it enables our right to live!" The Pretoria High Court ruled in TAC's favor, finding that government had unlawfully frustrated TAC's efforts to get information, and business and treatment plans.[31]

The rollout of ARVT continued, and with it the conflicts between TAC and the Ministry of Health. Until 2006, successful rollouts were largely the products of local and provincial political will—collaborations between TAC and other NGOs and committed managers and officials in the health system itself. Then, in October 2006, the minister of health, the living symbol of the government's ambivalence toward ARVs, fell ill with liver failure. As she lay in the intensive care unit of a private hospital, her deputy minister began meeting with Zackie Achmat and other TAC leaders to sketch the outlines of a new national plan for HIV/AIDS treatment in the public health system. Mbeki, embroiled in and weakened by a bitter succession race for leadership of the ANC, remained silent. A momentous change was slipping in under the radar.

Other cabinet officials also quietly entered the negotiations; the upshot was agreement that a new national strategic plan would be fashioned and that SANAC (the South African National Aids Council, the body charged with monitoring and oversight of the strategic plan) would be reconstituted. By the end of 2006, a new planning team was announced with several TAC allies from the public health field among its members, and SANAC was reformed, with TAC's Mark Heywood as deputy chair. The new plan was announced in March 2007.[32] It set the goal of ARVT to 80 percent of those who need it by 2011. Already by the end of 2008, roughly 600,000 South Africans were receiving ARVT in public healthcare institutions. The new plan broke sharply with the first one's emphasis on hospital-based, doctor-run treatment, providing instead that three-quarters of ARVT would be in nurse-run clinics. All treatment sites would have treatment literacy programs and support groups. The plan also provided for provincial and district AIDS councils, and it required that civil society and patients' organizations participate on these councils, supplying the latter with space and the potential to participate at several levels in the organization and implementation of HIV/AIDS treatment and prevention programs. The plan mandated community "outreach" with respect to sexual violence and women's equality as well as HIV/AIDS discrimination; mandated reform of social assistance programs to better support HIV/AIDS patients; and provided for a commission to draw up plans to bring greater equity of resources between the private and public health and health insurance systems.

Once again, a sea change in the politics around HIV/AIDS has occurred, and a new stage has begun. The hard-fought battle for free access to governmental information, combined with TAC's network of local branch, district, and provincial organizations, has enabled TAC to monitor the rollout and ensure continued expansion, keeping up pressure on the government and drawing attention to where provision is too slow or the process has broken down. TAC also has begun directing its strategic energies toward creating a dozen pilot site clinics and community centers in diverse urban and rural areas to model the possibilities of actualizing the various visionary elements of the national plan. As was the case with the Nevirapine pilot sites, showing that it can be done "within available resources" in these diverse settings may, once more, supply a basis for demanding comprehensive action and, if need be, going to court again.

After all, in the face of determined opposition from a president and minister of health who brooked no dissent on their HIV/AIDS policies, TAC and its allies and partners, including the nation's courts, fashioned a politico-constitutional strategy that has transformed South Africa's response to the pandemic, and has begun, finally, to bring to earth a social right to HIV/AIDS treatment in the public health system.

## TAC'S Treatment Literacy Campaign: Sustaining Social Movement Energy in the Process of Institutional Reform

Testifying in the U.S. Congress in June 2001, the head of the U.S. Agency for International Development (USAID), Andrew Natsios, declared that ARVT to combat AIDS in Africa was impossible, "because of lack of infrastructure, lack of doctors, lack of hospitals, lack of clinics, lack of electricity." Africans, he said, "don't know what Western time is. You have to take these drugs a certain number of hours each day, or they don't work . . . if you say, one o'clock in the afternoon, they do not know what you are talking about." How could they adhere to the rigid drug regimen? Failing that, treatment would only backfire as resistant strains of HIV multiplied. Apart from the inane and demeaning remarks about Africans and "Western time," this was not an outlier's view: Natsios's comments reflected prevailing opinion among U.S. and European HIV/AIDS scientists and doctors as well as policy makers at the time. ARVT for AIDS was a non-starter in sub-Saharan Africa. But Natsios's remarks were published, and they prompted this response from one TAC member:

> My name is Nontsikelelo Zwedala. I want to tell the world that I live in a shack
> in Phillippi in Cape Town. I do not have a degree from a university. But I [ . . . ]

know the names of my medicines. I received ARVs from a trial in Desmond Tutu Medical Centre. I take Nevirapine, AZT and 3TC. I know how they work. I know Nevirapine can cause liver damage so my doctor must monitor my liver function. I know AZT can give me anemia, I know all their side effects. Two months into my treatment I had liver problems. My doctor picked it up and managed it. I am alive today and didn't die. I know what the ARVs have done for me. I could not eat anymore with thrush and oral herpes. I was losing too much weight. I do not accept this insult from Mr. Natsios. That poor people cannot tell the time. That we are too poor to be able to learn how to look after our own health? That is an insult to us and we demand the Bush government to tell Mr. Natsios to apologise.

Ms. Zwedala was one of several hundred poor South Africans living with HIV/AIDS who were being treated with ARV medications at a Médecins Sans Frontières clinic in Khayelitsha, a black township outside Cape Town. The clinic was created in 1999, five years before the government finally began implementing ARVT in the nation's public health system. Zwedala was also a participant in one of TAC's early treatment literacy groups. Her words reflect something of the meld of biomedical knowledge and personal and political agency the Treatment Literacy Campaign has imparted to thousands of people living with HIV/AIDS. The Treatment Literacy Campaign (TLC) was born out of the MSF/TAC collaboration in Khayelitsha. The partnership yielded a model for providing essential ARVT in clinics across the nation; the TLC also may be useful as a model for methods of education, outreach, and institutional reform that help equip and enable the "clients" of social programs to participate in reforming and reshaping local state institutions and wider systems of social provision. By folding treatment literacy programs into the 2007 national ARVT plan, TAC and its allies aimed to build movement energy and actors into the institutional design of healthcare provision.

MSF doctors and nurses arrived in South Africa in 1999 determined to demonstrate that the then standard view of Western public health officialdom, echoed by Natsios, was wrong. That view held that (1) effective administration of ARVT demanded capital-intensive clinical resources and highly trained staffs with substantial numbers of specialist doctors at hand; whereas sub-Saharan African nations at best—as with South Africa—had rickety, understaffed public health systems, specialists at only a handful of urban hospitals, and precious few doctors overall; and (2) in any case, poor, ill-educated Africans simply would not be able to abide by the treatment regimen. There is no more demanding regimen: lifelong and fraught with grave side effects, if adherence falters at all (below 95 percent), resistance sets in, producing new virus strains and necessitating new arrays of ARV medications. Small wonder that policy makers and doctors were enormously cautious about providing treatment.

Against this view, MSF held that close access to hospitals, expensive equipment, and medical specialists was dispensable; doctors could ride circuit among clinics; specialists could remain at regional hospitals. What was essential was making the pills readily and regularly available far and wide, at clinics staffed by a few nurses and ample numbers of paraprofessionals and laypeople trained as adherence counselors and support group leaders. As for ill-educated Africans, they could be educated sufficiently about their disease and their treatment regimen, their meds, and their side effects, as long as the life-giving drugs were genuinely on offer, and support groups and community outreach were in place. It was a public health strategy that called for a social movement; TAC and MSF in South Africa were made for each other.

MSF set up a pilot clinic in Khayelitsha, where TAC had been founded the previous year. TAC's Zachie Achmat had just made his first "HIV POSITIVE" T-shirt, inspired by the Danish king's legendary Yellow Star—save that Achmat was in fact HIV-positive, while the king was a Gentile; the star was about solidarity, and the T-shirt (now worn by tens of thousands of HIV-positive South Africans) stood for collective self-assertion as unafraid, worthy members of society—when he met with the MSF doctors and began mapping out a "treatment literacy" program. It would meld lessons about HIV and AIDS, ARVs, side effects, and opportunistic infections with lessons about safe sex and women's rights; about exploring the ESR provisions in the South African Constitution and the meaning of rights for healthcare, dignity, and equality in the context of the HIV/AIDS pandemic. It happened that the lead MSF HIV/AIDS doctor, a white South African named Herman Reuter, had been a Trotskyist ANC comrade of Achmat's throughout the 1980s.

Reuter and Achmat found inspiration for treatment literacy from the work of AIDS activists in the United States. Already in the mid-1990s Achmat had forged links with the Gay Men's Health Crisis (GMHC) and ACT-UP, and in 1999 Greg Gonzales of GMHC helped lead TAC's first treatment literacy training sessions. Soon Reuter and Sipo Nthathi produced TAC's core treatment literacy teaching materials, *ARVs in Our Lives* and *Opportunistic Infections in*

*Our Lives*. At the clinic in Khayelitsha and elsewhere in townships around Cape Town, the first treatment literacy groups were created, and the idea took shape of embedding treatment literacy programs in clinics, hospitals, and community organizations and making treatment literacy and support groups the organizational link between the worlds of the clinics and that of TAC's local branches.

Over the next two years the MSF clinic in Khayelitsha made ARVs available to several hundred poor black patients with HIV/AIDS. MSF-hired lay counselors and TAC volunteers unfurled the treatment literacy program. TAC volunteers drawn from the initial treatment literacy and clinic support groups were trained as treatment literacy practitioners and support group leaders themselves. Adherence rates proved remarkably high, surpassing those in much of the United States. But all agreed that Cape Town might be unique: it was cosmopolitan, had hospitals and doctors nearby, and enjoyed plentiful urban recruits for TAC.

In 2001, then, MSF and TAC set up a handful of ARVT programs in village clinics across Lusikisiki, a rural region of the East Cape with as shaky a public health system as anywhere in South Africa. Along with MSF lay personnel, TAC volunteers—most of them young, unemployed township blacks with secondary educations—in their HIV POSITIVE T-shirts and jeans came regularly to the villages. They set up treatment literacy workshops and support groups, doing the painstaking, delicate work of breaking down the walls of shame, anger, and self-loathing that attend the disease, persuading villagers to go to the nearby clinics and be tested, get meds, participate in support groups, and learn and talk about AIDS and ARVT in a realistic and remarkably informed way.

Treatment literacy and support groups met outdoors, in full view. On folding chairs, improbable assortments of people made common cause: middle-aged gold miners in overalls ("retrenched" from the mines when they fell ill, and returned to their villages), village women in traditional dresses, urban youths. Daunted by the new responsibilities of administering ARV meds, overworked public health nurses resented, but came to depend on, the MSF-trained pharmacist's assistants, TAC volunteers, the literacy and support group leaders, and on Dr. Reuter as he made weekly rounds across Lusikisiki. Poor, physically and spiritually debilitated villagers stricken with AIDS began to participate in, make demands on, and embrace responsibility for their own treatment and care.

Journalist Jonny Steinberg spent weeks observing events at the village clinics in Lusikisiki during this period. Steinberg wrote that the "social movement to which AIDS medications and TAC's treatment literacy and support groups have given birth is unprecedented and novel." Steinberg described one support group as the members discussed their clinic pharmacy's vexing lack of the medication co-trimoxazole, how it affected them, and how their complaints to the pharmacist had been unavailing:

> It was time to broach the matter with the clinic head, a white nurse practitioner. The members turned to the TAC group leader, but she demurred. It was better, she suggested, for some of the quiet members of the support group to get some practice speaking. So, a black villager, a "peasant-miner" approached the white clinic head on the group's behalf and explained their grievance and their demand for improvement,

enacting, in Steinberg's words, "the most innovative social action of his times," a "previously unheard of relationship between rural blacks and South African state institutions."[33]

Reading the handful of ethnographic studies of TAC's treatment literacy work in the context of HIV/AIDS as lived in the township and village, one finds an untidy, uneven, many-layered process of new rights-bearing identities in the making. Religious structures of thought and feeling and customary local knowledge, witchcraft, and spirit worlds merge and jostle with medico-scientific "enlightenment" and liberal and social rights consciousness. For a great many participants stricken with HIV/AIDS, the extraordinary experience of feeling and being seen by others as "near death" or the "walking dead" and then regaining health, strength, and vigor by dint of ARVT was like nothing so much as being "born again." And having been harshly shunned and stigmatized by their communities, then embraced by TAC, was like being "born again" into a new and higher self—a conversion experience, in other words, brought about and made known, in important part, by "rights."

Many in the townships and villages found the new TAC-based, "HIV POSITIVE" community off-putting; like the evangelical churches, it seemed pious and preachy. Many villagers combined the clinics' ARVT with traditional healers, weaving back and forth between "science" and "tradition." Many refused to test. But four years out, in 2002, some thousands of poor South Africans in Khayelitsha and Lusikisiki were receiving ARVT; what was more, TAC and MSF had lit upon a model of treatment literacy that not only helped deliver effective ARVT and sustain high adherence levels but also produced knowledgeable and inspired social movement activists. The Treatment Literacy Campaign proved a renewable source of political energy from below—equipping poor black South Africans with HIV/AIDS not only for "taking responsibility" for their healthcare and making demands on local clinics but also for engaging the politics of health policy, countering denialism with detailed understanding of biomedicine, and demanding social rights from an obdurate national government. It was a fortunate development in a dark time, for as we have seen, many more years of bitter struggle separated the demonstrable successes of the MSF/TAC clinics in Khayelitsha and Lusikisiki from the creation and rollout of an adequate national plan for confronting HIV/AIDS. And that struggle demanded a large cadre of activists, which the TLC produced.

During those early years, between 1999 and 2001, public health officials like clinic and hospital managers and nurses had ample reasons to be apprehensive and resentful about MSF's (and a few other NGOs') introduction of taxing and complex HIV/AIDS ARVT into their routines, although most managers and nurses probably didn't share the president's denialist outlook on ARV medicines. Still, it was one thing for them to accommodate these demanding but life-saving pilot projects in their hospitals and clinics; it was quite another to welcome the young "hot-headed" TAC volunteers, who aimed to "educate" and "empower" their patients. *Ex ante*, they had every reason to share the president's and minister of health's well-publicized loathing for TAC as troublemakers and subversives.

TAC had to have something significant to offer the hard-pressed clinic and hospital authorities, or it would have been shown the door, as it was at some clinics during the early 2000s. But most nurses and managers, to their surprise, found TAC volunteers and TAC treatment literacy and support groups useful, not only in encouraging patient responsibility and treatment adherence but also in creating new clinical resources, removing community obstacles, and enlisting community support for treatment and prevention. "I have been a nurse for 21 years," reports Sister Mbatha of her experiences with TAC at a public health system clinic she directed in the Western Cape.

> I consider myself very experienced. I've worked in government clinics and hospitals most of my life. I have also worked in the private sector. When this young woman wearing an HIV-positive T-shirt first came to introduce herself at our clinic I thought, here we go again, another TAC person. I told her, "Listen, if you've come to march again, just do your march and get it over and done with and leave us to do our job. I am sick and tired of you people marching and complaining. We have problems here too you know."

Some of us try to do our best. We never get thanked, just told how bad we are . . . No one ever bothers to say, when last did you go on leave? I have not taken leave for a year. As a sister in charge I can't go on leave when we are just three people in the clinic that caters for hundreds of people.

But this girl Nomalizo, she was very patient. She explained the HIV lifecycle to me. She explained how ARVs work. I felt angry at first, because I thought, how can she know so much, what she says can't be accurate she's just a lay person, I am the nurse. She watched me get angry and just continued her explanation. Then she said, well, if you feel there's a way we can help, this is my number. I didn't call her for three weeks. But every day when I opened the clinic and people came streaming, every time we tested a person with HIV, I thought imagine if this person could hear that information that girl gave me. It could help so much.

It was when I tested a girl of 15 years who it seemed had already started getting sick that I decided, I have to swallow my pride. She was a young woman but all I could see was a child. I am a mother you know. So when I see a young girl with problems I think of my girls. I thought, I couldn't send this child home without knowing someone will sit her down and explain things to her which can give her hope. So I called this woman. Then she comes wearing her positive T-shirt and I think I want to kill her. How can she wear this T-shirt when there's so much stigma if she expects people to speak to her. But she came, she spoke to Nozipho and they both left the clinic together. A few weeks later Nozipho came back and asked me for Cotrimoxazole. Then I said, what you are talking about. She said I want Cotrimoxazole and I want to know which stage I am in and I want a CD4 count. She didn't even wink when said this and I thought, how cheeky! But she was a completely different person from the weeping girl who fainted when I told her she had HIV. We had Cotrimoxazole but had just run out of B-Co so I sent her with a letter to Mzamomhle clinic and she got vitamins and started her Cotrimoxazole. I used to hate these people with their HIV-positive T-shirts. Now I cannot imagine our life at the clinic without them. They have brought the community to us. Now the community helps us. They trained our clinic committee. They have established a support group at the clinic and have given treatment literacy training to all of them. They still make me angry because we order condoms and they take them all. Then they come back and say: "Sister Mbatha, when are more condoms coming, the community needs them?" At first I thought, they must be selling them to someone, we used to order a box of condoms and it can stay here for three weeks, now it doesn't even last a day.

I know what people say about this TAC and how they think it is fighting government. But here in NU2 clinic we have a different experience. ("A nurse's story: Sister Mbatha," *ARVs in Our Lives*, 80)

As Sister Mbatha's account suggests, public health officials like clinic and hospital managers had many reasons to be suspicious and hostile toward TAC's empowerment-based model of treatment literacy. But many, like Sister Mbatha, found that this model does important work, not only in encouraging patient responsibility and treatment adherence but also in creating new clinical resources in the form of counselors and support groups, in "bringing the community to us," and in striving to bring safe sex practices to the community.

Just as frontline public health officials were finding common ground with TAC's treatment literacy and support group work, so public health scholars and policy makers in South Africa and around the world had begun thinking that the MSF/TAC model of clinic- and community-based ARVT had legs, and that the standard views about poor sub-Saharan Africans and ARVT were wrong. Five years after the launch of the Khayelitsha clinic and four years out from the start of the Lusikisiki clinics, painstaking studies showed that adherence rates were high by any standard, including that set by sophisticated, hospital-based treatment programs in the United States and Western Europe. Based on the experience of these clinics and kindred ones in Haiti and elsewhere in sub-Saharan Africa, calls for "scaling up" the MSF/TAC model began to ring out of policy journals and international HIV/AIDS organizations. Far-flung, nurse-led clinics could sustain effective ARVT as long as the pills were on offer and the "empowerment" programs in place.

During the 1990s, public health experts and policy makers across the globe had come to embrace "contract"-based models of clinic-patient relations, demanding a host of commitments on patients' part in exchange for treatment. Such contractual models were after all a staple of neoliberal social policy. Thanks to the 1999–2004 MSF/TAC collaboration, however, the model that South Africa's leading public health scholars and medical journals promoted was one that emphasized not only "individual responsibilization" but individual rights, group empowerment, and community engagement. TAC's treatment literacy campaign was shaping policy discourse:

Alternative approaches to the traditional management of chronic diseases [ . . . ] are needed if the stringent adherence requirements of ART (anti-retroviral treatment) are to be achieved. The evidence from pilot projects is that high levels of adherence stem from "a new kind of contract between providers and clients." The contract is premised on very high levels of understanding, treatment literacy and preparation on the part of users, the establishment of explicit support systems around users, and community advocacy processes that promote the rights of people living with HIV/AIDS. The responsibility for adherence is given to the client within a clear framework of empowerment and support. This is very different to the traditional paternalistic and passive relationship between health care workers and patients—changing this represents the key innovation challenge of an ART programme. (David Coetzee and Helen Schneider, Editorial, *South African Medical Journal* 93:10 [2004]: 1–3)

Shaping professional policy discourse was not enough, though, if government remained obdurate. MSF could not bring about the broader institutionalization of the innovative treatment model it had helped fashion. It lacked both authority and resources for that kind of undertaking; it was in the "demonstration" business, not the "scaling up" business. MSF was closing down its South African HIV/AIDS clinical operation. It was time for the national public health service to take over. MSF hoped that the national government would heed the lessons of Khayelitsha and Lusikisiki. But even in 2004, the government remained in the grip of denial, resisting the implementation of the flawed national plan that TAC and its allies had wrested from it.

During that long contest, fortunately, TAC held hundreds of treatment literacy workshops, building up and sustaining the base of activists in treatment but also expanding the TLC's ambit from clinics and hospitals to churches, schools, workplaces, and union halls. Treatment literacy methods and materials were retailored to provide "scientific and medical literacy" and "HIV/AIDS literacy" to schoolchildren, teenagers, and the general public about the biomedical workings and transmission of HIV, the onset of AIDS and the operation and exigencies of ARVT, and about safe sex and respect for women's rights. In this fashion, treatment literacy helped to produce not only knowledgeable activists but also a broader knowledgeable public, where otherwise—in view of the government's wildly ambivalent and confusing messages about HIV/AIDS—none would exist.

The titles of articles in an issue of TAC's journal *Equal Treatment* illustrate the step-by-step way in which TAC's literacy efforts set about refuting the government's claims against HIV/AIDS science: "How We Know That HIV Causes AIDS"; "How HIV Works"; "How We Know HIV Tests Are Accurate"; "How We Know There Is an HIV Epidemic in South Africa"; "How We Know That Antiretrovirals Save Lives"; and the list goes on, giving clear scientific explanations of every aspect of the epidemic, from prevention (how condoms work; PMTCT) to treatment (ARVs in the developing world; opportunistic infections). Bringing these lessons via literacy workshops into the nation's churches and trade unions was, according to Achmat, TAC's "greatest victory," creating a broad and mobilized base of popular support for TAC in its contests with government, and gradually changing the public outlook in the nation's urban areas about HIV/AIDS treatment and prevention. By the time the deputy minister of health began her meetings with Achmat, in 2005, to create a new national plan for finally confronting the pandemic in a concerted and responsible fashion, it was understood that treatment literacy on TAC's model would be an essential element.

Today, as the national rollout proceeds, there are TAC-led treatment literacy and support groups in clinics and hospitals around the country; these in turn generate new rank-and-file members, volunteers, and activists for TAC's local chapters. These TAC groups and chapters are invaluable in the clinic and community-based work of HIV/AIDS treatment and prevention. They have changed power and authority in relations across patients, healthcare workers, nurses, and doctors, as well as across family, community, and gender relations. They also engage HIV/AIDS patients and communities in broader policy issues regarding biomedical resources and HIV/AIDS policy. The national plan also provides for treatment literacy programs for healthcare workers and schoolteachers. Meanwhile, these local TAC groups also have proved essential in deepening TAC's alliances with hard-pressed public healthcare workers, nurses, and doctors by mobilizing political support for the public healthcare unions' demands for better wages, salaries, and working conditions.

TAC and its allies have thus built into the emerging institutional design of the public healthcare system for HIV/AIDS a renewable source of political energy from below, at the grassroots level. This is a means of producing movement activists to carry on the tasks of continued organizing and campaigning for new resources and policy initiatives, such as the campaigns for basic income grants for poor patients as well as better wages and salaries for healthcare workers, for research and development initiatives aimed at cheaper and simpler CD4 and viral load testing, and for cheaper and better tuberculosis testing and medicines.

## Conclusion

Treatment Action Campaign's political and legal strategies present sharp contrasts with the classic NAACP civil rights model, and with the prevailing local-global strategic outlook among international human rights and antipoverty advocates. TAC's strategies don't fit the latter's staunchly antistatist, decentralizing emphasis on local communities and global aid. While plowing local, grassroots, and international terrains, TAC also built itself into an oppositionist movement in the national polity, with strategies directed at protesting, challenging, and changing state policy, and enlisting and collaborating with allies in the state and party apparatus and in the national trade union federation.

TAC made securing the constitutional social right to HIV/AIDS treatment the core of its efforts. Yet in contrast to the classic twentieth-century struggles for constitutional rights, constitutional *litigation* has played a subordinate, supporting role in TAC's work. In this supporting role, litigation and formal legal advocacy of ESR proved a good deal more valuable in bringing social rights to earth than many ESR scholars and activists believe possible. Because it put aside the court-centered model of rights advocacy in favor of a politics-centered model, TAC never made court victories the object of its campaigns; nor did it try to use the courts as the central arena for initiating or shaping pro-poor state policies. Instead, as we've seen, TAC used litigation in service of many-sided strategies to open up policy-making processes, to reshape programs and policies in democratic and pro-poor directions, and to prod government to implement them. In this context, ESR litigation and court victories provided invaluable political leverage and moral authority.

Thus, the policy-shaping and policy-changing work of the 2002 Constitutional Court decision on Nevirapine and PMTCT was largely done outside the Court via pressure, protests, proposals, and alliances, with reformers inside government, before the litigation even got under way. What's more, TAC never brought to court its broader claim for a national ARVT plan in the public health system. Instead, TAC chose the public political sphere as the arena for pressing the case for the social right to adequate healthcare for HIV/AIDS: holding workshops and conferences; preparing studies and proposals; monitoring government's performance at local, provincial, and national levels; educating the lay public; and at the same time, building a social movement, staging dramatic public protests and demonstrations, and several times resorting to civil disobedience to dramatize the government's death-dealing failure to develop and then implement a responsible program.

Paradoxically, although TAC never brought the case for the national treatment plan to court, its strategists saw the Constitutional Court as an essential partner in this campaign. The Court's 2002 ruling on Nevirapine and PMTCT proved a crucial turning point in the broader struggle. Even though, as we saw, the president and minister of health remained obdurate on many fronts, the Court's intervention brought invaluable strategic and moral assets: emboldening reformers within government to reach out to TAC; providing an incentive to continue the kind of painstaking nonjudicial efforts to persuade government to adopt responsible policies, efforts that had laid the groundwork for the 2002 PMTCT decree; and creating a credible threat of going back to court, which TAC did twice during the later struggles around implementation. From 2002 onward, the Constitutional Court decision served as a "legal and moral anchor" for the struggle for a robust and democratic national HIV/AIDS treatment plan.

Much that is said about Treatment Action Campaign and South Africa's Constitutional Court emphasizes the distinctiveness of South African experience. But it would be a mistake to overlook the more generalizable features of the story we've told. Start with the Constitutional Court. Several of its justices have revolutionary pasts, but on the bench they have proved anything but freewheeling radical reformers in robes. Committed to the constitution's promises of social citizenship, they also are acutely sensitive to practical and political limitations of judicial power. Like many constitutional courts around the globe, this one prefers to husband its political capital, to intervene modestly and in "compelling" cases, and to shun sweeping programmatic decrees. It prefers to help and rely upon civil society organizations and reform-minded political actors to develop the political and institutional contexts that make relatively modest, episodic, and iterative judicial interventions yield maximal effects. This vision of judicial collaboration with civil society organizations and reform-minded state actors comports with what constitutional courts elsewhere seem willing to hazard in the service of ESR. Thus, this context-creating craft is worth cultivating in many places; by recounting TAC's and the South African Court's collaboration in some detail, we have tried to convey what we have learned about that craft.

We've sketched the development of some of TAC's key ESR-based reforms and the manifold strategies used to promote them in cultural, public, political, and administrative arenas. And we've suggested that this kind of extrajudicial work supplies not only a basis for litigation, as occasions for litigation arise, but also a basis for swaying popular and elite opinion and mounting protests and civil disobedience campaigns, where these seem essential, with maximum moral and political warrant and effect.

Also generalizable, we think, are some of the lessons learned in the Treatment Literacy Campaign. Countless social provision and social assistance programs all over the globe today aim to "activate" or "contract with" individuals and make them "take responsibility" for their own health, education, or welfare; community housing; or economic development projects. This "responsibilizing" mode of social provision often proves fruitless or deeply unfair, shifting on to poor people responsibility for market failures and infrastructural and institutional infirmities that impede them from fulfilling their end of "the bargain" with social agencies. But in some settings, this "responsibilizing" mode can allow opportunities for genuine empowerment, concerted action, and even movement-building on the part of poor people who had been merely clients of government programs.

Wherever social programs call for educating and training poor people to participate in their own healthcare or economic or social uplift, needs arise for educational and training methods, materials, and practitioners. These various resources may be authoritarian; they may cultivate individualistic notions of self-help and self-blame; they may be impractical, inaccessible, unhelpful, or ill-suited in many ways. But they also may be practically and politically inspired; they may democratize expertise; make technical and scientific knowledge accessible and usable for poor people who have little formal education; and impart new rights- and knowledge-and-power-bearing identities, as well as lessons in mutual aid, problem solving, negotiation, and collective action.

Of course, the kinds of knowledge and skills training a given social program requires will vary with the design and aims of the program. The extent to which a rights- and empowerment-based approach seems either essential or "just a political add-on" will vary too. But this will depend less, we think, on the subject matter of the program—healthcare versus childcare versus community economic development, say—and more on how the program's goals and strategies are defined. Furthermore, starting with a modest conception of "empowerment" or "rights education" in the creation of methods and materials can provide the seedbed and entry point for social movement activists, who in turn may bring broader goals and strategies to the enterprise over time.

Certainly this was the case with the Treatment Literacy Campaign. MSF's approach to delivering ARVT to poor South Africans, we have seen, demanded that HIV/AIDS patients gain an active understanding of their illnesses and treatment in order to monitor adherence to drug regimens, side effects, and opportunistic illnesses in a setting where professional monitoring was inevitably in short supply. MSF and all African HIV/AIDS experts also agreed that effective treatment and prevention entailed extensive community education to overcome stigma and women's oppression and thereby encourage testing and safe sex. Thus, to a certain extent, as we've noted, the MSF model for delivering ARVT to poor South Africans included a rights- and empowerment-minded educational and support group element in its conception. It was the efficacy of TAC's educational methods and materials in these respects—encouraging treatment adherence, testing, and safe sex—that led the World Health Organization to adopt TAC's treatment literacy program in its array of "best practices" for HIV/AIDS programs in Africa. It was partly the happenstance of TAC having gotten there first with an effective method and body of materials that led in this case to the best practices including a more expansive than usual democratic and rights-claiming educational repertoire.

It's also possible for treatment literacy or any other literacy and training program to be (re)packaged and practiced in ways that leech out radical democratic features. For example, we've seen that South Africa's new National Plan envisions TAC-style treatment literacy and support groups in clinics throughout the public health system, and provides for the participation of community organizations and associations of people living with HIV/AIDS in framing and reframing provincial and national policies and goals—building on the information and insights about problems and possibilities generated from below via these local groups. But there are afoot many rival treatment literacy materials and methods with a narrower vision; meanwhile, pressures from above and burnouts from below can shut down the fragile circuits that enable bottom-up political energy and reform impulses to guide and propel a process of revising institutional arrangements and opening political economic arrangements (of healthcare, in this case) to deepening democratic reforms. Even "responsive" and "participatory" state institutions and social bureaucracies tend to grow resistant toward social movement actors; and they tend to co-opt the machinery that institutional designers hope will continue generating movement energy "from within." TAC will thus need to keep up its varied means of disruption and continue finding new ways to bridge the incommensurable but indispensable worlds of social movement and social provision.

## Chapter 3

# The Evictions at Nyamuma, Tanzania

## *Structural Constraints and Alternative Pathways in the Struggles over Land*

Ruth Buchanan, Helen Kijo-Bisimba, and Kerry Rittich

The event that gave rise to the inquiry in this chapter occurred in a village known as Remaining Nyamuma, which was located on the border of the Ikorongo Game Reserve, immediately adjacent to the Serengeti National Park in Tanzania.[1] Sometime in October 2001, district officials informed the villagers by loudspeaker that they must leave the area and return to their original villages within four days.[2] Two days after the notice period had ended, the district commissioner himself set fire to a house belonging to one of the villagers, initiating a violent eviction of the villagers by the burning of their houses and fields. In the course of the evictions, 132 households were displaced; villagers were injured; livestock were killed; and families were scattered. No alternative land or housing was allocated to those evicted. Indeed, officials subverted their efforts to find housing elsewhere by encouraging neighboring villagers to report their presence to district authorities.[3] Evicted villagers were harassed by officials and prevented from conducting business, effectively becoming internally displaced people.[4]

The case of the Nyamuma evictions is both tragic and illuminating. It is tragic because despite all the efforts on the part of the Tanzanian Legal and Human Rights Centre (LHRC), an education- and advocacy-oriented NGO based in Dar es Salaam, nearly eight years later there is remarkably little to show for it all. Since the burnings and evictions, the LHRC has worked to publicize the plight of the affected people, to characterize both the acts and their consequences as human rights violations, and to utilize the new institutional mechanism that was expressly designed to address human rights violations for redress; yet, eight hundred people remain homeless and without compensation. The remarkable resistance of the Tanzanian government to sustained and vigorous advocacy efforts in the court of public opinion as well as in various legal arenas sends a daunting message to funders and advocates of human rights throughout the region. However, we do not understand the lesson of Nyamuma simply as a "failure" of the human rights frameworks and mechanisms to redress the harms done in this instance. Rather, we read this event as deeply entwined within a tangled web of issues, some reaching back to colonial times, concerning development and land policy in Tanzania. A study of the evictions also discloses a more recent local history of displacement and a shrinking supply of land, as well as complex interconnections with international actors, multilateral institutions, donors, investors, and tourists. For these reasons, the tragedy of the Nyamuma evictions represents an opportunity for broader reflection on the factors that enable, or that block, the realization of the goals that human rights entitlements seek to secure, both within and beyond the state.

In this chapter we use the Nyamuma case as a starting point for just that type of broader reflection. In the next section we begin with a general consideration of some of the challenges that face economic and social rights (ESR) advocacy in Africa today. In the following section we return to the Nyamuma evictions through a consideration of the report of the LHRC on its advocacy efforts in that case. The ensuing three sections seek to deepen our analysis by considering a series of relevant contexts: property law reforms; changing land uses, including the growth of tourism and mining in the area; and issues relating to the funding of the newly created Tanzanian Commission on Human Rights and Good Governance, and the LHRC itself. The penultimate section presents the results of our analysis through a series of further questions about the complex social, economic, and institutional embeddedness of human rights strategies. Rather than understanding the evictions at Nyamuma as an unfortunate but isolated incident, our analysis leads us to the conclusion that it exemplifies much that has gone awry with Tanzania's development policies from the perspective of the poor. The final section, a postscript on a series of evictions that have occurred since Nyamuma and the responses to them by local communities and advocates, underscores our argument and provides an opportunity to consider possible strategies for the future.

## Challenges of Economic and Social Rights Advocacy in Africa

The evictions at Nyamuma and their aftermath exemplify the phenomenon of structural violence in an extreme form, and place the challenges of obtaining structural justice in stark relief. The evictions also demonstrate the complex and contested relationship between human rights and development, particularly in Africa. The focus on civil and political rights that even up to the present dominates the human rights agendas of the international advocacy community has rarely been seen as responsive to the predicaments of disempowered groups, or well-targeted to the challenges faced by developing states.[5] While the "right to development" was crafted specifically to respond to these challenges, as well as to the political and economic position that newly decolonized Third World states occupied within the international order, the status of this right remains contested. Despite receiving formalistic recognition within the international order, the right to development has suffered from its connection to a particular idea of the dirigiste or developmental state that has been under sustained ideological and institutional attack since the end of the Cold War. But economic and social rights, too, often sit uncomfortably within institutional reform agendas in the international order that are designed to further development by enabling foreign investment and facilitating transborder transactions.[6]

"Rights-based approaches" to development represent an attempt to both mediate these tensions and secure a foundational place for human rights within these development and broader institutional reform agendas.[7] And at least since 1999 the idea that development itself must be conceived in ways that incorporate human rights has been uncontentious. Yet despite the incorporation of human rights into the development agenda, and efforts to represent the promotion of human rights and development as fundamentally coterminous enterprises,[8] it is clear that many questions concerning the links between ESR and the trajectory of social transformation and economic development policy remain. How economic development priorities are identified, which groups are consulted in the process of formulating them, how policies are implemented and risks and entitlements allocated, and how the associated costs and benefits are distributed are all questions with profound implications for the realization of economic and social rights. Moreover, general assessments and predictions about the relationship between human rights and development, on their own, say little if anything about the prospects for particular groups. Although those prospects can sometimes be positive, as the Nyamuma evictions make clear, they can also be dire.

The Nyamuma evictions, particularly when contextualized within broader Tanzanian economic development policies and the recent history of displacement and dispossession from land within the region, illuminate just how complicated and contested the realization of economic and social rights is likely to be. They also provide a sobering check on an increasingly common narrative, which holds that the road to economic and social rights lies through development. By indicating how competing state objectives and pressures are likely to operate on human rights objectives, the evictions also provide a revealing guide to how and where conflicts and human rights violations are likely to arise elsewhere.

Nyamuma provides a number of vantage points from which to consider the relation of the inside to the outside, and the national to the transnational and international, in struggles for economic and social rights. For example, it illuminates some of the ways in which popular power might be constrained and democratic institutions turned in the service of projects that, while favored by powerful international institutions and forces, have a more uncertain grounding in local or national political choices and priorities. The case also provokes hard reflection on the roles, for better or worse, that even "friendly" or well-meaning outside groups and institutions play in advancing the human rights of those they purport to aid. For the irony of Nyamuma is that outside actors and institutions, some of whom claimed special knowledge and expertise in the field of human rights, seemed at best naïve about what was involved in designing even a marginally effective national human rights regime, and at worst "part of the problem."[9]

Nyamuma also provokes reflection on the practice and challenge of ESR advocacy itself, in particular what constitutes "success." Is it possible to read Nyamuma in a more positive light notwithstanding the manner in which the campaign has so far unfolded? In addressing this question, it seems important to emphasize that the actors within the LHRC were very sophisticated: in their appreciation of the potential problems with the human rights machinery at their disposal; in their use of publicity; in their assessment of the strengths and weaknesses of courts versus the human rights tribunal as a venue for litigation; in their knowledge of what was afoot at different levels of government; in their knowledge of customary law and traditional dispute resolution processes and how they motivated the villagers and affected their interactions with officials; and in their knowledge of the international actors and their particular projects and interests. This suggests that those within the LHRC may have had multiple objectives, some of which could well have been furthered in the litigation process, even in the face of their inability to prevail on the specific question of relief for the people who had been evicted. It is also important to look beyond the litigation process, however, in seeking to understand the lessons of the Nyamuma evictions. While analyses of economic and social rights often default to accounts about litigation, should human rights advocacy be understood first and foremost in this way? Is advocacy only about courts and tribunals? Or can it be more securely linked to popular mobilization on the one hand and democratic transformation on the other?

Our aims in this account are threefold. The first is to expose more fully some of the underlying systemic and structural sources of the dispute at Nyamuma. The second is to consider the constraints on more democratic futures and the obstacles to "alternative pathways" to development, alternatives that might have made the dispute more tractable and avoided some of the problems and abuses already described, even if they did not eliminate the underlying conflicts themselves. The third aim is to situate Nyamuma in the wider scheme of global governance. We are interested in the events at Nyamuma not only in their particularity; to paraphrase Gayle Rubin,[10] we are also interested in their monotonous similarity to conflicts and predicaments that have been documented elsewhere in recent years, particularly those that touch on land.

## Framing the Issues: The Role of the LHRC

The evictions at Nyamuma stand as an important test case of ESR advocacy, one that deserves to be more widely publicized. However, the LHRC has already issued a report detailing all the ways in which the evictions, which the LHRC rightly call a "calamity," directly violated human rights.[11] This report also documents the extensive advocacy efforts undertaken on behalf of the displaced villagers. Revisiting this story in the context of this project and book, as we've noted above, reveals both the structural violence that is a feature of the development landscape in Tanzania, and that landscape's inhospitability to human rights advocacy.

The LHRC made a strategic decision to bring the case before the newly created Tanzanian Commission on Human Rights and Good Governance ("the Commission") rather than before the courts.[12] Other options were available—it could have been brought as a criminal case, for the acts involved included arson and assaults as well as the deprivations of property. However, to prosecute government agents appeared rather too politically risky, and the likelihood of the proceedings being stalled at an early stage seemed high. A second option would have been to pursue a civil case, but this also faced the same set of concerns about the political nature of the proceedings and the possibility that progress would be stalled. Finally, a constitutional case might have been brought, for example, invoking the protections provided by the Bill of Rights against arbitrary deprivations of property without compensation. However, these cases must go to the High Court, which is located some distance away from the Serengeti District where the events occurred, and are certain to be more procedurally involved. A test case for the Commission appeared to be the most attractive option, not least because it promised to be faster and more independent from the government than the court system. The Commission, in addition to looking at the Tanzanian constitution, could also look at international principles, such as those elaborated in the Convention on Economic, Social, and Cultural Rights.

The Commission investigated the case, and although it dismissed the initial complaint (which had been filed in June 2002), after an intervention from the LHRC in May 2003 it convened a hearing, which commenced in August of that year. A report on the evictions was issued by the Commission in December 2004. The report was highly critical of the government, stating that numerous violations of human rights had occurred and ordering adequate and fair compensation to be paid to the villagers. In particular, the Commission determined that over the course of the evictions, the government had committed a number of human rights violations, including arbitrary deprivation and uncompensated expropriation of property; physical assault, which led in one case to a miscarriage and in another to serious injury; intimidation and confinement of those from the LHRC who initially investigated the circumstances surrounding the evictions[13]; loss of livelihood and failure to provide humanitarian aid to those who were summarily cast out of their homes; denial of education to the affected children following the eviction; and subjection to cruel, inhumane, and degrading treatment, which the LHRC concluded amounted to torture. The Commission's report also detailed numerous procedural irregularities and contraventions of quite ordinary principles of administrative justice that surrounded the evictions. Finally, it identified the government's obstruction of the Commission inquiry as itself a violation of human rights.

The LHRC's own report documents this series of events, including the complaint, the investigation, and the Commission report. However, the LHRC report also repeatedly touches on issues that did not form part of the core of the Commission inquiry but that seem clearly relevant to the evictions and to the human rights violations that ensued. Indeed, woven throughout the account of the evictions are suggestive, even tantalizing, references to issues and policies that formed the ground out of which the events at Nyamuma emerged and that influenced the disposition of the human rights complaint itself. A salient, recurring issue is conflict around land, of which the evictions at Nyamuma are one of the most dramatic instance, though hardly the only one. Although for lack of witnesses two related incidents never formed part of the official complaint to the Commission, the LHRC report mentions the killing of eight "poachers" and the injury of a ninth by game wardens in the Serengeti National Park in 1997, and another shooting in which four hunters were killed in the same park in 1998.[14] These incidents were intimately tied up with changing land use and new "security" concerns in the Serengeti and the wildlife management areas.

Another set of concerns that emerges in the LHRC report relates to the structure of the Commission and to the role played by outside agencies—whether national development agencies, private foundations, or NGOs—as funders and arbiters of human rights policy. These agencies and actors not only alternatively provided and denied funding to the Commission and the LHRC at crucial junctures; some also had competing projects and concerns, such as wildlife preservation and the promotion of ecotourism in the Serengeti.

So far, the government has failed to pay the compensation required by the Commission. But it has also refused to accept the findings of the Commission, alleging that they were "based on fabricated evidence," notwithstanding that they were the product of a public hearing at which the government itself was represented.[15] The Commission then requested the LHRC to take the case before the courts in order to enforce the Commission's recommendations against the government; the case has been mired in appeals and jurisdictional disputes ever since.[16]

The limits to what has been attained from six years of skilled and sustained advocacy both before the Commission and the courts are revealing and sobering. Our hypothesis is that these limits are most usefully explored not as failures attributable either to any strategic decision that could have been made differently by the advocates or indeed to the decisions made within the Commission and the court system. Rather, the challenges to the effective realization of economic and social rights here appear to emanate from much deeper structural and institutional features of Tanzanian society and economy, as well as to the specific preoccupations of those within the wider human rights community, the international community in particular. Investigating these issues, accordingly, requires longer, and different, histories as well as a broader context than conventional litigation-oriented accounts of human rights advocacy usually provide. For Nyamuma not only suggests that, as Issa Shivji puts it, "a court is not the most appropriate forum for resolving fundamental policy issues such as the problem of land tenure"[17]: when we bring this broader context—development policies and priorities, and the path of land reforms, for example—into the foreground, the evictions at Nyamuma and their unhappy aftermath no longer look like isolated, disconnected instances of human rights abuse. Instead, they seem inextricably connected to other disputes and to wider social and economic developments within Tanzania, particularly the forced evictions and growing pressures on traditional villages brought about by development, tourism, and land reform projects, which are increasingly common in many parts of rural Africa.[18] Similarly, once we consider the preoccupations of the international human rights advocates and funders, the disposition of the case of the Nyamuma evictions within the national human rights machinery no longer looks so surprising, nor does it seem unique.

## Reforms to Property Law

At the center of the Nyamuma evictions is a series of interlinked issues: land shortages; conflict over land and changing land use; growing impoverishment, unemployment, and economic insecurity of the people in the Mara region; increasing levels of violence and a deteriorating security situation, some of which is attributed to the return of decommissioned soldiers and an influx of guns; and the intensification and reorganization of traditional activities.[19] These issues themselves are connected to governance reforms in two areas: land reform and development policy, both centered on attracting foreign investment, particularly in the mining and tourism sectors (which we discuss in the following section). Further, it is possible to identify a relatively discrete set of laws and policies concerning land entitlements and land use, implemented in recent years, that in conjunction with other developments, such as a rapidly expanding population, markedly exacerbate the likelihood and intensity of conflicts and set the stage for the types of violations that arose at Nyamuma.

The roots of the conflicts over land in Tanzania arguably date back to colonial rule of Tanganyika first by Germany and then Britain.[20] More proximately, while land shortages seem to originally have been provoked by land reforms beginning in the 1970s,[21] recent land reforms and decisions on land policy have clearly exacerbated the shortages and engendered new conflicts around land use. Beginning in the 1980s, a number of developments, including the expansion of the land reserve surrounding the Serengeti National Park; an influx of international investors in mining, notably the Canadian-based Barrick Gold; and very recent developments in the privatization of titles to land, provide a wider context for the conflict we document here. We would note also that the growing pressures on governments for land reform come from different sources and pull in different directions. For example "the external donor[-]driven pressures are aimed at facilitating the operation of a market for land, while some, at least[,] of the internal pressures pull in the direction of strengthening the security of tenure of those already on the land."[22]

The starting point for the present analysis is a set of policy shifts around land in Tanzania that commenced in the early 1990s. At that time, a presidential commission chaired by the well-known academic-lawyer Issa Shivji was convened to undertake a major investigation into the shortcomings of existing land policies and practices. Although the commission reported in 1992, the government failed to follow many of its recommendations in its drafting of the National Land Policy, which was enacted in June 1995. The passage of the new land policy was not without controversy. After farmers, pastoralists, and other civil society groups mobilized in opposition to some of its proposals,[23] a petition was circulated and the process was slowed down to facilitate more careful consideration of issues such as gender and the role of customary law. However, after Patrick McAuslan, a UK-based property law expert with extensive consulting experience in other African countries, was hired to assist in the drafting of new land law, the process was quickly, and controversially, concluded as Parliament rushed into passage two major new acts in 1999: the Village Land Act, and the Land Act. However, popular reaction was at least partly positive, as the reforms promised local power through village assemblies and recognized land ownership by women. Most important for our purposes is that both acts expressly direct authorities who have any reason to acquire land to give notice to the people using that land, and provide that the people will be required to move only after an agreement for appropriate compensation is reached and the compensation is actually paid.

Notwithstanding the passage of these acts, little progress was made in terms of the implementation of land reform until 2003. In April 2003, after Hernando de Soto met with the Tanzanian president, a project on the formalization of property—*mkurabita* in Swahili—quickly followed, funded by the government of Norway as well as the World Bank. Since 2003, however, progress on titling has been slow; although an office was opened in 2005, titling has only proceeded in a few villages since that time. Around the same time, the Norwegian People's Aid, an NGO, began a pilot project to determine how best to ensure that titling benefited the communities in which it was introduced. This organization also conducted a follow-up study in a few villages to assess how well individuals understood the implications of the formalization of titles. Its conclusions suggested that in general, people did not understand the full implications of the new property rights they were being granted. The report is consequently critical of the way in which land titling has proceeded in Tanzania.[24]

It seems important at this point to say something about the specific rationale behind land titling, and to identify the significance of Hernando de Soto to current approaches to land reform, those promoted by the World Bank included, because both the motivation for and the structure of the reforms in Tanzania resonate with the dominant approach to land reforms for development within the international financial institutions. The now widespread efforts to promote land titling rest upon de Soto's argument that titling is a means to convert otherwise "dead capital" into new sources of wealth.[25] Under this theory, once title is formalized, land can and will be deployed by the owner in service of wealth generation and greater productivity in a variety of new ways.[26] For example, it may be used to secure loans either to improve the land itself and generate higher-use values from the land or to engage in other economic ventures. However, land titling is also intended to create new markets and facilitate the transfer of land. The point of titling is thus not merely to formalize existing entitlements and establish secure and unambiguous ownership. Rather, it is to move toward a regime of property in which land is largely freed of the encumbrances of complex use rights, and the owner, as the unchallenged and unfettered sovereign, is able to dispose of land and exercise the full panoply of rights with respect to the land under his control. For this reason, titling ideally involves not merely land registration but registration in the name of a single owner as well.

The World Bank has made land titling a centerpiece of development policy in recent years, arguing that land titling promotes both growth and the alleviation of poverty.[27] Indeed, at virtually the same time as the 2003 titling initiatives were introduced in Tanzania, the World Bank released a policy research report that contained both a stylized analysis of the question of land reform in developing countries and a template for reforms that has since been widely disseminated. The reform template has three dimensions: formalization of title, individualization of ownership, and the commodification of land. Adopting this strategy, it is argued, will spur economic development that would otherwise not occur; through titling, communities can expect to accrue the full range of benefits that come from the conversion of land into a highly fungible and tradable commodity.

What matters for the purposes of the Nyamuma case study and the other conflicts that are emerging around land in Tanzania is that these reforms are not indifferent to all possible uses of land, nor are they neutral among the affected parties or actors. They are particularly uncongenial to "traditional" land ownership patterns, entitlements, and uses in Tanzania and elsewhere. These include arrangements in which many persons have entitlements to access; land is not designated for a single use but serves multiple different functions; and land may be held an inalienable source of wealth and security for a clan or other entity over generations.[28] Indeed, it bears emphasizing that land titling reforms are often explicitly designed to interrupt such uses and entitlements, and for this reason they systematically disfavor subsistence activities and non-tradable production as compared to commercial ventures that are measurably growth-enhancing.[29]

In addition, a well-documented set of risks is associated with such land reforms, risks that tend to be systemically underplayed by those who stress the benefits of land titling for poverty alleviation.[30] These include dispossession of those with interests under customary law; loss of land due to forfeiture for non-payment of loans; and sales of large tracts of land from the economically less sophisticated or desperate to the financially savvy or well positioned.[31] The net result may be widespread changes to land access and ownership in a relatively short period of time, leading to far-reaching dispossession of groups who have traditionally held land and to erosion of economic and food security for groups or nations as a whole.[32] In short, land titling creates the risk that rather than assist the most disempowered it will enhance the economic opportunities of those who are already more advantaged.

In the face of such risks, the point is not that traditional land entitlements must reflexively be defended or that traditional uses are entitled to automatic priority over new ones. There may well be a range of arguments to revisit both, and appropriate outcomes will likely be differently configured in different parts of the country. It is clear that in Tanzania there was already a complex and contested process of land reform well under way when titling was initiated, some of which was almost certainly motivated by a desire to facilitate new or different economic activities. Nor, as the events at Nyamuma disclose, is the preservation of "traditional" entitlements and uses necessarily even an option; entire villages had already been relocated, and the evictions themselves emerged out of conflict over land that was already an entrenched feature of the social and political landscape.[33] In short, it is not change or the attack on tradition per se that seem problematic about the titling initiative. Rather, what leaps out is the lack of weight given to distributive considerations in the reform calculus, and the absence of plans to compensate those who lost out in the titling process; the markedly foreign or external impetus behind the reform, and the displacement of local or national imperatives and input into land titling laws, despite the already extensive debate and study on these questions; and, especially evident in the speed in which the land titling was introduced, a puzzling blindness to the social disruption and upheaval that significant land reform almost certainly entails, and hence to the possibility of conflict and suffering.

## Changing Patterns of Land Use: Tourism, Mining, and Wildlife Protection

In addition to the general aims of land reform described above, in Tanzania the land reforms are also intended to enable more intensive exploitation of land for tourism and mining; both are designed to attract greater foreign investment and foreign exchange. One key illustration of the "open for business" approach of the Tanzanian government would be the work of the Tanzanian Investment Center, which "is reported to have identified some four million hectares of land under its Land Bank scheme" that is deemed "suitable for investment" and is then made available to potential investors under a type of derivative title or lease found in the new land laws.[34] A seemingly inevitable side effect of the aggressive promotion of land for development by the government of Tanzania, however, has been the widespread dispossession and evictions of peasant landholders and subsistence farmers or miners in rural areas.[35]

The land reforms were paralleled in the mid-1990s by the development of a Tanzanian tourism policy. In 1996 a master plan for the implementation of the new tourism policy was announced. In 1999 an updated tourism policy was adopted by the Ministry of Natural Resources and Tourism, and in 2002 an updated master plan was published.[36] It is noteworthy that the 2002 plan comments briefly, but critically, on the recent land reforms: "The new land laws in Tanzania will place considerable importance on liasing/getting agreement with local communities regarding land use for tourism purposes. However, there appears to be lack of clarity with regard to the interpretation and implementation of these laws."[37]

The Serengeti is located within the Northern Wildlife Area, which has long been a focal point of these activities, because it is an internationally known tourist attraction and because traditional uses of land are perceived to conflict, or do in fact conflict, with the objective of expanding the revenue generated by tourism. While the policies contain some requirements for community-based ecotourism initiatives, the evidence so far suggests that these provisions have provided little assistance in minimizing these conflicts, nor have they led to significant benefits to communities. Such benefits are often merely cosmetic, like the building of a classroom or some other small piece of infrastructure. Where communities are given a more meaningful opportunity to be involved in the development of local integrated conservation and tourism programs, these benefits may well increase. However, there are countervailing concerns that the overall trajectory of development, including the privatization of control over the wildlife areas described below, will continue to subvert these efforts or push them to the margins. As the LHRC 2005 report noted, it is "easier to relocate people rather than animals."[38] Both the structure of the land reforms and the explicit embrace of tourism and mining as development strategies suggest why any conflict over land use has usually been resolved in the animals' favor, and people have increasingly found themselves at the losing end, facing either eviction or punitive measures from officials for engaging in traditional activities such as hunting.

It is not clear whether the people in the Serengeti District have ever been able to live compatibly with wildlife. This is not surprising, given that their practices are largely restricted to hunting small game for food.[39] However, as both the local population and the wildlife management areas around the national park have expanded over the past several decades, access to traditional sources of sustenance and livelihood have been curtailed or eliminated. As part of this intensifying pressure on land use in the area, the Ikorongo Game Reserve on the northwest border of the Serengeti National Park was substantially expanded in 1994 and its status upgraded from game-controlled area to game reserve. The expansion of the reserve (along with other park and reserve expansions in the area) reduced the land available for cultivation and pastorage. It has also intensified the risk of disease transmission from wildlife to people. It was this expansion that originally led to the eviction of most of the village of Nyamuma, for which the former residents continued to seek compensation until the time of the Remaining Nyamuma evictions in 2001. Another eviction, of the nearby village of Nyanguge in January 2000, also increased the pressures on land in the area, as some of those villagers settled in Remaining Nyamuma; they too sought compensation from the government.

Game reserves and game-controlled areas are both managed by the Department of Wildlife. However, while the residence of people and their livestock is prohibited in game reserves, local human activities (apart from hunting) are allowed in game-controlled areas.[40] For this reason, the 1994 shift in designation of the Ikorongo reserve from a game-controlled area to a game reserve, in order to facilitate other activities, was a significant step in dispossessing the local communities, hunters in particular. Hunting in game reserves is allowed by permit issued by the Wildlife Division of the Ministry of Natural Resources and Tourism. Hunting outfitters gain exclusive access (concessions) to specific game reserves from the director of wildlife. The director exercises considerable discretion in granting these concessions, which effectively take the form of leases permitting exclusive access to a specific wildlife management area for a specified period of time (generally five years).

The Ikorongo reserve is located within a unique and globally remarkable migratory corridor, between the Serengeti National Park and Kenya's Maasai Mara National Reserve. It is this factor that may have prompted its expansion and upgraded status in 1994. Government records from the Wildlife Division's hunting section in 2003 reveal a hunting concession over three areas, Ikorongo, Grumeti, and the Fort Ikoa Open Area, registered to a company named VIP Hunting Safaris Club.[41] VIP Hunting Safaris is the former name of the company Grumeti Reserves, Ltd., which is currently the holder of the concession in these three areas. Grumeti Reserves is wholly owned by the American financier and commodities trader Paul Tudor Jones. Although its access to the land is held in the form of a hunting concession, Grumeti discontinued hunting on the property sometime in 2002, and instead has developed the property as a wildlife viewing area. The three areas over which Grumeti now appears to exercise exclusive access total approximately 136,000 hectares (340,000 acres), and the area, with its three high-end lodges, stables, tennis courts, and spa, is now being marketed as "one of the world's most luxurious eco-tourism resorts."[42]

Given the exclusivity of the tourism that is now being marketed in the very site, or very close to the site, of the evictions, it is easy to see why these people and their activities might have become an issue for the government in 2001, if the Grumeti venture were at the proposal stage at that time. Despite the fact that both the people and their subsistence activities have long coexisted with wildlife in the area, the activities are increasingly construed as a threat to the wildlife and to the tourists who come to view it, while the villagers themselves are styled as "poachers," "vagrants," "criminals," or simply as a "security risk." These villagers were also sometimes referred to as "Kenyans," a rhetorical move clearly intended to call into question their entitlement to anything at all, despite the fact that their citizenship has never seriously been an issue. It would seem that here, however, the real source of the current conflict is not between the local people and the animals but rather between the locals and outside interests, as well as perhaps national elites, both of whom stand to profit from the abundance of wildlife in the area and the extraordinary spectacle of the annual migrations. Tanzania's tourism policies reflect the importance of investors and tourism to its foreign exchange revenue. Yet despite the tendency to conflate these policies with the national interest, the question of whose interest is served by such policies remains, for the costs to local inhabitants are clear while it is uncertain whether they will derive any countervailing benefits. The representation of locals alternatively as criminals or as outsiders is a discursive strategy designed to delegitimate or exclude their concerns and opposition in the policy-making process; the effect is to exacerbate their disadvantage.

In addition to tourist development related to wildlife viewing in the Serengeti District, two other significant external drivers of development in this region are gold mining and hunting. Although they don't appear to be directly implicated in the evictions in this case, they are certainly implicated in a pattern of evictions in the region and in the rest of the country. Recently Tanzania has seen a number of incidents of forcible dispossession of locals related to mining operations, and violent conflicts between small-scale miners and residents, on the one hand, and multinational companies such as the Canadian-based Barrick Gold and Placer Dome, on the other. A legal advocacy group based in Dar es Salaam, the Lawyers Environmental Action Team (LEAT), has been investigating the complaints of local communities displaced by mining and has advised locals, with some limited successes.[43]

The most egregious incident occurred in 1996 at the Bulyanhulu Gold Mine, now owned and operated by Canadian-based Barrick Gold (then operated by Sutton Resources), where at least thirty thousand small-scale miners were forcibly evicted, and more than fifty of them killed, buried by a bulldozer in the process of the eviction.[44] No compensation has yet been provided to the displaced in that instance, notwithstanding ongoing domestic and international NGO mobilization concerning the issue.[45]

More proximate, geographically and temporally, are evictions related to two gold mines located in Tarime District (next to Serengeti District): the North Mara Gold Mine (also operated by Barrick) and the Africa Mashariki Gold Mine (parent company Placer Dome). The North Mara mine commenced operations in 2001, after the forced evictions of local villagers. Since that time,

village leaders and prominent locals have been harassed, arrested, and imprisoned; further village lands have been appropriated by the dumping of waste
and rubble onto those lands without notice or compensation; and up to six
villagers have been shot by company security guards (one was shot on the
grounds of the local primary school after he allegedly stole some gas or oil from
the company; the most recent victim was shot in the back by a security guard
in June 2006 after he allegedly entered the mine complex). After complaints at
the Mashariki Gold Mine related to inadequate compensation paid to evicted
villagers, in 2003 LEAT was successful in obtaining an order for an injunction
against the mine from the Commission.[46]

## Funding Issues: NGOs, Bilateral Donors, and the Human Rights Commission

A final set of issues relates to the structure of the Commission on Human
Rights and Good Governance and the role of outside funders in its creation
and operation, and in the work of NGOs such as the Legal and Human Rights
Centre (LHRC) within Tanzania. The Commission was created in 2000 following pressure from the Citizen's Coalition for a New Constitution ("the Coalition"), a group of over fifty Tanzanian NGOs organized for the creation of
a body to address human rights complaints.[47] The catalyst for the formation
of the Coalition was the fiftieth anniversary of the Universal Declaration of
Human Rights. However, it was also greatly facilitated by the provision of funding to the Tanzanian government earmarked for the establishment of just such
a commission, including the building to house it. The government originally
proposed to simply rename an existing inquiry body, one that was designed
to deal with administrative malfeasance and other complaints against government functionaries. Although the body was redesigned somewhat as well as re-
named in the face of a counterproposal from the Coalition, concerns remained
about the capacity of the Commission to effectively deal with human rights
complaints articulated by the LHRC and others. For example, there were no
human rights specialists on the Commission and there was no secure, independent source of funding for its work that could be insulated from government
pressure and spending priorities.

The adequacy of the Commission's structure was a source of dispute between the internal human rights groups and external funders in the Nyamuma
case, the first human rights complaint to come before the Commission. At the
same time, the reaction of the government to the results of the inquiry suggests

that it remained resistant to the mandate of the Commission. These disputes and differences provide a point of entry into the question of what the different groups hoped to achieve through the Commission; they also open a window on their possibly diverging aspirations for the human rights enterprise as a whole.

One issue is the degree of naïve "rights formalism" exhibited by international human rights funders and NGOs. The LHRC was concerned from the beginning about the structure of the Commission and whether it would provide an avenue of real redress for victims such as those at Nyamuma. The funders by contrast insisted that all that was necessary for the Commission to function well was to staff it with "good people." The actual path that the Nyamuma case took suggests that the LHRC's concerns about structure and funding were not misplaced: the first "inquiry" by the Commission, a cursory review that involved no public hearings, determined that there was no factual basis for the claims and that the people had not been evicted but had moved voluntarily. Even when the second, "real" and "public" inquiry was convened after interventions from the LHRC, the problems were not over. While it was possible to find funding for the Commission itself, it proved impossible to extract resources from either governments or NGOs for basic humanitarian relief to the villagers evicted from Remaining Nyamuma. This was not because the plight of the villagers lacked either urgency or severity—villagers were already dying, some from hunger, others from lack of medical care. In addition, funds were required to enable the villagers to testify at the inquiry. This too was not a minor issue. The villagers who had been displaced from Remaining Nyamuma were located in the far western part of Tanzania. Even when the hearing was convened in a town closer than Dar es Salaam, considerable funds were still required to enable the villagers to travel the 110 kilometers to the hearings and to ensure them basic accommodation while they were there.[48] Although the government had been involved in setting up the Commission, it not only failed to provide the funding needed to adequately conduct the inquiry but rejected the Commission's findings in the Nyamuma case on the theory that it had been "misled." Moreover, it refused to provide alternative housing or any other form of humanitarian relief to the displaced people, as the report had required; the LHRC's effort in the courts to force the government to comply with the Commission's recommendations is ongoing.

Resistance on the part of governments to inquiries that place them in an unsympathetic light or cost them money is neither unusual nor difficult to understand. In addition, resistance through bureaucratic and procedural subversion is a common reaction to institutional reforms that are unpopular, especially those that are externally imposed.

What of the external funders?[49] Why did the failures—whether measured in terms of the suffering of the affected people, or the deficiencies of process that were evident throughout the Nyamuma inquiry—not evoke a more sympathetic response, especially given that such issues typically lie at the center of the concerns of human rights groups? Did the mere *existence* of the Commission constitute a victory for human rights in the eyes of foreign donors?

Another possibility is that the funders themselves harbored some degree of ambivalence, if not conflict of interest, around Nyamuma, at least to the extent that addressing the concerns of the LHRC in that case required them to confront government actors directly over their actions and (non)responses. In general, outside funders, especially other national governments, do not speak out on controversial issues, for fear that they will be perceived as interfering in domestic affairs. Individual ambassadors may be willing to act or to speak out on certain issues; when the LHRC ran short of money, it was the Embassy of Sweden that was forthcoming with some limited funds. The "diplomatic" role adopted by most state funders may also explain why it was so much more difficult to obtain funds for humanitarian relief, to provide food and housing for the displaced people, than it was to obtain funding for legal actions.

Should the other, nonstate outside funders have weighed in at this point on the side of the Commission? On the side of the LHRC? In the name of human rights? On behalf of the villagers themselves? It is worth considering why they might have been reluctant to do so. Outside funders typically depend on the sufferance of the government to remain in the country. Unless they have points of leverage that they are willing to use, this is likely to restrain them from engaging in open conflict with the government. This is especially true if they have a number of projects ongoing. In such cases, they may be unwilling to jeopardize them all for the sake of one, no matter how compelling it may seem on its own merits.[50]

Foreign funders may also have goals and aims that diverge from or actually conflict with those of local human rights activists, a possibility that emerges especially clearly in the context of the uninvestigated killings of "poachers" by the wardens in the wildlife management area around the Serengeti National Park. These "poachers" were locals who had traditionally relied on small animals in the park as a source of food. With increasing emphasis on the park as a site for international tourism, however, there was growing pressure at the national and international levels to "make the Park safe for tourists." It is this perceived conflict between tourism and local subsistence activity that seems to have set the context for the shootings of nine alleged poachers in the wildlife management area just outside the park in 1997.[51] The LHRC had commenced an investigation of the shootings and, despite difficulties in obtaining funding for this particular case, did bring the complaint to the newly created Commission. However, the complaint has not proceeded, in part for lack of witnesses but also, it seems, because of political sensitivities. There were only two survivors, one of whom was age fifteen at the time, and their whereabouts are not known. Further, the LHRC received an unprecedented visit from the German ambassador shortly after the killings, in which he commented on the negative publicity that had been received by the Frankfurt Zoological Society connecting it to the incident.[52] In the meeting, he made reference to "basket funding" offered for the election year 2000, which was essentially a pooled fund available to NGOs from a number of state donors, including the Germans, and asked whether the LHRC had applied. Although the LHRC had up to that point generally been successful in its funding applications, following the ambassador's visit, the LHRC discovered that it had now been unsuccessful in gaining access to that pool of funds.

Domestic NGOs and activist groups are almost invariably engaged in conflict and contestation with governments; indeed, they are often organized precisely for this purpose. However, as is the case with foreign governments, it is not atypical for international human rights or humanitarian groups to try to avoid issues that are perceived to be "political," either on the theory that such issues would jeopardize their neutrality or out of pragmatic concern for their capacity to continue doing the work they want to do. This may cash out in a variety of ways. Such groups may prefer to focus on one issue and avoid another; they may prefer more narrowly targeted campaigns rather than campaigns that aim at broad social or political transformation.[53] In addition, they may have an eye on the international stage as much as the domestic audience, if only because they may have donors or backers of their own that they seek to satisfy or placate.

What is more, external funders may simply have different priorities and projects than local human rights groups. Well before they become involved in a particular dispute in a given country, external organizations are likely to be in possession of a well-elaborated sense of what it means to promote human rights or humanitarian goals; they may also have entrenched ideas about how to go about doing so; and they may already have a conception of the "problem" that they must address in any given country or context. For example, international actors, whether international NGOs, international institutions, or states, may be as interested in establishing a "culture of human rights" and implementing human rights processes and institutions as in responding to any particular issue or abuse. One reason is that objectives like promoting human rights and the rule of law are increasingly part of broader governance projects to which such actors may be committed. For a range of reasons, outside funders typically come armed and girded for particular types of battles and are prepared to face some enemies but not others. Hence, some human rights issues may register more powerfully on their radar screens than others, and notwithstanding the capacious reach of human rights norms at the formal level, some concerns may not register at all. It may be very difficult to alter or dislodge prevailing ideas and intuitions about how to engage in human rights work, even where evidence on the ground suggests something sharply at odds with these premises. Instead, initial assumptions about what human rights "are" in form and content are likely to powerfully shape the agenda and may simply function to screen some issues out or render them invisible within the framework of human rights entirely.

This concern is especially salient with respect to economic and social rights. Because they so often touch on distributive conflicts, economic and social rights are often perceived to be "political" per se—that is, inextricably connected to popular and legislative choices and processes. Notwithstanding the Vienna Declaration and the supposed indivisibility and interdependence of human rights to which the international community is now committed, the geopolitical battles that marked the field of human rights until the end of the Cold War continue to leave their mark. There is still a hierarchy among rights, and Western foundations and human rights groups, the source of most human rights funding and influence in the international arena, continue to prioritize those rights enumerated in the International Covenant on Civil and Political Rights. As a result, many economic and social conflicts and crises simply do not evoke a response framed in the language of rights.[54]

It is worth observing that international NGOs and funders are not simply autonomous decision makers with respect to human rights; rather, they themselves may be hostage to some degree to projects, priorities, and trends emanating from other institutions and actors. Because they themselves operate in a complex international environment, these NGOs and funders may be channeling rather than authoring concerns about corruption and human rights abuses, or reiterating "common sense" about human rights and good governance, now in wide circulation on the international plane. Where the funders are, as in the case of the LHRC, governments or international institutions, the likelihood that external influences and complex motives are part of the decision-making process is still greater. Even assuming agreement on what constitutes the proper focus of attention, here human rights are likely to be only one concern of many, and moreover one that takes a backseat to others. Whatever the reasons, it is clear that in the case of Nyamuma, the LHRC found it much more difficult to get funds for humanitarian relief than it did for human rights advocacy.

## How Institutions Matter to Human Rights Strategies

If one of the challenges of economic and social rights is securing substantive relief and resources rather than mere "process" rights for those who are dispossessed and disempowered, another is institutionalizing what often seem like fragile and contingent victories. Here the hope is that rather than merely local and evanescent, success can be structurally grounded in order to carry some promise of broader, and lasting, transformative change. Nyamuma reminds us that in order to realize this aspiration we may be compelled to reflect, in the most basic and thoroughgoing ways, on what institutions matter to human rights and why. For many things were indeed being "institutionalized" in the run-up to the Nyamuma evictions, including the Commission, a variety of land reforms, and new development strategies concerning tourism and mining. Although land reforms and development strategies may seem marginal or irrelevant to the realization of human rights and did not, in any event, form any part of the inquiry process, this analysis points to a quite different set of conclusions: land reforms and development strategies set in motion a series of events and, in so doing, appear to have played a significant and sometimes pernicious role in the violations that occurred at Nyamuma. And while human rights institutions are often styled as "the answer" to abuses in cases such as Nyamuma, it is clear that that would be an unsafe conclusion too.

Nyamuma also raises the relationship of critique to reconstruction. It seems fruitless to try to imagine full-scale alternatives that could reliably have prevented the evictions and subsequent violations from occurring. But the institutional discussion need not end there. On the theory that alternative pathways don't come from Mars, that it is indeed possible to "hew stones of hope" from present conditions and possibilities, part of the task must involve identifying the concrete decisions that were made about institutional design; the alternatives that were available and in some cases even on the table; and the consequences of choosing one route versus another.

There are also the questions of who controls or influences the land reform process, and how it is that revolutionizing land policy comes to have the priority that it now so often has. How, for example, did it come to pass that land reforms were instituted by the Tanzanian Parliament so shortly after de Soto's visit in 2003? Where did those reforms engender conflicts with other government policies, and what might have been done differently if those conflicts had been recognized? How carefully, if at all, was the full range of consequences considered? And if such reforms are retained, what might need to be added to the regulatory and policy agenda to forestall or ameliorate problems such as occurred at Nyamuma?

Whether, and to what extent, these reforms and policies will result in any larger benefits for Tanzanians as a whole still remains in question. However, it is already clear that they are creating profound, and growing, disparities among different groups. It is these growing disparities that seem likely to generate ongoing human rights conflicts, conflicts that will not be remedied by attention to conventional human rights norms, objectives, and institutions alone. The central issue here is the distribution of the costs and benefits of Tanzania's path to development. At present, the vast majority of the costs of development are being imposed on subsistence-based local communities in areas such as the West Serengeti, groups of people who can least afford to bear them. Up to the present time, little or no effort has been made to mitigate these losses, either by the government or by the other parties who are now benefiting from the changes. Instead, beneficiaries of the new policies, whether they are foreign investors or merely better-positioned Tanzanians, are now able to call on the state to enforce and sometimes, as Nyamuma illustrates, to assist in the practice of evictions and dispossession.

Inherent local challenges arising from the limited land base and the growing population are likely to put continuing pressure on subsistence activities and to generate further conflict over access to land. However, it is clear that both the land reform and development policies, some of which were the result of outside pressure from commercial interests and multilateral agencies, have exacerbated the intergroup conflict within Tanzania. As a result, there is an immediate need to deal with the local resentments and distrust bred from years of disenfranchisement, as well as those arising from the generations of resettlements that have occurred. The characterization of particular locals as lawless and dangerous to tourists and animals, or both, covers over a set of conflicts, real and imaginary, over land use and development policy. Efforts to criminalize these actors merely obscure rather than address issues that are likely to persist, generating further human rights concerns and violations and intensifying rather than ameliorating the harm to those who are on the losing side of the deal. It seems unlikely that these conflicts can be successfully addressed without revisiting some of the basic decisions about land reform and development policy and probing the consequences, both expected and unexpected, that they have generated so far.

Land reforms in the style of de Soto are now repeatedly sold as "pro-poor" policy. Yet as the struggles over land document, the routine experience is that as previously "valueless" land becomes recognized as an investment opportunity, most Tanzanians see little benefit. Indeed, despite the promise of both growth and poverty alleviation, such reforms create the very risks of dispossession that are now so clearly materializing in Tanzania, risks that are intensified when particular plots of land are specifically identified for development and banked for future exploitation by outsiders. The consequence is that land reforms persistently generate not widespread empowerment and engagement in more sophisticated and remunerative economic activity on the part of the economically disenfranchised, but the perverse consequence of greater concentration of wealth and power in the elite.

There are alternatives, and they need not be understood simply in terms of the choice between reform and stasis, or between development and tradition.[55] Consider, for example, the other land reform proposals in circulation, such as those tabled in the Shivji Report. They may very well have been more attentive and sensitive to the interests of those who are now being dispossessed; in any event, it is certain that land reforms *can* be made more attentive to those interests. If the effect of such alternatives is to restrain the easy alienation of these lands or prevent their use and development without wider consultation and agreement among the affected parties, then that may be the point: securing agreement for new land uses under different legal and institutional arrangements may compel concessions and compensation to those who would otherwise simply lose out.

It is worth recalling that until recently, land reform for development was primarily about the *distribution* of land. By contrast, land reform in conjunction with contemporary development policy almost invariably means reform to land *law*. Given that legal reforms often effectively redistribute land, the question of distribution may need to be put back on the agenda explicitly. The argument for doing so seems compelling where, as in Tanzania, land and other reforms lead not only to the "hard" evictions such as occurred at Nyamuma but also to what might be called "soft eviction," that is, the effective expulsion, through urban upgrading or other policies, of communities from the land they have traditionally used.

Real consultation, and substantial control of the decision-making process, is also key. Although it has officially been part of Tanzanian law for some time now that communities be given a meaningful opportunity to participate in the development of the lands on which they reside, and to thereby directly reap some of the economic benefits of that process, these laws have not been implemented effectively to date.[56] Notwithstanding token efforts at the implementation of "benefit-based" approaches to development, locals (rightly) believe that the gains they are receiving are far outweighed by the costs that are being imposed on them. How different this picture might look in the Serengeti if the requirements for real consultation and participation were taken seriously is something we can only guess at, although there are real lessons from other contexts that are surely of use here.[57] As the more recent history of land struggles in Tanzania discloses, the extent of countervailing pressure and the bargaining power of the groups—and hence the outcome of conflicts such as Nyamuma—can sometimes be successfully altered by factors such as the disclosure of previously hidden information; collective learning, leading to organized rather than sporadic responses; and shifts in external alliances and the tactics those alliances enable.

## Postscript: Hope After Nyamuma?

As the people of Nyamuma have struggled in court to have their rights to their land recognized and compensated, unauthorized takings of land by the government for a variety of purposes—foreign investment, environmental protection, or conservation—have continued to occur throughout the country. However, there has been a significant change in the ways that both local communities and advocacy organizations have responded to these events. Tanzanians are now more likely to vigorously contest such dispossessions, and are more empowered to do so, while advocacy groups like the LHRC are more strategic in how they are intervening to assist the people affected. It is in these developments, detailed below in the context of several recent disputes, that it is possible to identify a ray of hope emerging from the ongoing tragedy of Nyamuma.

The following five scenarios detail some of the ways in which the experience of the Nyamuma evictions has changed peoples' responses to conflicts over land. In general, they reveal greater strategic engagement with both legal and political processes, from selective use of court processes to parliamentary interventions; increased reliance on media to publicize disputes; continued advocacy on the domestic and international fronts; and no small amount of direct action against officials who formerly used force against local populaces with impunity.

The first concerns the Hadzabe in the Yaeda Chini Valley in the Mbulu District of the Manyara Region, internationally recognized as the oldest group still living traditionally in the Rift Valley. The Hadzabe's ability to maintain their traditional hunter-gatherer way of life is increasingly under threat by the incursion of other groups into their traditional territory, as well as by the granting of hunting permits in the area by the government. Recently, the district commissioner, working with other groups who have settled in the valley, attempted to enter into an agreement with a foreign investor for an exclusive lease for big-game hunting. This would have left the Hadzabe people without access to the land for hunting or gathering and, consequently, entirely without sustenance. When they first became aware of the proposal, the Hadzabe contacted the media and international organizations that work for minority rights in order to publicize their opposition to it. A commissioner from the Commission was sent to investigate, and after meeting with the district authorities he became persuaded of the merits of the investment, and subsequently convened a meeting in which he encouraged the people of Yaeda Chini to support the investment. That meeting was disrupted by protest. The abortive meeting and the very public protest was then publicized in the national media, which facilitated efforts by the Hadzabe to secure more support from advocacy groups both within and outside the country. The vigorous advocacy on the part of the Hadzabe leaders led to the arrest of their two spokespersons on a charge of inciting the people. However, the arrests silenced neither the Hadzabe nor the advocacy groups, including international NGOs and faith-based organizations working on their behalf. Instead, a further onslaught of urgent appeals to both the government and the investor on behalf of the Hadzabe eventually led to the withdrawal of the proposal by the investor.

Two differences from the Nyamuma case are worth noting here. First, the government did not use force to evict these people but rather attempted negotiations through the district commission and then the Commission itself with the less affected villagers in the area. Second, and perhaps as a consequence of this approach, the people were made aware of the looming threat of dispossession, and with this knowledge and the support of NGOs and the media were able to successfully challenge the authorities, even when other groups were already siding with the government.

In another area, known as Kiteto, in the same region of Manyara, the district council decided to earmark an area in and around a cluster of seven villages as a village conservation area. According to the Village Land Act, it should be the villages, through their village assemblies, that decide to demarcate such areas. The law further allows several villages to agree among themselves to demarcate land for certain common uses among the villages. In this case, however, the villagers were not consulted. When they were asked to move to give way to the conservation area, they refused and turned to the media and to the LHRC for legal support and intervention with the regional police. Notwithstanding these efforts, a forced eviction was subsequently conducted. The immediate response from the villagers was to seek further publicity in the national media and to seek an injunction against the evictions while they filed a suit challenging the process of demarcating land as a conservation area without their involvement, and their subsequent forced eviction. The injunction application was successful, allowing the people to stay on their land until the main suit is determined. The greater effectiveness of legal advocacy in this instance can be traced to the greater awareness of the potential for a legal challenge on the part of the villagers. While the people in Nyamuma sought help only after they were already out of their area, the villagers of Kiteto acted immediately in approaching the media and the LHRC. For its part, LHRC was willing to take on this case and successfully argued the injunction application, thus ensuring that unlike the villagers of Nyamuma, who have remained homeless and dispossessed throughout their lengthy court battle, these villagers will be entitled to remain on their land until such time as the government is able to make its case for the eviction successfully to the court, which given the clear violations of provisions of the Village Land Act, seems unlikely.

A third episode concerned a group of pastoralists who had moved to a valley known as Ihefu, which is also a water catchment area. The authorities decided, rather abruptly, that cattle grazing had been responsible for environmental degradation in the area and ordered thousands of the Ihefu to move within a very short time. The affected people were required to hire trucks at their own expense to move the cattle, and the scale and speed of the demanded relocation caused significant expense and loss of livestock. This relocation, like the others, incited an active opposition. More than twenty pastoralist groups came together to challenge the government's actions. They informed advocacy groups and sent petitions to their members of Parliament, leading to a discussion of the matter in Parliament. The groups are also pursuing a legal challenge in the courts to seek compensation for their lost property.

While the preceding examples emphasize the prompt and effective pursuit of legal and administrative advocacy strategies, aided by publicity, in a growing number of instances the people are prepared to articulate even more directly their opposition to proposed government actions to remove them from their land. In a suburb of Dar es Salaam known as Chasimba, a legal dispute is currently before the courts between the residents and a company over title to the land. Before the legal proceedings were concluded, the district commissioner held a meeting with the residents, in which he attempted to convince them to prepare to move from the area. Although the residents were angered by what they took to be the assumption that they would lose in court, the district commissioner persisted in claiming that they would need to move, thereby inflaming the group. The meeting became so hostile that the district commissioner had to be rushed out of the area. This type of confrontation of a political leader by the people is unprecedented in Tanzania, and is evidence of a new level of empowerment of the people. Fortunately, such encounters do not always end with the threat of violence. In two other recent examples, meetings between the people and high-level political figures have led to successful resolutions of the conflicts in question.

In Misenyi, a group of people were being requested to vacate to give way for a proposed (international) investment in a ranching enterprise. Although the groups opposing the investment were pursuing various channels to have it shut down, it was not until the president of Tanzania, Jakaya Kikwete, visited the area in person that a successful resolution for the people was obtained. On hearing of the difficult situation from the people themselves, and how they were exhausting their meager resources in order to defend their lands in court, the president publicly declared that they should be left alone. A similar encounter took place in another area of Dar es Salaam known as Kibamba. Here, residents had originally agreed to relocate for some development initiatives but had not been able to reach agreement on a fair compensation. The matter was heavily reported in the media and eventually came to the attention of the minister for lands, who then decided to hold a meeting with the residents. At the meeting, when an official report was read out that the people claimed contained inaccuracies, they shouted down the official and provided their own evidence directly to the minister. The meeting led the minister to order that the residents be allowed to stay on their land until adequate compensation was decided upon and paid out, and to order a police investigation against his own officers.

All of these incidents have occurred in the years after the evictions at Nyamuma. As awareness of the illegality and the political resistance to the perceived injustice of these acts has grown, it has become more difficult for the government to simply displace people from their land by force. Tanzanians who are adversely affected are actively resisting these evictions through recourse to administrative mechanisms, the courts, international civil society alerts, domestic and international media outlets, and even "shouting down" local officials. Perhaps because the pressure exerted through these means has become more common and more organized, higher authorities such as the president and the minister have been willing to intervene in some of these cases.

This new mobilization, some of which has prevented planned evictions altogether and some of which has merely altered the terms in which they occur, represents a significant achievement in itself. Yet the evictions are merely the most visible, and extreme, consequence of a larger set of transformations, raising a further question: What are the prospects that this mobilization will, on its own, come to exert pressure on the larger regulatory and policy initiatives behind the evictions?

Here the issue is complicated. When the 1999 land laws were enacted, the popular reaction was positive, as the reforms promised power to the people through the village assemblies, and recognized land ownership by women. The challenge now is to unpack the constellation of concerns occasioned by a larger set of laws on investment and development, including the development of land banks, as these laws collectively provide the legal basis for evictions. In addition, a hidden time bomb is now on the horizon: *mkurabita*, or land registration.

The LHRC is currently engaged in outreach work to sensitize people to the risks entailed by land registration. This has not been easy: fed a steady diet of claims about its benefits, people are anxiously awaiting registration in order to access the capital that it may provide. Moreover, registration has some undeniable attractions. The new land laws have made it possible to register customary land, something that is appealing to customary landholders who had sometimes faced the onerous task of claiming back land from individuals who had attempted, and sometimes succeeded, in registering land individually.

Especially attractive is the idea that when land is registered, not only will title be secure, but land can be used to obtain cash.

The main concern of the LHRC has simply been to caution people about the dark side of these developments, however obscure the risks may seem. As the LHRC has discovered in two districts, Handeni and Bagamoyo, in which *mkurabita* has been attempted, people are not generally aware of the ultimate implications of registration. In the excitement over the prospect of obtaining loans, they typically fail to appreciate that they could lose their land if debts remain unpaid, and they may not consider that although registration entitles them to sell their land, the result may be that they then have no alternative land to cling to. Most Tanzanians are poor; they will be tempted to take out loans or even sell the land in order to pay for necessities such as school fees or to engage in petty business ventures. In most cases, it will not be easy to repay the loans. Thus, the specter of permanent indebtedness or dispossession looms. Apart from the risks to individuals, there are systemic risks to communities as a whole as a result of alienation of land on a widespread scale. Pastoralists, in addition, face distinct threats to their way of life. Not only is the idea of individual title alien to these groups; land registration is very likely to force pastoral groups to give up access to the lands on which they have traditionally hunted and to settle for a mere piece of land in exchange.

The weapon at hand to contest the manner in which land registration is proceeding may be the very empowerment that has come out of the mobilization around the evictions. Once land registration is recognized as a matter of economic security and even survival, those with stakes in the reform process can be expected to organize and to resist, as they have in the case of evictions. However, given that registration is at a relatively early stage in Tanzania and that concrete internal illustrations of the risks are few, effective mobilization will almost certainly require activists to draw lessons from other contexts, where the experience with registration is more advanced. This suggests new, and different, roles for international advocacy groups: the provision of information about other contexts in which land registration has been introduced, and the consequences that have ensued; the identification of the actors behind these initiatives; and the sharing of strategies for engagement, and if necessary, resistance to these processes, ideally in advance of their introduction rather than after the fact.[58]

Yet there is a further question: can local action on its own, even assisted in this manner, be expected to disrupt the overall project of transforming land uses, especially the trend toward rewarding foreign investors with large land grants? Mobilization sometimes stops the evictions; it may impede the implementation of land policies in particular locales; or it may mitigate the effects of reforms. But so far, it is not altering the general drive to commodify land in the name of greater productivity and growth. Nor has it yet defeated the campaign, waged both directly and collaterally, against those engaged in subsistence activities wherever those activities are perceived to conflict with initiatives to foster market-centered investment and growth.

This is where the conflicts continue. Although the normal expectation may be that a government has the interests of its people at the forefront, what we observe in some of the examples is the government acting against its own people, in some instances even contrary to the law. For example, even the Commission, which is supposed to guard against government violations of rights, was used against the people in the case of the Hadzabe. It is clear that the government and particular populations may have divided interests, although reforms are typically couched in terms of economic benefit to those populations. To use the words of one minister interviewed by the LHRC, "The Arab is coming there to put up a camp for his leisure, to rest and to do some small hunting, as there is not much in terms of animals to hunt. But it will be for the good of the people, as he will make a road and build a school which is needed by this people." Roads and schools, however, are of little interest to people who have lost their land.

The government of Tanzania remains under a clear inducement to facilitate foreign investment because the revenue that it generates enables the reimbursement of loans. Yet while we may assume that either government or some government officials are excited by the possibilities offered by openness to foreign investment, it is also worth considering the external groups and institutions driving this venture forward. As indicated by the widespread introduction of land reform projects looking much like those now operating in Tanzania, whatever the government's own desires and responsibilities with respect to land policy and land use are, it is caught up in a development trend not entirely of its own making. To the extent that they are part of the equation, ultimately the external forces that have proved to be such powerful catalysts to land reform may have to be engaged as well.

What would an international campaign challenging the forces promoting such policies and reforms look like? Could we imagine an international campaign, for example, that eschewed selective advocacy on behalf of the environment and wildlife and, instead of positioning those engaged in traditional economic activities as a threat, or even as a development problem to be "solved," imagined them as the very parties to be supported?

Would such a campaign still be framed in the language of human rights? If so, in the name of what rights would it be advanced? At this point, we can safely say that any such campaign, because it is destined—even designed—to engage dominant ideas of property rights and development, could expect to meet either countervailing rights claims or competing interpretations of what respect for those rights entails. If so, would prevailing in the end require recuperating other vocabularies of struggle—solidarity, self-determination, socialism,[59] or even sustainable development, for example—or inventing new ones not yet on the horizon?

Beyond the vocabularies of moral responsibility, political struggle, and economic development, on what regulatory and policy territory would such a campaign rest? What positions would it advance with respect to land and development, for example? Might it endorse heterodoxy rather than orthodoxy in law and policy, thereby sanctioning greater diversity and experimentation and empowering those at the local and national levels who have reason to prioritize other legal rules and policies?[60]

Moving into this territory engages a host of interconnected issues about growth and distributive justice. It would almost certainly involve new analytic and discursive work, as well as engage types of knowledge and expertise—collective, professional, and political—that lie largely outside the purview of the human rights community as it is currently constituted. In short, it would be a big step, especially for international human rights advocates. Moreover, the complexities of effective and sustained ESR advocacy are not to be underestimated, as this and the other chapters in this volume have illustrated. However, the LHRC has already signaled that in Tanzania this is where at least some of the important action now lies. In their own actions, local activists and advocates have issued a clear challenge to advocates and actors on the international plane as well.

## Chapter 4

# Freeing Mohammed Zakari

*Rights as Footprints*

Jeremy Perelman and Katharine Young,
with the participation of Mahama Ayariga

So the Zakari case has been one of the biggest achievements of what legal aid has done in this community. And because everyone, almost all the community members were involved, it became like a footprint in everybody's mind: anybody you ask around knows the story.

*Nihad Swallah, Community Organizer, Legal Resources Center*

This chapter begins and ends with a metaphor. The metaphor is not our own; rather, it was first articulated during an interview with Nihad Swallah, a community organizer with whom we had worked on the Zakari case. We use it as a metaphor of rights, as "footprints" of remembered facts and values, rather than as normatively charged interests or as bundles of entitlements. This metaphor helps us to understand the process of rights-claiming in a new way. The Zakari story—and with it, the story of a community's battle for "access to healthcare" in Ghana—serves to illustrate the meaning of the footprints metaphor and its departure from current representations of rights. It demonstrates how multiple communities assimilate and incorporate ideas of "rights" and how this assimilation works over time.

This story features a series of encounters. It involves an encounter between a legal norm—encapsulating the internationally recognized "right of everyone to the enjoyment of the highest attainable standard of physical and mental health"[1] and the constitutionally endorsed "right to good health care"[2]—and the community in Nima, Ghana. It describes encounters among subsistence farmers, innovative Ghanaian lawyer-activists, community leaders from organizations of mothers and youth, as well as foreign law-student interns and their professor. It also speculates about encounters between rights and collective memory, and between pessimism and hope. Finally, it seeks to make sense of encounters between writers and the fields of action in which they participate.

The case of Mohammed Zakari began and ended formally in one month, but its significance lies in a pursuit of rights-claiming that is still under way. The chapter is organized into two parts. The first part tells the story of Mohammed Zakari, an elderly subsistence farmer detained in a public hospital for failure to pay his medical expenses. In this part, the story is told through four significant moments, which represent the choices and turning points of advocacy and mobilization.

The second part of the chapter uses three analytical lenses to explore the significance of rights-claiming to the social movement to which the Zakari case gave rise. In this part, we show how the "rights as footprints" metaphor allows us to emphasize three characteristics of rights claims that move beyond conventional conceptions.

First, the footprints image helps us to see that the meaning of a right can endure. As the community repeatedly recalls the history of Mohammed Zakari's rights struggle, the meaning of that memory will change over time.[3] Such symbolic work done by rights is not a new idea.[4] Yet the footprints image shows how the symbolic meaning of a right can both anchor and transform legal consciousness, at the same time. To get at this doubleness of rights histories as remembered, we explain how "footprints," which both move and stand still, are more like fluid memories than the more rigid concepts of precedents or covenants.

Second, the footprints metaphor emphasizes the tension between the universality and particularity of human rights values. Thus, the image invokes the way in which rights language makes meaning in multiple ways. At the same time, rights stories like Mr. Zakari's have a specificity. They are not merely anecdotes. Instead, the retellings replay more or less constant features of the rights stories they represent.

Finally, the footprints image helps us to envision law, law reform, and lawyering in more open ways. More open lawyering tactics might enable more situated, thoughtful, and also fluid dynamics of change. Thus understood, rights practice can create new pathways of social innovation and institutional change that respond to people's expression of justice.

## January 7:
## Agitation at the Mothers' Club

The story begins with the Mothers' Club of Nima, a somewhat unusual source of the political agitation and protest against Ghana's system of healthcare.

The mothers of the Mothers' Club are no strangers to rights articulation and defense: they meet regularly in the conference room of the Legal Resources Center (LRC), a Ghanaian human rights organization based in Nima, a small, crowded community wedged in central Accra, Ghana's national capital. The LRC employs an expansive definition of "legal resources," which includes conventional legal aid, dispute resolution, and importantly, the use of its office space for local groups to meet. During these meetings, community groups are able to trade local stories and advice, and warnings and complaints—and sometimes all of the above—under the heading of "human rights education." With this format, the mothers of Nima, with the help of the LRC, have managed to draw attention to the lack of street lighting in Nima, the pitfalls of the open drain that snakes its way between their homes, and the refusal of the public works to remove rubbish from the Nima streets. On the meeting of January 7, 2003, the agenda for the meeting was hardly unrelated: it was to address the problem of Health.

Nima is a well-studied place. For Ghanaians, the term refers to the crammed urban communities of Nima and neighboring Mamobi and New Town. About 150,000 people live there, compared with 2.4 million in Greater Accra. Many of Nima's residents are migrants from other parts of Ghana, mostly from the impoverished north. The majority of Nima's population belongs to a Ghanaian minority: it is Muslim and speaks Hausa. Nima is known as one of Accra's poorer districts: it provides the domestic labor for the rich communities that reside in the lower-density, leafier parts of Accra; the informal labor for the administrative and business districts that encircle it; and the unskilled labor needs of local industries. Crowded arterial roads track the boundaries of Nima, and few non-Nima residents seem to venture in. Yet the main street is often crowded, serving as the entry to Nima's market, where cheap Chinese gadgets are hawked—along with oil, flour, vegetables, and meats. Petty traders, tailors, and artisans attempt to make a living in the midst of crowded buses, political slogans, and large advertisements for beauty products or American sodas. In these six square kilometers, development concepts like "rationing," "planning," and "provision" reveal their foreignness at once. The concept through which Zakari's case was framed—the concept of "human rights"—would do the same thing.

"The Right to Health" was on the agenda for the Mothers' Club meeting on January 7. The meeting was coordinated by Auntie Rahina, a knowledgeable member of the community, who wore didactic Oxfam T-shirts over her elaborate African dress. She sat in the back of the room, with mothers on either side. Nihad Swallah, a young organizer at the LRC, sat in the front. This was the first meeting of the winter with the visiting student interns from Harvard Law School—six foreign student interns, accompanied by their professor, were thus also present in the room.

Before coming to Ghana, the interns had studied Ghana's "user fee" system of healthcare, which required patients to pay for their treatment before it could be administered by doctors or nurses. They had a rough understanding of how the user fee system (known as "cash and carry") was introduced in Ghana. They knew something about the hospitals and clinics of the British-colonized Gold Coast, the high ideals of free public healthcare within the ambitions of the first decolonized country in Africa, Ghana's gradual commitment to fees for services commencing in 1971, the descending ideals matching descending realities during Ghana's economic decline in the 1980s, and the extreme "rationalization" of health programs under structural adjustment policies in the 1990s.[5] They also knew something about the orthodox ideas of neoliberalism: distrust of the state; trust in the rational, decision-making subject; and the consequent role of incentives, preferences, and efficiencies. They had read the text of the legislative system of "exemptions," which seemed to make "user fees" less discriminatory and regressive. Their legal analysis had told them that user fees would be waived for particular classes of people—for public servants, for instance, but also for the elderly, children, pregnant women, and those "unable to pay those fees on the ground of poverty."[6] But they knew, from their contacts in Ghana rather than from their reading, that the legislative exemptions were rarely, if ever, enforced. Only public servants were in a position to demand their exemptions in the clinics that treated them: other users either did not know of them or did not have the clout to request that they not pay any fees. Even the process of determining who, "on the ground of poverty," would be "unable to pay"—key to the operation of this provision—was unspecified. This clause, described by the LRC lawyers as "the pauper exemption," lacked any regulatory definition.

By 2003 health was a very familiar topic for the LRC. In keeping with its focus on economic and social rights, the center had launched a "right to health campaign" several years earlier. Established by two law students at the University of Ghana, Raymond Atuguba and Mahama Ayariga,[7] the LRC had already set its ambitions on difficult campaigns for socioeconomic provision within Nima. Their model of legal aid was informed by the study of legal aid in many settings, especially across Africa and the Americas. Indeed, the Legal Resources

Center had borrowed its name from the famous public interest law organization in South Africa, which had evolved from anti-apartheid advocacy to constitutional rights litigation. Mahama Ayariga had interned at the South African Legal Resources Center, and both he and Raymond Atuguba had undertaken, in separate years, graduate study at Harvard Law School, where they had established links with its faculty and students.

So far, the right-to-health campaign had involved an exemptions education campaign, which aimed to inform community members of their rights, in the hope of ensuring that their demands for exemptions would be made and met. Interns from prior years had helped put up posters in the local clinics, and had held meetings with pregnant women to advise them of their rights in childbirth and in postnatal care. They had gathered affidavits from community members who had been patients in local clinics and from the nurses who had treated them. They had also engaged with local chiefs, imams, and others about their experience under the user fees regime.[8] But despite these efforts, these educative strategies had not resolved the basic structural problem of healthcare. Even when patients—acting as "consumers," as the legislation intended—knew to demand their exemptions, local clinics or even hospitals did not have the resources to grant them. To do so would deplete these public facilities of their drugs and dressings and physicians' time, since there was no framework within which they could seek reimbursement. The right-to-health campaign had reached a stalemate.

Knowing this history, the students went to the Mothers' Club meeting of January 7 half expecting another round of human rights education to begin. They did not predict that a very different script was waiting for them, and how it would unfold. Auntie Rahina and Nihad Swallah sat among a room full of women in colorful dresses and headscarves; the students, most of them *Obrunis*,[9] were dressed in khaki. There were probably twenty present at this meeting; all the heavy wooden chairs were occupied, and the younger women standing. The room was both hot and noisy from the street outside: the air conditioner corrected the heat but exacerbated the noise, and closing the windows operated in reverse. The group compromised with slow-moving ceiling fans doing very little above them.

A translator provided instantaneous—and disconcertingly shortened—introductions from Hausa to English and back again. Students were invited to call the elder women "Auntie" and were graciously welcomed into the community. After this welcome, they began a small presentation of their research on health. Building on the notes taken at previous workshops, they had listed eight "strategies for action" for health in Nima, and planned to subject these to a ranking after the mothers' input. But after the strategies were listed on butcher paper, and before the priority-setting had begun, their professor invited each woman around the circle to describe her experiences with the health system.

The mothers first seemed surprised at this shift in gear, but the question ignited a small cluster of women sitting at the back of the room, one of whom could hardly hide her impatience. When it was finally her turn—her name was Salima—she related her information swiftly. She had a cousin at Ridge Hospital. She didn't want a strategy so much as to raise money for him. The students' reaction was exasperation: of course, everyone needed money, but they were here to give legal expertise, not charity! Auntie Rahina explained what the woman was asking for: the money was not meant for the cousin's treatment—it was meant for his release.

It came to light that the hospital was detaining Salima's cousin—Mohammed Zakari—until he could raise the money for his treatment. He would not be allowed to leave the hospital until his bill was paid. The LRC lawyers instantly saw the potential of a legal claim, combining basic habeas corpus rights with other rights denied by the health system. As the lawyers and students' enthusiasm about the legal potential of the case grew, so too did the women's indignation at Mohammed Zakari's treatment. Indignation fueled enthusiasm, and vice versa. The footprint was taking shape. The LRC decided to take on the case.

## January 17:
## Notes from a Crowded Taxi Parked in a Hospital

Exactly ten days later, two students, one from Australia and one from France, found themselves at Ridge Hospital, where Mohammed Zakari was detained.[10] The scene was pivotal. Prior to the interview, the students had researched Ghana's habeas corpus laws and other human rights provisions and talked at length with the LRC's attorneys. The interview occurred in the cramped interior of a Ghanaian taxi, parked on the hospital grounds. In order not to arouse (too much) suspicion, and to keep the conversation private, the students decided to interview Mohammed Zakari this way, with a translator sitting on one side of him and one of the students twisting back from the front seat. Auntie Rahina, who had brought them to the hospital, looked on.

When they found him, Mohammed Zakari was wearing a long white Islamic tunic and a cap. He was tall and thin, and his manner was gentle. He spoke in Hausa with the translator but answered the students' questions without hesitation. He wept during the interview, most notably when he was describing the problems he was causing those around him, especially his wife.[11]

As the affidavit would record, Mohammed Zakari was sixty-two years old and worked as a subsistence farmer in Ghana's impoverished north. With this occupation he commanded a yearly income of 500,000 cedis (or about 20 U.S. cents per day). This he earned from selling the cassava and maize crops that he farmed. On this income he supported his wife and three school-age children. Living with the day-to-day insecurity of this minimal income, Mohammed Zakari did have one thing in his favor: he had a cousin living in the city of Accra, in Nima.

On a Friday in November 2002, just before afternoon prayer time, he had felt a sharp pain in his abdomen and asked that a call be made to his cousin. His sister, realizing the seriousness of his condition, took him directly to his cousin's home in Nima. One day after his arrival, he was taken to Ridge Hospital, the closest public hospital, where his cousin registered him. There he underwent emergency hernia surgery, and three weeks later had a second operation. After his recovery, he was discharged and handed a bill, which included the cost of his dressing, injections, laboratory, theater, sanitation, and accommodation. This bill totaled 2,396,000 cedis (about US$240).

This amount was more than three times Mohammed Zakari's yearly income. After telling the hospital's administrative staff that he could not afford to pay this bill, he was told he could not leave the hospital until it was settled. For the next six weeks he was detained within the boundaries of Ridge Hospital, boundaries guarded by private security personnel and a high fence. During this period of detention, Mohammed Zakari was allowed outside the fence only under the supervision of hospital staff, and in this case only to buy plantains to eat. He paid for these with donations from the Nima community: the hospital refused to provide him with regular meals after the date of his "discharge." His only source of food, apart from the leftovers the hospital handed out sporadically, was brought in by his wife, who had to leave their children in the care of relatives and could only occasionally do so. During this time, he slept on a bed on the porch of the hospital ward, for which he was charged a daily fee of 15,000 cedis (about US$1.50).

During this time, Mohammed Zakari was not aware of the exemptions formally provided for "paupers" within the Ghanaian health system. Neither the hospital's administrative staff nor any nurse or doctor with whom he came into contact had informed him of the potential for people living in extreme poverty to be exempted from this financial burden, as provided by the letter of the law. With no means to challenge this situation, he was left to wait for outside assistance. His relatives in Nima were the only plausible source.

Something else happened the day the affidavit was collected. As a result of economic restructuring policies, fuel prices in Ghana were raised by 80 percent. The fuel crisis would have an impact on all sectors of the economy. It would also affect the mobilization strategies of the Zakari case.

## January 13–21:
## The Litigation, the Petition, and the Plan to March

The affidavit had been taken for the purposes of filing suit. And yet this was not the only action pursued by the LRC. Simultaneously, the lawyers and organizers had decided to circulate a petition about Mohammed Zakari's release, with the help of the Nima community, and present it to the Ministries of Health and Finance, the Commission for Human Rights and Administrative Justice, and the Health Committee of Parliament.

### The Litigation

Because of Mohammed Zakari's detention, the strategy of litigation was a promising one. The lawyers could seek a writ of habeas corpus on the grounds that the detention of Mohammed Zakari in the public facilities of Ridge Hospital, without first charging him with a crime, was patently illegal. Stripped away from the hospital context, the state would have to show due cause for the deprivation of liberty. Even a letter of demand to the state could have brought about the release of Mohammed Zakari: filing a lawsuit before taking this less adversarial step would seem, to the experienced lawyer, an overkill. Nonetheless, they decided to join the habeas corpus claim with a human rights claim that challenged the illegality and inequity of the system of health financing in Ghana. They therefore used the complaint as a vehicle for drawing attention to norms protecting health, both in Ghana's constitution and international human rights instruments. This required research into Ghana's constitutional law, as well as comparative interpretations of similar constitutional protections elsewhere. The right to health, even if it was set out as a "directive principle of state policy" rather than a "justiciable right" in Ghana's constitution, could still be significant.

The remedies they sought were expansive because they decided to go beyond Mohammed Zakari's individual complaint. Indeed, they crafted the lawsuit as a challenge to the entire structure of Ghana's healthcare cost recovery system, on the basis of how that system impacted the poor. The complaint stated four claims, each with its own remedy. Taken together, these remedies combined traditional common law relief like habeas corpus with more far-reaching efforts to coax the Ghanaian judges to deliver structural remedies that would address the inequities of the healthcare system and prevent the reoccurrence of hospital detentions.

The first remedy sought an order of "mandamus," which would require the Ministry of Health to set up and implement a procedure for sorting out, at the time a person sought hospital admission, the "paupers" from those who could pay. It demanded that other actors be consulted by the ministry in this process. The second remedy sought an order requiring "the authorities of the Ridge Hospital to exempt Mohammed Zakari from payment of his medical costs on the grounds of poverty." The third remedy asked the court to declare that the hospital's refusal to release Mohammed Zakari violated his constitutional right "to be free from unlawful detention." And finally, the fourth remedy asked the court to declare that the hospital's failure to define the pauper exemption and then grant it to Mohammed Zakari was a "simple and egregious violation of his right to health," his right to be free from discrimination on grounds of poverty, and his right to administrative justice under Ghana's constitution.[12]

The first claim, for "mandamus," focused on the Ministry of Health rather than the public hospital where Mr. Zakari was detained. Departing from individually focused common law remedies, the LRC sought an order that would compel the Ministry of Health to commence an administrative process that would finally define and implement the pauper exemption. Furthermore, it requested that the judge require the Ministry of Health to structure that process in a consultative way. Even further, if the proposed remedy were granted, the Ministry of Health would be required by the court to include specific groups in that consultative process, including people like Mr. Zakari.

This idea of "stakeholder consultation" borrowed heavily on U.S. legal literature on regulatory negotiation.[13] Drawing on participation, the practice of regulatory negotiation convenes interest groups that are sharply divided in what they want regulations to accomplish. Regulatory negotiation also enlists private actors to work with the state in the administrative realm. Finally, regulatory negotiation sets in motion a learning process for all participants. Transplanted into the Zakari remedy,[14] a court order requiring regulatory negotiation could launch a new process for reforming Ghana's healthcare system.

The other remedies were not quite as ambitious. The second remedy—the mandatory injunction—constituted a more straightforward demand to formally exempt Mohammed Zakari from the payment of his medical expenses. The third remedy tied the hospital's refusal to release Mohammed Zakari with the constitutional right to be free from unlawful detention. Finally, the lawyers sought to name the lack of exemption as a violation of the right to good healthcare.

## The Petition

In addition to the litigation, the lawyers and students worked together in drafting a petition for the community to sign. The petition was titled "Petition for the Right to Health" and read like a second-generation civil rights plea. Many of the student interns spent several days walking the streets of Nima, accompanied by a member of the Youth Group, in order to collect signatures and publicize the campaign. Like the Mothers' Club, Nima's Youth Group is a community group that meets and works with the LRC. The Youth Group members were mostly males between fifteen and twenty-five, and they were eager to work with the interns. However, the relationship between the Youth Group members and the interns was very different from that between the interns and Nima's mothers. The two groups of youth were from the same global generation. In spite of their differences, they shared a common interest in the latest pop charts, international soccer triumphs, and fancy mobile phones.

Before being asked to sign the petition, community residents were asked a series of questions about their experience with exemption from user fees. They were also informed of the exemption policy and the plight of Mohammed Zakari. Finally, they were told about plans to march to Parliament to deliver the petition. Afterwards, they were invited to sign their name at the end of the following statement:

> We, the people of the Nima, Mamobi, and Newtown communities, believe that our right to health is being neglected.
>
> We know that paupers, pregnant women, the elderly over 70 years old, and children under 5 are legally exempt from medical fees. However, this exemption policy is not enforced.
>
> We often do not go to the hospital when sick or injured because we know that we will not be able to afford medical care there.
>
> In emergencies, we should always receive medical care even before we are asked to pay.
>
> Finally, like Mohammed Zakari, we should never be detained in the hospital because we cannot pay.

The petition was met with a significant community response. During its cir-culation, it triggered many conversations between interns, Youth Group mem-bers, and other members of the Nima community. It was signed by some fifteen hundred people between January 13 and January 21, 2003. As well as circulat-ing the petition, the teams also prepared a press statement and invitations to the press officers of Ghana's main television stations and newspapers. One team designed a banner with the slogan "Health Regardless of Wealth" painted in big purple letters.

This petition seemed to present a different form of politics to the people of Nima. Of course, politics was ever present in the community. Political advertise-ments and billboards could be seen all through the streets; a constant stream of political announcements was heard on the radio. Indeed, during the interns' visit, a National Reconciliation Commission event, meant to apply the balm of "transitional justice" to the wounds of Ghana's former military rule, took up much of the radio air. Many of these attempts generated only cynicism and in-ertia in Nima itself. The petition, however, seemed to have the opposite effect.

## The March

After five days of signature gathering, a noticeable air of expectation hung in the LRC conference room on January 18 as interns, Youth Group members, mothers, and lawyers met together. All who were present seemed invested in the next steps. (This can be contrasted with the meetings held during other parts of the campaign; for instance, when the progress of the litigation was reported to the community, which evoked only patient passivity.)

The question for the meeting was whether to march on Parliament on the same day of filing the suit in court and the petition in Parliament. The march was consistent with the overall right-to-health strategy, which was to make the community's outrage about the health system as lucid and loud as it could be. Nonetheless, the group faced two problems. First, the LRC had not informed the police about the demonstration in due time, which meant that the demonstra-tion would be outside the law. And second, it recognized that the march might be joined by people violently protesting things other than health—most rele-vantly, the staggering hike in fuel prices. The message of indignation over health-care could be co-opted by others; and worse, a more chaotic unrest might ensue.

The decision to march was put to a vote. Members of the Youth Group, buoyed by their work in collecting signatures and educating interns, were intent on doing something. Yet the mothers were worried about the consequences of violence, and some of the lawyers were worried about the fine line between democratic self-expression and violence.[15] Mahama Ayariga wished to picket Parliament and gave an impassioned speech invoking "courage" and "justified, non-violent illegality." Nonetheless, it was decided almost unanimously—with the exception of Mahama Ayariga and one of the students—to cancel the march and proceed with a press conference staged outside the LRC offices in Nima, followed by a bus ride to Parliament to present the petitions.

## January 22:
## Mohammed Zakari's Release and Performance

A key part of the Zakari case was then to allow the three "rights" strategies— the litigation, petition to Parliament, and press conference—to occur on one day. The three branches of government (the judiciary, the executive, and the Parliament), as well as the press, were therefore all targeted at once as a single moment of rights-claiming. In staging it this way, each action was meant to lend greater symbolism to the others.

Everyone expected that the campaign would be successful: it would either shame—or force—the government to grant Mr. Zakari's release. They were thus surprised, and even somewhat disappointed, to learn, on the morning of January 22, that he was a free man. No one ever found out how this had happened. Did the government release him to avoid a scandal, or did someone step up at the final hour to pay his illegal fees? When Mahama Ayariga went to the hospital to examine Zakari's bill, it did not indicate whether anyone had settled it. In any event, he had been "released" at two that morning and was at the moment staying with Auntie Rahina.

The student interns came to the project of social movement lawyering without much experience; therefore, they had mixed feelings about Mohammed Zakari's release. They could not help being disappointed that he had not been forced to stay—at least one more day—in his hospital-qua-prison. They did not want their legal brief to be rendered moot. They did not want to lose the opportunity to develop precedent, air the grievance, shine the light of the judicial system onto the case. They did not want the community's energy to dissipate, the people's attention turned to now more urgent claims. Of course, they were glad that Mohammed Zakari was free, but couldn't this wait!?

In fact, the momentum built up around the right-to-health campaign could not be so easily quelled. The lawyers of the LRC—most explicitly, Mahama Ayariga—immediately recognized the potential for bringing Mohammed

Zakari himself to the press conference and having him speak in front of the community about what had happened to him. Just as the script of the press conference had to be improvised, so too did the legal claim: it no longer demanded the release of Mohammed Zakari through a habeas corpus action but instead sought damages for wrongful imprisonment.

By the time of the press conference, the interns had become used to Nima's rhythms. They were familiar with the city taxi drivers who refused to deliver them to Nima; they had eaten at the best and cheapest chop bars; and they had begun to understand the peaks and troughs of Nima's market activities. They had an inkling of what an outdoor press conference would look like on a busy market day on Nima's main street. The LRC had invited members of the press, and had attracted community residents with loudly blaring "high life" music, sodas, and plastic chairs. Undoubtedly one of the best attractions was the coterie of white faces and bland dress, as foreign as the Chinese gadgets for sale on the road.

Before the crowd gathered, Auntie Rahina had arrived with Mohammed Zakari. The big conference table was taken from the LRC offices and set up in front of the audience. A few chairs were arranged behind the table: there sat Mahama Ayariga and Nihad Swallah, as well as a Muslim cleric and a couple of interns, all flanking Mohammed Zakari. Behind them the huge sign was propped up: "Health Regardless of Wealth."

Nihad began by reading aloud an official statement describing the LRC's litigation and petitions. Nihad was a young Muslim woman, an articulate speaker, and well attuned to local cultural practices as well as to the problems with healthcare provision in Nima. Her speech became a singular memory in Mohammed Zakari's case. Indeed, it was Nihad's speech that was reported in the local press.[16] In it, she claimed that the exemptions were rarely enforced in Ghana's public hospitals and that if they were provided, would strain the Ministry of Health's capacity to reimburse hospitals for the exempted services. She was therefore careful not to vilify the Ministry of Health for violating human rights.

After Nihad's speech, Mohammed Zakari was asked to tell his story. In front of scores of people—the men, women, and children of Nima, student interns, television camera crews, and journalists—Mohammed Zakari was introduced. As he called on the audience to pray, he couldn't hold back his emotion. The community immediately responded, all in prayer, many in tears. Standing tall behind the press conference table, he related what had happened to him, in Hausa. This was a story of misery and miracles, of faith and uncertainty. He explained that now he was a free man. The community responded with jubilation. The high life music returned to full volume.

Members of the press, who had been waiting for hours and had impatiently demanded more sodas to withstand the heat, seemed curious about the direction the press conference was taking: they were surprised at the pamphlets the students had been handing out. During the question period, several journalists asked why community members hadn't engaged in a protest and marched to Parliament. They tried to get the students' inside story: hadn't they brought all of this strange legalese straight from their foreign law school? The press seemed not to trust the authenticity of the occasion, despite accepting the genuineness of Mohammad Zakari and Nihad Swallah's words.

Six days later, the same reporters reported the following:

Three billion cedis will be disbursed this year to the country's hospitals to settle bills of the needy and vulnerable under the exemption policy of the Ministry of Health. The amount represents a 100 per cent rise over last year's figure of two billion and forms part of the government's plan to increase the funds to cover all beneficiaries under the scheme. The Deputy Ministry of Health [ . . . ] made that known in Accra yesterday at a meeting with community leaders from Nima and Mamobi to dialogue on how best to operate the exemption policy in the two communities. The people had earlier in a petition appealed to the ministry to put in place workable mechanisms to ensure the effective operation of the system in the hospital and clinics in the two areas. The Deputy Minister said apart from the delays, the funds made available are inadequate to cater for all the beneficiaries and most health institutions are not reimbursed for the treatment of beneficiaries of the scheme.[17]

## Rights as Footprints

Since Zakari's story was first recounted, it has been retold to the Nima community, to new generations of student interns, to Ghanaian communities outside of Nima, and to audiences outside of Ghana. By retelling the story yet again in this chapter, we, the chapter's authors, seek to convey how it lodged itself in the community's collective memory and gave shape to an emerging social justice movement. As participants in the story, we witnessed the power of rights to move people in multiple ways. The image of "footprints" can help explain how.

As we said earlier, it was Nihad Swallah who first used the image in an interview with us three years after the case had originally transpired. She noted how the case had become "one of the biggest achievements of what legal aid has done in this community." Two years after the case had concluded, she attributed this achievement to the fact that "everyone, almost all the community members were involved." It had thus become "like a footprint in everybody's mind: anybody you ask around knows the story."[18]

Importantly, Nihad Swallah did not see Mohammed Zakari's situation as atypical; rather, she attributed the power of the case to the uncommon way in which the activists and community members had responded to it. In her words:

> It is not that we went for this case and wanted to use it and for it to become a hit and everyone wanted to talk about this case, no. This case came up and we think that the way we dealt with it and type of community lawyering that we did around it was special and uncommon and captured the attention of all therefore we tell the story. Otherwise we don't see it as so unique.[19]

In seeking to uncover the meanings of these "footprints," we now consider the ways in which the footprints image moves the ways we imagine rights beyond other conceptions. We offer contrasts with images of rights as precedents, covenants, anecdotes, and blueprints. Each of these aspects is discussed in turn, and related back to the moments—or retellings—of the Mohammed Zakari story.

## Footprints, Not Precedents

The image of rights as footprints may be contrasted with the legalist understanding of rights as precedent, which evokes the legal advocate's preference for institutionalizing victories in court. In contrast, the footprints image enables us to envision rights as decentralized and democratized, as making meanings outside of the institutionalized normative system of legislation, regulations, and adjudication.[20] This contrast is one of emphasis rather than dichotomy: the footprinted rights practice may locate itself in the conventional forums of positivist law (courts, legislators, agencies) and its conventional texts (human rights instruments, constitutions, and legislation) in order to enact its meaning. Nonetheless, the primary focus of the rights as footprints is on meaning-making by and for communities themselves.

Legal precedent is usually embedded in a judicial decision operating as a source of law for subsequent cases of a similar kind. In generating precedent, lawyers often strive to create favorable legal terms, not only for their own clients, but for those in the same situations in the future. In this way, new norms, or different areas of law, can be drawn into legal claims, pushing settled areas of law in new directions. Much of the current scholarship on social and economic rights operates precisely at this juncture—where constitutional protections of rights result in judicial revision of legislation, executive power, or common law principle.[21] While this attention to precedent is certainly critical, we focus on an extrajudicial feature of lawmaking that is obscured by attention to precedent.

This is not to suggest that the images of footprints and precedent are not related. Both admit a diachronic pathway for law, allowing for present-day activities to shape the future. Both involve elements of narrative and retelling, and selectivity and change. Both rely on certain rules to persuade and operate through time. And each may mirror or even constitute the other.[22] Nonetheless, while precedent requires the imprimatur of the court for its existence, and indeed draws on the power to coerce just as it draws on the power to persuade,[23] the footprinted right requires a community: voices to remember, listen to, and retell the tale. The contour of the right and its very longevity is filtered, not through courts but through the social relations that bind communities. Nihad Swallah, remembering Mohammed Zakari's story three years later, starts by articulating it as a legal construct—a "case" of "legal aid." Even while thus implying that Mohammed Zakari's story created a precedent, making law as a legal construct, she interpreted and expressed the event through "what [it] has *done in this community*" (emphasis added). For her, the case was a moment of meaning-creation that was grounded in community norms. Further in the interview, she adds:

> For me, this is one of the cases the LRC has dealt with and people talk about it because they were directly involved—it is in their memory and they want to talk about it every now and then.

Although the Zakari case involved lawyers, courts, and remedies, its locus remained with the community of Nima. Its central physical location was not a courtroom but a crowded conference room; its central players were mothers, young men, *Obrunis*, organizers—as well as lawyers. The story was also enacted in a taxi, in a makeshift podium, and in the streets of Nima beyond. Although it was a case that was strengthened by the presence of formal law—habeas corpus, statutory entitlements, and multiple constitutional provisions—the norms that lodged in the community's own expression of the case were not restricted to law. Indeed, at the moments when formal law was discussed, the community members were at their most passive; at the moments when Zakari's rights were expressed as instances of justice, members were at their most engaged.

For example, in the first scene of agitation at the Mothers' Club meeting, a key moment occurred when the preestablished human rights script of "participation" was disrupted and the women were invited to speak out.[24] The narrative space, unexpectedly opened up to express individual grievances, operated as a space in which a politics of justice was able to develop.[25] The impatient, emotional storytelling by Mohammed Zakari's cousin, the excited looks among the lawyers, the mounting rumble in the back of the room—all incrementally transpired to produce a collective indignation. The footprinted language of rights functioned not only outside a courtroom but also, crucially, inside the minds of those present. Moreover, the language of rights allowed different perspectives to develop in each participant—and, it should be emphasized, the presence of the interns meant that the perspectives were extraordinarily varied—and created an altogether new horizon of action.[26] In a fluid back-and-forth effect, rights talk interacted with preexisting social meanings (grief, suffering, law, action) to generate this politics of justice.

## Footprints, Not Covenants

The footprints image may also be contrasted with another legalist image, that of covenants. Human rights declarations and instruments, as well as under-enforced constitutional text, often enjoy a status as "soft" law in contradistinction to the "hardness" of legal precedent. They may harden over time, or have elements of justiciability that provide a particular legal enforceability akin to precedent, but they also generate a range of declaratory normative texts upon which rights practice can rely. In the Zakari story, "declaratory principles of state policy" in the Ghanaian constitution, as well as "progressive realization" formulas, taken from international covenants and comparative jurisprudence,[27] were important features of the claim.

The rights-as-footprints image does not discount the importance of covenants; nonetheless, the emphasis here is different. Instead of seeking to generate additional covenants or normative development of existing covenants, in the way that often characterizes the work of international human rights activists,[28] the footprints image connotes smaller-scale ambitions, focusing foremost on the generative engagement of the community members themselves.

In this sense, the footprints image is "glocalized" rather than "globalized," retaining a strong local character.[29] Admittedly, there is a tension here, because the language of rights already suggests the universal, but the footprints image explicitly locates this universalization in local places—the Mothers' Club meeting, the taxi, the petition, the vote, the press conference table—allowing the interpretation of rights to settle and resettle.[30] This localized usage differs from any official or nationally fostered account of rights, such as was occurring during the contemporaneous National Reconciliation Commission, which had had little traction within the community.

Unlike covenants, which purport to entrench general statements about rights, the footprint may fade over time, thus requiring social action to keep it meaningful and reshapings and retellings in light of different contributors, audiences, and contexts. The story is one of action that works for, rather than assumes, an agreement.

This contrast explains, for example, the part played by the petition-gathering process. The fifteen hundred signatures each brought about an important encounter between community members, youth groups, and interns. Before the signature or thumbprint was given, the intern read out the statement, which described both the community's continuing situation with respect to user fees and the plight of Mohammed Zakari. One intern would later describe this experience as "hugely important. The international covenants had never seemed meaningful until that moment, when we tried to translate it into something that would move people."[31]

As Mahama Ayariga would describe, "the petition signing created an important space for the interns and the people to agree on rights." Along with the press conference, the petition became a central tool in the mobilization and involvement of the broader community.

## Footprints, Not Anecdotes

Nonetheless, the particularist image may go too far. Just as the rights-as-footprints practice is wary to adopt too globalist and general an articulation of rights, it seeks more than an anecdotal understanding of particular losses, traumas, or triumphs in social histories and actions.[32] Like legal pluralism, which emphasizes the way that alternative conceptions of rights and law take shape in different communities through time, the footprinted image provides a frame for alternative readings of legal orders in history.[33] The image of footprints suggests how collective memories of political mobilization, repeatedly retold through shared but shifting frames, generate multiple pathways toward justice.

Such stories may be the most important for the marginalized groups themselves, expressive of important "truths" about their historical experiences and their current social relations.[34] As oral historians have noted, "the strongest communal memories are those of beleaguered out-groups."[35] These expressions of rights—existing beyond "law stories"[36] into the realm of a group's identity and its oral history—reach outsiders as well. For outsiders, they may make new groups of people visible.

Such effects do not operate in a singular, triumphalist course but subsist in expressive spirals, which are transmitted in different times and places by different actors, often undergoing a change in meaning according to the forum and the community.[37] The progression of a story has its own phases. Thus, psychologists Gordon W. Allport and Leo Postman identify three mental processes common to memory retention, which taken together, may transform a story or rumor into "a shorter, more concise, more easily grasped and told" version over time.[38] The first phase, which is termed "leveling," denotes the sharp decline in the number of details in a story until its stabilization in a brief report. Next, the process of "sharpening" prepares for the "selective perception, retention and reporting of a limited number of details from a larger context."[39] Leveling tends to continue through this sharpening phase, "thus resulting in multiple versions of the 'truth.'"[40] Finally, "assimilation" describes listeners' own attraction to the story through their own intellectual and emotional context.[41] In our account, the framework and language of rights provides a crucial backdrop and context for the story to be shaped and to hold.

The memory allows the community to coalesce and sustain a localized movement. In the Nima case, the assimilation of the right to health with community notions of justice succeeded in part because of the intellectual and emotional context linking modernity, colonialism, and development. That is, the right to health seemed to challenge market efficiency and commodification as a prerequisite of development, and suggested a return to different considerations of how healthcare should be provided—more accommodating, as it turns out, with status-based views of justice.[42] It remains to be examined, however, how successful such assimilation of rights discourse would be for a different set of rights, such as gender rights. This point shows the contingency of the footprinted rights practice; for example, that social and economic rights may have a greater prospect of success than rights against discrimination on grounds of gender, a type of discrimination that might be justified by customary norms.

Yet this collective memory was not exclusive to the geographic community of Nima, for it carried significant meaning for other participants in the rights campaign who were themselves mobilized outside of Ghana. For instance, a participant in the campaign retold the story at Stanford Law School, in 2005. Mohammed Zakari's story was a central part of a presentation to law students about human rights in Africa, leading many to sign up for further work in Ghana. What was retained by the students was not identical, of course, to what was remembered by the community; and yet the rights idea was mobilizing.[43] For example, the talk to students emphasized the moral dimensions of the case:

> The work we did around the case of Mohammed Zakari . . . led to the first ever right to health case ever started in a Ghanaian court. It was about the international and constitutional legal standard that says that everyone—no matter how poor—has a universal right to access the best possible health care. It was about the idea that you should not *die*, you should not be left untreated, you should not be deprived from your liberty—because you are too poor to pay a medical bill. For Mohammed Zakari, that humble, religious, dignified man had been locked up—and I mean *LOCKED UP*, with guards in arms at the door and a high metallic fence!—in a public hospital simply because . . . he couldn't afford his bill. He was locked up, *for simply being too poor.*

Yet the moral dimension was not the only animating idea. The spontaneity and intrigue kept the story vibrant and also accessible to a new audience:

> Because of the mobilization and the "hype" in the community around his case, and although Mohammed Zakari's bill was mysteriously paid (by a government agent) in the middle of the night—like in your best Hollywood movie . . . our action helped start negotiations with the government to have the community *itself* involved in shaping [healthcare financing in Ghana] and make it more accessible to the poor.

Of course, the community of Nima experienced the memory differently, in critical ways. Theirs was an almost "eye-witness" account; the students received a different "word-of-mouth" version of the events. More importantly, the community of Nima experienced Mohammed Zakari's injury firsthand and would have lived with the ongoing injustice if the healthcare system remained unchanged. Nonetheless, the currency of Mohammed Zakari's story for remote audiences is another vital part of the footprints effect.

## Footprints, Not Blueprints

A contrast between rights as footprints and blueprints also emerges from the Mohammed Zakari story. This contrast operates not merely at the point in which legal consciousness is changed by rights, as our previous contrasts have emphasized, but in how the change in consciousness is embedded in the demand for a change in institutional practices. In other words, the contrast between footprints and blueprints establishes the metaphor in its institutional setting. It does not suggest that this setting can be fixed by a formula of either litigation or institutional reform. The image of the footprint retains the potential of rights to be disruptive, creative, and locally responsive. It connotes an opened-up, open-ended process of communities' engagement with other relevant actors in changing present institutions.

This stands out against the familiar image of the "blueprint" in human rights and development commentary. In these fields, the blueprint offers a standard means of planning a set of institutional reforms from previous practices that suggest a plausible assertion of success.[44] For development economists, a current example of an institutional blueprint is the Poverty Reduction Strategy Papers (PRSP) framework, in which low-income countries are required to develop their own plans for reducing poverty.[45] For lawyers, an example might resemble efforts to develop a "minimum core" of economic and social rights.[46]

The PRSP exercise offers a "chastened" blueprint for development, chastened in that it recognizes the value of participation and national-ownership, as opposed to the "top down" version of previous best practices.[47] Thus, the World Bank's current blueprint on reducing poverty invites civil society and the private sector to participate in the development of an appropriate national strategy. Strategies from differently situated countries are then compiled and compared. As much might be said of our footprinted rights practice.

But going further, evidence on the PRSP suggests that in reality it is nonparticipatory for certain groups, such as local parliamentarians, trade unions, women, and the marginalized groups who actually represent the poor.[48] In content, the PRSPs have curiously replicated earlier structural reform programs, endorsing financial and trade liberalization, privatization, and in the case of curative healthcare, cost recovery mechanisms. Some commentators have suggested that the fact that PRSPs are compulsory for countries seeking to qualify for debt relief, and must be developed quickly, limits the opportunity for local participation.[49]

Like the proceedings of the newly institutionalized National Reconciliation Commission that we had encountered during our rights campaign in Ghana, the PRSPs have taken on a "one size fits all" shape, which fails to resonate locally. In Ghana, reporters on the PRSP process suggested that "community consultations did not feed into the analyses and recommendations." Instead, the authors of Ghana's PRSP were reluctant to second-guess the wisdom of the financial institutions.[50]

In contradistinction to this image, our examples of rights as footprints show a strategy that is constitutive of, rather than formally reliant on, community participation, and responsive to local agency, creativity, and uncertainty. The example of the press conference is one in which a highly disruptive practice emerged from a seemingly conventional human rights medium. This event, to which members of the community were invited to participate, and in which their own members spoke from the podium, was crucial in formulating the rights footprint. In contrast to blueprinted rights strategies, in which formal authorities are engaged, the press conference represented the community's ability to voice their claim in the terms of their own choosing.

This strategy also supported the remedial claim for inclusion and voice in the lawsuit itself. As discussed, the LRC sought creative remedies to end Mohammed Zakari's detention, pressing the Ghanaian courts to devise a process by which the Ministry of Health, the Ministry of Finance, and health consumer groups could negotiate a solution to the punitive effects of user fees. This tactic responded to the inertia of public institutions to the problems of health financing, and attempted to dislodge their entrenched position of deciding health issues for Ghanaians.[51] If representatives from the Nima community were to be included in a negotiated process of defining future exemptions, the resulting regulation might offer clear distributional as well as political benefits for the poor.

Importantly, the footprint was neither normatively nor institutionally empty. By responding to the memory of injustice embodied within the right, the campaign around the right introduced a particular direction to the development path on which future changes would depend. Mohammed Zakari had been detained in a hospital for being poor and sick. Any healthcare scheme that would allow this situation to repeat would violate the collective understanding of the right.[52]

## Epilogue

Nihad Swallah has spoken of Mohammed Zakari's experience as one with religious significance for himself and others in the community. Six years on, we are no longer able to ask him directly about his own views of what happened to him, and we wonder where he is. He may have decided to withdraw because of fear that his good luck might reverse one day. He may be living in good health, without fear—*Insha'Allah*.

The Legal Resources Center continues to engage in mobilization around the levels of socioeconomic provision in the Nima community, although its new status as a leading national human rights organization and a partner to legislation drafting has limited its ability to engage in litigation and community petitions. Its main office is now located considerably far from Nima.

The Ghanaian user fees model of health financing that was the focus of this campaign is no longer in effect. Since 2003 it has been replaced with the gradual phasing in of a national health insurance system.[53] The user fees model fell out of favor with liberal economists and the international financial institutions, although it would take some time for new models to replace it in national policies.[54] The campaign in Nima was one example of a voice against user fees, locally expressed. In the end, the LRC, along with community representatives (including the Mothers' Club), carried this voice throughout the reforming phases, in which the alternative model of health insurance was developed. The role of the LRC was in representing how the interests of the poor would be catered to in the future health financing system. This included a role in the design stage for both legislation and follow-up regulations.

The replacement of user fees with national health insurance has not put an end to the practice of detention. The LRC's repeated surveys reveal that in fact this practice is still a part of the revenue-raising activities of cash-strapped hospitals, particularly in rural areas of Ghana.[55] Insurance premiums do not resolve the financial shortcomings in the system: the story of Mohammed Zakari is therefore not to be understood as a triumphant success for the right to health.

Mahama Ayariga is no longer the executive director of the Legal Resources Center but served as Ghana's youngest member of Parliament and as spokesperson for the president, before assuming his current position as Deputy Minister of Trade and Industry. In looking back at the Zakari case, Ayariga now sees instances of success but also "gaps and failures." While a parliamentarian serving on the Health Committee, he identified parliamentary alliances and international institutions that had been outside of the LRC's advocacy arsenal in 2003. Raymond Atuguba, now a legal academic at the University of Ghana, remains closely involved in research, advocacy, and policy making around Ghana's new health insurance system. As the Legal Resources Center's executive director, he launched in 2004 two sister "human rights cities" projects in the rural north of Ghana, which aim to generate grassroots-based, human rights-infused pilot schemes within the National Health Insurance framework.

At the end of this long exercise of retelling, we see how the shaping of the rights footprint continually looks back upon itself. The forward-looking progression of human rights advocacy can be intimately related to the experience of reflection. Collective memory plays a powerful role in a dynamic, community-focused, and community-reinforced practice of hope. It involves telling and retelling, forgetting and remembering, all in a spirit of reflective critique.

# PART II

# Theoretical Essays

## Chapter 5

# Stones of Hope

*Experience and Theory in African Economic
and Social Rights Activism*

Jeremy Perelman and Lucie E. White

The case studies in this volume feature African lawyer-activists who shape economic and social rights (ESR) "campaigns" around broad justice issues like the right to health, shelter, sanitation, community integrity, freedom of movement, and personal security. Each campaign centers on the situation of a particular person, a local community, or in the case of South Africa, an entire nation. Each advocate whose work is featured here has a signature working style. Yet common strategies of engagement, normative commitments, and prefigurative practices repeatedly emerge.

## Strategies of Engagement

We noticed two strategic patterns of engagement. First, these advocates are *pragmatic* in three ways that we articulate below. Second, they stage *performance* in powerful and creative ways.

### These Advocates Are Pragmatic

The human rights activists featured in this book start with a keen understanding of the limits to the traditional human rights game. This perception could have led them to spurn human rights language and tools altogether. And indeed, as we have noted in the Introduction, some Third World social justice scholars encourage activists to think carefully before they embrace human rights discourse in their work.[1] Yet the activists in the Stones of Hope project did not make this choice; instead, they devised a new kind of ESR practice that in more robust and realistic ways has successfully framed public debate, challenged political will, and sparked social movement around issues of extreme deprivation. This practice is characterized by gritty pragmatism, in which the lawyer-activists push beyond formalistic notions of what human rights advocates should do.

**They Use Litigation but Do Not Privilege It**    The advocates in this volume do not privilege litigation or other win-lose procedures in their human rights work. Formalistic versions of the human rights game typically start from positive law—an official human rights covenant, a domestic statute, a constitutional mandate—and then search for an instance of state action that defies that command.[2] To face radical poverty head-on, these African advocates start not with the black-letter law but rather with the predicament of people who live and describe that situation on the ground. Furthermore, these activists move beyond the adversarial remedial paradigm that dominates domestic justice, at least in the common law nations. They do not consider adversarial procedures and court orders to be the best methods for challenging ESR violations and enforcing ESR mandates.[3] But neither do they avoid such advocacy tools when appeal to the courts will build their campaigns' strategic power. When they do go to court, their reasons may have less to do with the potential effect of the judgment than the expressive force of the lawsuit or the potential to create a public spectacle or spark public movement at a press conference.

In addition to exploiting the indirect opportunities that litigation presents, these lawyers also stretch the potential of the litigation process itself. They craft structural remedies that enlist judges and stakeholders to redesign entire governmental systems—of housing construction, HIV treatment, or food distribution, for instance—to make those systems consistent with human rights values like inclusion, distributional equity, and voice.[4]

At the same time that they litigate, these advocates use all of the other familiar lawyering tools, plus more. They use formal human rights instruments and appeal to official human rights forums. They also do grassroots organizing, community development, policy advocacy, and global networking. They use the media. And they often orchestrate such tactics in sequence, to leverage great power. For instance, consider the case of Mohammed Zakari, the Ghanaian man featured in Chapter 4 who found himself detained in a public hospital because he could not pay his bill. There, the lawyers used a carefully orchestrated sequence of grassroots organizing, a petition drive, a press conference, lobbying, *and* litigation, in order to build power. They filed a lawsuit to document, investigate, educate, engage, perform, entice, compel, inspire, as well as to order the release of a detainee, reform the administrative process, and change the black-letter law. The advocates did not use these tactics in isolated, scattershot ways; rather, they artfully combined them into powerful ESR campaigns.

They Engage Multiple Public Actors in Every Domain of State Power    Human rights advocates often use the language of economic and social rights to focus attention on the nation-state's deliberate indifference to human deprivation. These advocates might compare one nation to another. Thus, they might argue that in contrast to other, equally positioned nations, their own nations have shortchanged the health sector by allocating it an inadequate share of their national budgets. However, they do not track the global contexts, micropractices, or development pathways in the shadow of which exchanges between the individual and the nation-state take place. In reality, African nation-states, for whatever reasons, are often cash-strapped. They often lack the funds or governmental capacity to solve such big-ticket problems as healthcare without help from other sources. Because of this occasional limit to the African state's capacity to provide, this book's ESR scholars and advocates are engaged in a debate about whether the nation-state should sometimes be bypassed in favor of deeper pockets and more powerful actors, wherever they are found. For instance, while William Forbath and Peter Houtzager take the position that the nation-state should be the primary target of ESR advocacy,[5] the Lagos and Tanzania case studies make global forces a major focus of analysis and advocacy.[6]

All of the activists and scholars, however, regardless of the position they take in this debate, recognize that in some cases it is appropriate to engage in advocacy in multiple domains. Thus, these lawyer-activists seek hearings in international human rights bodies, negotiate with multilateral organizations, forge links with international NGOs, take part in transnational social movements, challenge the governments of rich nations, as well as seek hearings in domestic courts, national human rights commissions, and local government forums. These practices may help to strengthen the resolve and capacity of nation-states to respond to ESR delivery challenges. At the same time, however, they reform nonstate institutions, forge advocacy networks, and mobilize social movement by engaging a range of other sources of money, other resources, and political power. Thus, the practices that the advocates engage in blur the boundaries of the academic debate.

A case in point is that of the collaboration between the activist founder of Nigeria's Social and Economic Rights Action Center (SERAC), Felix Morka, and members of the Ijora-Badia community in Lagos. Working with

Morka, residents of Ijora-Badia organized themselves to defy the state's effort to remove them from an increasingly valuable tract of land. Their campaign interwove grassroots organizing, political maneuvering, social-movement building, and multitargeted litigation around the right to housing. This campaign successfully postponed the residents' mass eviction, at least for the moment. The advocates pragmatically used legal, educational, and organizing tactics to target multiple public actors. They leapt over Nigeria's domestic government to challenge the World Bank's administration of an informal-sector infrastructure improvement loan. This tactic did not write off the importance of the Nigerian state to their problem, however, because bringing in the World Bank put pressure on the Nigerian government, from above, to cease its own efforts to clear the vulnerable residents from their homes. When the group finally got the World Bank to include them in managing a subsequent loan, the residents came to the table cognizant of the political challenges and confident of their political competence to take the World Bank on.

These advocates did not place all of their hope in this single tactic. At the same time that they mobilized the World Bank's resources and influence, they did not let the Nigerian government off the hook. Stubbornly pragmatic in that work, they followed the traditional legal dictum to target the national state only if it *unilaterally* held the power to deliver the goods. Thus, the Nigerian activists did not hesitate to petition the national government to force it to block the regional government from going forward on a massive eviction. But before they settled on this tactic, they mapped out the flow of governmental power above and around the national government, as well as within it.

**They Engage Both Private and State Actors**    These advocates work both with and against all sources of oppressive power, from multinational conglomerates to governmental institutions to family patriarchs. They reject the idea that only the state and other sites of public power can be called up to help address ESR deprivation.[7] Not only do they push beyond the adversarial paradigm; they reject the moral logic of the public/private divide. Thus, in a campaign to claim the human rights of workers and residents in Ghanaian mining communities, not featured in this book, the advocates targeted and engaged with both multinational mining conglomerates based in Canada and the Ghanaian government's ineffective Chamber of Mines. In the Treatment Action Campaign's effort in South Africa to secure antiretroviral treatment for pregnant women, the activists targeted both the state and multinational drug companies. And in their campaign to bring down the cost of drugs for HIV/AIDS patients, they both targeted the drug companies in an adversarial process and negotiated with them over the price of the drugs.

**Putting It All Together**    What might pragmatic human rights activists do in the face of Abdullah Muman's fear that his house would collapse in Nima's big gutter?[8] First they would map out the sources of power to make change, both their own and those of their adversaries and potential allies. Then they would devise specific tactics to leverage their power to entice or coerce those actors to use their own clout to help solve the problem. They might target the bilateral donors that have made specific commitments to upgrade drainage infrastructure. They might first negotiate with these donors to live up to their promises and then shame them through media pressure in the donor's own nation and their own. If aid contracts had been signed, they might file official complaints to internal monitors in the host nation or bring the breached duties to the attention of watchdog groups. They might link up with activists in other countries who face similar problems.

With this foundation laid, they might target their own nation's relevant ministries for failure to make plans and seek funds to do their statutory jobs. Where there was potential for domestic litigation, they might file. At the same time, they might organize their own communities to monitor the local government's failure to collect the garbage and sewage on a regular basis, as their constitution's decentralization provisions require. They might bring a parliamentary committee into the community to hold a fact-finding hearing at which families living on the banks of the ditch can testify. They might then mobilize people—the entire community—into a political force that could leverage the government's fear that "unrest in the slums" might drive potential foreign investors away.

Thus, lawyers and organizers working in the pragmatist spirit of the Stones of Hope's activist team *could* shift power toward Abdullah Muman and others in his situation. They *could* mobilize political will and amass material resources for cleaning up the ditch that cuts through his community. They *could* open up a space for political contestation about the causes and remedies for his situation. And out of this discussion, new ways for the state to tackle the challenges of urban infrastructure could be devised.

### These Advocates Stage Performance

These advocates do more than break the rules of traditional practice in pragmatic ways. When tactical openings arise, they identify and then choreograph public performances that manifest the injustice they are fighting and enlist the empathy of multiple audiences with the people and communities they represent. These performances evoke all of the usual expressive effects that law scholars have described.[9] But more striking are the ways these performances can sometimes disrupt or reverse entrenched power hierarchies. Because of the deep penetration of those hierarchies into the subjectivity of those at the bottom,[10] however, such disruptions seldom last.

Yet several case studies, especially the one that features Mohammed Zakari,[11] show how those moments of power reversal get *remembered* and *retold* in ways that sustain their politicizing effect over time. In that case, Mr. Zakari spoke with great emotion at a press conference that took place soon after he was mysteriously released from illegal detainment in a public hospital. The story of his dignified—yet also disruptive—appearance has been repeatedly retold, both within his community and farther afield. Indeed, the story as retold in this book is one of the Zakari story's most recent iterations. As an organizer in his community describes it, the community's collective remembrance of his release and subsequent public appearance inspired community members to challenge other injustices after his case was resolved. Their collective remembrance made the force of his resistance persist long after the event itself had transpired. Thus, because of their recollection of Mr. Zakari's performance, Nima residents challenged further injustices with a sense that they were part of a powerful, historically rooted social justice movement. A single real-time performance sparked multiple memories of its disruptive shock, setting loose a sustained ripple that shifted power, emboldened community members, and enabled episodes of political contestation and experimentation over the longer term.

Another campaign, not featured in this volume,[12] presents a similarly remembered performance. The scene is the northeast coast of Kenya, where the salt-farming industry poses a threat to the livelihood of workers and residents of the Malindi community. Here, a lawyer-activist on the Stones of Hope team organized community members to pressure the Kenya National Human Rights Commission to hold a public hearing investigating the salt-farm owners' practices, at the very site of the farms. In the hearing, community members, ESR activists, public officials, *and* representatives of the salt-farming corporation all testified. The community members' performances leveled the power gap between the corporation and themselves. At the same time, the corporate representatives' own performances revealed their position to be implausible. For a moment, the community members were in command of the situation and could forcefully assert their common sense of injustice. It was the replaying of that moment in people's shared stories that gave it empowering force over time.

In the case of Abdullah Muman, his reading of his affidavit at a community-based public hearing enacted a similar moment of disruption. Before his performance, the experience of living beside the gutter was not accessible to elites, even if the public health effects of the gutter on the community had been extensively documented in both expert reports and, indeed, his own written testimony. When his experience was reported in a written text, it became a passive description, accessible, if at all, through the reader's empathy alone. For even the most empathic reader is likely to focus on the show-stealing actor—the gutter itself—which threatens to suck up Mr. Muman's house and then snake its way inside the high-end gated enclaves that abut it.

When Muman performs that text on a stage built by a grassroots social movement, however, his voice becomes powerful and alive. He becomes defiant rather than pathetic. Through his performance in a space of social movement, he wrestles the emotional meaning of his experience free from elites' fears for their own health and toward his fury about his children's terror. When his performance is staged at a public hearing that attracts media coverage, it momentarily brings elites perilously close to that anger. He can give them the gift of nightmares.

## Normative Commitments

The pragmatic and performative strategies of engagement deployed by the lawyer-activists featured in this volume constitute a common thread of ESR practice. Our inquiry revealed that this practice is embedded in three common normative commitments: critical liberal legalism, pluralism, and distributive politics. We explore these normative commitments in the following sections.

### Critical Liberal Legalism

This normative perspective refers to an engaged but critical stance toward liberal values and human rights practice.[13] More specifically, it denotes a reflexive, politically progressive interpretation of liberal legal norms and a corresponding set of recognizably legal, but also explicitly political, advocacy strategies. Both this interpretation of liberal values and these politicized advocacy strategies challenge the version of liberal human rights practice that limits itself to protecting vulnerable people against "negative" rights violations by the nation-state. In  contrast, what we call "critical liberal legalism" implies a politically committed, interpretatively grounded politics that identifies itself with a fair redistribution of wealth and power between rich and poor. This politics is given substantive content, and gains legitimacy, through democratic deliberation that is guided by politically valenced interpretations of liberal procedural values, such as fairness, inclusion, and voice. In a sense, then, the rock-bottom foundation for critical liberal legalism, in our sense of the term, is itself *always already* grounded upon a *politically committed and democratically deliberative* interpretive practice.

As a normative approach, this critical liberal stance wholeheartedly embraces the idea that material goods such as food, health, and education anchor any person's active engagement in a liberal democracy, no matter where that system falls on the deliberative/electoral spectrum.[14] For as so many democratic theorists have noted, you can't deliberate if you are sick or hungry. Nor are you likely to resist selling your vote if it can buy you food.

As an advocacy style, the critical liberal stance is both partisan and pragmatic. Critical liberal advocates make use of public institutions such as courts, the media, and philanthropies to claim expansive entitlements to basic social goods.[15] Yet all the while they realize that such claim making will work, if at all, only in specific political contexts and limited ways. They see how liberal legal systems are structured by background rules that hide—and tilt—power, predictably against the poor.[16] They know firsthand how such skewed rules routinely constrain the scope of progressive human rights practice in uncertain but nonetheless loosely structured ways.[17]

Critical liberal advocates use liberal rhetoric to describe economic struggles as crusades for justice rather than squabbles over rents. They use rights tactics to embolden disenfranchised peoples to claim political agency and equal citizenship. They invoke rights language to move well-off people to share their own wealth in favor of the poor. But where such efforts fail to engender solidarity, these advocates do not recoil from pushing elites into fractious alliance with the poor. Thus defined, a critical liberal approach to ESR practice pushes formal liberal values as far as possible toward the progressive end of the interpretive spectrum.

A case in which this approach features prominently is that of the Ijora-Badia anti-eviction campaign in Nigeria. In their grassroots and social movement organizing, the lawyer-activists engaged community members and others to analyze the crisis through a lens of critical liberal values and methods. Thus, they challenged community members to consider rich-to-poor redistribution and institutional change as proactive responses to the repeated eviction threats that they were forced to endure. In doing so, they recast "strategic planning" as political debate. They maintained community members' *political* passion even as they took their fight into Nigerian courts and the World Bank's internal inspection panel. Indeed, SERAC consciously drew on this political passion to motivate community members to come into court to witness the performance of an uncertain liberal justice.

Another case in which this approach features prominently is that of Mohammed Zakari. In that case, the lawyer-activists also drew on formal liberal values to mobilize force for structural change. They did so by filing a legal claim of habeas corpus, alleging the unlawful detainment of a person by the state. The right to habeas corpus is one of the most fundamental liberal rights in the Anglo-American canon. Furthermore, the right not to be imprisoned for debt, though lacking the same historical pedigree, is explicitly enumerated in the International Covenant on Civil and Political Rights.[18] The lawyer-activists then linked this alleged violation of Zakari's formal "negative" right to freedom from unlawful detainment to a more controversial claim, with inevitably deeper distributive and structural dimensions, for his right to health. Through this linkage, they invoked, reinterpreted, and politically "activated" this liberal right to advance their movement-based claim to challenge structurally based and distributively manifested health inequality.

### Legal Pluralism

The second normative perspective that both emerges from and informs the lawyer-activists' practice refers to the way these actors engage with multiple lifeways and hybrid legalities. This perspective is best captured by a body of work, found largely in socio-legal anthropology, called "legal pluralism."[19] In broad terms, this school claims that the "law" which shapes people's legal consciousness and sociocultural fabric does not merely consist of the jurisdiction's formal legal rules. Rather, multiple legal and normative orders coexist in interwoven patterns.[20] Taken together, these coexisting legal orders produce intricate webs of constraint and opportunity for progressive politics and legal activism, particularly in the context of developing countries and in the areas of economic and social rights.

The work of several scholars offered our group maps of such constraint and opportunity. The work of Boaventura de Sousa Santos and César A. Rodríguez-Garavito highlights "subaltern" local and transnational activism that undercuts the official legal institutions of neoliberal globalization by endorsing alternative "legal orders."[21] Such social projects draw on what are formally labeled legal, illegal, and nonlegal elements to advance their causes. They expand the notion of liberal individual rights to incorporate "solidaristic understandings of entitlements grounded on alternative forms of legal knowledge." They highlight the importance of sustained political mobilization for the long-term success of grassroots legal strategies. Finally, they operate pragmatically by using political and legal tools and by mobilizing state and nonstate legal orders in every geographical and institutional niche.

A related perspective is that of postcolonial political scientist Partha Chatterjee as he explores bottom-up politics and deliberation of formally disenfranchised "populations" in postcolonial democracies.[22] Chatterjee suggests that the growth of such popular democracy depends on the increasing entry of the poor into a kind of politics that uses direct mobilization, rather than conventional electoral channels and formal legal institutions, to pressure the state to expand their share of social goods.[23] Chatterjee sometimes appears to focus only on a politics of zero-sum rent-seeking by the poor. At other times, however, he envisions a form of democratic politics grounded on informally and sometimes illegally mobilized demands, which reshapes delivery systems to engage and include their sustained presence as well as episodic demands.

Throughout the case studies featured in this volume, legal pluralism emerges as a distinguishing trend and a common normative commitment in the African activists' practice, one that responds to the deepest tension in their work. On the one hand, as we have seen, those featured in this volume embrace universal liberal human rights values like dignity, inclusiveness, and voice, at least in their most critically elaborated, politically tilted—"transformative"—valence. On the other hand, they are equally committed to engaging the plural lifeways and multiple legalities that prevail on the African continent and indeed across the globe. This tension is most intense in postcolonial settings, where "indigenous" lifeways can never be accepted as authentic or pure. Rather, those cultural practices and normative worlds are always historically shaped by a colonial past.[24]

Thus, these activists are determined to stand up to injustice while questioning *both* Enlightenment values *and* plural alternatives. In the face of this conundrum, any activist would be tempted to charge ahead in his work while keeping his head in the sand. Yet the activists featured here do not make this easy choice; instead, a signature moral theme of their practice is to work through that tension rather than around it. Like the pragmatists that they are, they work through this tension by continually reflecting, with others, about the values, both chosen and taken for granted, both formally liberal and fluidly plural, that guide their work.

Yet it is not the abstract commitment to reflection that is important. It is the way that such reflection is *practiced* when particular tensions arise between universalist liberal values and alternative ways of life. Where in the case studies can we see such reflection? The case studies show two scenarios when liberal/pluralist negotiation takes place.

The more familiar scenario is that in which the "rule of law" commands one action and an alternative legality warrants another.[25] Here the activist must choose between unquestioning conformity with the conventional, politically dominant, and officially state-sanctioned legal order, on the one hand, and an alternative legality, perhaps based on religious values, that deviates from it. Or the alternative legality might base itself on what it espouses as "higher principles" of justice. In either case, such alternative legality might endorse actions deemed illegal in the dominant order. This gap between the dominant order's law and alternative notions of legality or justice challenges pluralist human rights activists to engage in ongoing reflection on their own actions. It is not enough for those actions to be guided by positive law; rather, to be true to their pluralist commitments, the lawyers must respect all subordinated legal orders while still grounding their own actions on a considered judgment of which among these multiple legal orders most closely responds to their sense of justice.[26]

Several of the case studies demonstrate activists negotiating this "conflict of laws" scenario. For instance, in the case of Mohammed Zakari, the community split about whether to stage an unlicensed protest march demanding his release. Those who wanted to march viewed the state to be acting outside of the law when it refused them a license. To them, the public march was a moral imperative rather than a tactical trade-off. Others in the community felt that the rule of law demanded that they defer to the state's legal rules and bureaucratic power. The lawyer-activists involved in this case did not consider liberal legalism to be the only version of law with moral traction or everyday sense. Rather, they considered a range of different legal logics to occupy the same social space, commanding legitimacy and eliciting allegiance with different groups of people, all at the same time. Regardless of which choice the group eventually made, however, the important point is that the activists and community members took this clash of legal orders seriously and deliberated among themselves about the right thing to do. They did not dodge the moral decision by pleading "relativism": you can have your own legal order and I'll take mine. At the same time, they understood a commitment to pluralism as holding them to a more demanding version of moral responsibility than a compulsion to follow what "the" law would require. For in moments of conflict among legal orders, a plural sensibility required them to exercise their best moral judgment without the safe guidance of hard legal rules.

A second scenario in which lawyer-activists must negotiate a pluralist challenge involves the way that they use an awareness of plural legal orders to help them envision alternatives to "neoliberal" legal arrangements. Consider the case of the Nyamuma evictions, in which Tanzanian pastoral people were violently displaced from their grazing lands to make way for wildlife reserves and ecotourism enterprises. This strategy might look like an exemplary approach to "rights-based" development: it protects wildlife; promotes environmentally sound, participatory tourist development; and raises the nation's GDP. Yet the strategy requires that the pastoral people, who formerly used the land, be relocated to bounded tracts poorly suited to grazing their cattle. Thus, from the pastoral people's perspective, the development strategy was flawed because it threatened their livelihood by valuing wild animals over people, and the global tourist industry over their established way of life.

Here a pluralist perspective offers an opportunity to negotiate a more nuanced development and land-use policy. The pastoral people's "traditional" ways of valuing land suggest strategies for mediating between a rigid development formula that calls for the eviction of pastoral peoples from their traditional grazing land, on the one hand, and no development at all, on the other. Activists who understand how the pastoralists traditionally relate to large animals might ask whether these animals need to be "protected" from pastoral peoples in a fenced-in, people-free reserve. How can species protection be ensured without fencing pastoral peoples off of their land? Indeed, might the targeted pastoral people be engaged in *shaping* animal conservation policies rather than criminalized for performing the practices they had followed for centuries?

A pluralist imagination thus motivates the Nyamuma activists to push beyond the current vogue in land reform, which is to grant Western-type individual land rights in order to promote economic growth.[27] This policy tends to explicitly exclude both "traditional" forms of land ownership and alternative policies for redistributing land. By taking the pastoralists' landholding practices seriously, the Nyamuma activists think beyond this dichotomy between "neoliberal" and "traditional" landholding regimes. They break loose from the "modern" landholding paradigm, opening up multiple possibilities for configuring markets, land rights, and democratic governance practices.[28] Thus, through their pluralist orientation, the Nyamuma activists begin to envision alternative trajectories of development. Critical reflection on the apparent clash between liberal values and traditional practices opens up new ways to embed a progressive version of liberal values into social policy.

At the same time that they "listened" to what the pastoralists had to teach them about land use, the Nyamuma lawyer-activists were counseled by their pluralist commitments to remain skeptical about the "authenticity" of what they heard. Yet this skepticism was not the same as postmodern paralysis. Rather, their skepticism about the idea of authenticity led the activists to explore the *colonial* histories of the values and practices that had been labeled traditional, indigenous, or authentic. How did colonization affect the pastoralists' land use practices and "indigenous" values with respect to the animals they used?[29]

In the Nyamuma eviction case, for instance, the activists questioned the colonial history of communal land ownership at the same time that they used those forms of ownership to break out of the neoliberal property order. For instance, an investigation of colonial and postcolonial history might show that in some times and places colonial forces would fabricate an account of indigenous communal land use to rationalize the removal of settled people from valuable arable land into unproductive land in remote areas.[30]

As another example, consider one historical context for the setting of Accra's "Big Gutter" near Abdullah Muman's home. The history underscores the political and distributional dimensions of the gutter's location, factors that might heighten residents' political energy for demanding that it be either relocated or cleaned up. In the colonial city of Accra, the Europeans' science taught that malaria was caused by toxic vapors that rose from low-lying areas. Thus, the British built their own houses, but not their servants', on concrete pilings. They took the highest ground for their own dwellings, leaving the "natives" to the low-lying land, the very areas where the disease was believed to fester and within which infected people, so the thinking went, could be contained.

Our understanding of the cause of malaria has become more "scientific" in recent years: now it is the mosquitoes that are bred in the low-lying standing water rather than the vapors that arise from it. But the path-dependent geography of residential space has not changed. Predominantly white elites live and work on the city's high ground, in neighborhoods with evocative names like "Ridge," while their subjects are spread about in low-lying informal settlements without the infrastructure to drain waste water or prevent flooding. Because of a shortage of personnel, facilities, and drugs, the residents of these informal enclaves have no access to primary healthcare unless they can pay for it in cash. Without such access, when the "weaker" children get malaria, they die. It's that simple.

The colonial history was different in the rural areas. There, indirect rule prevailed. Thus, missionary clinics gave care to indigenous elites but not to the most disadvantaged. This colonial manipulation of health access enticed—or bribed—elites to play their assigned role in the regime of indirect rule, wielding delegated state power to control their own subjects on behalf of their colonial masters. Meanwhile, colonial health officers, missionaries, and others in alliance with them condoned and even spread "traditional" theories of disease causation, prevention, and cure, which blamed the natives for making themselves vulnerable to endemic disease through lifestyles of filth and sin.[31] Such myths discouraged the nonelite indigenous peoples from making demands for better healthcare from colonial authorities. This uneven distribution of healthcare for native subjects ensured, through a Darwinian logic, that only the strongest workers would survive the "malaria test," to toil in the mines and plantations, build the railroads, and fight in the Europeans' wars.[32]

This sort of historical research can help advocates negotiate with the claims of traditional medicine in an ESR campaign. Rather than dismissing "nonliberal" traditional practices, advocates negotiating the pluralist challenge through a historical lens might work with community members to trace the roots of those practices. They could then focus their campaigns on enduring patterns of skewed political insight and resource distribution suggested by those histories. For instance, in the health example, such work might raise questions about the distribution of hospitals and clinics, and the patterns of access to them. Where do these patterns come from and how can we change them? What control do local elites continue to wield over health access? How do regional and national governments, as well as international donors, shore up this power? What resistance would we face if we tried to challenge that spatial distribution? Why do politicians continue to claim that their constituents' lack of hygiene and moral deviation is a major part of the problem? How can such myths be dislodged from the minds of those they were crafted to shame? And why are the dominant centers of research on tropical disease not located in the former colonies instead of large Northern cities like London, Amsterdam, Berlin, and Boston?

On a more fundamental level, such historical analysis puts into question the authenticity of what are often considered to be traditional theories of the origin of malaria or HIV and traditional practices for its prevention and cure. Thus, human rights advocates' lingering reservations about promoting the hegemony of Western science can be situated in a new context. Consider here the case study in this volume about the Treatment Action Campaign's efforts to secure HIV treatment for all infected people in South Africa. In this case, the government refused to provide antiretroviral HIV treatment to infected South Africans, choosing instead to let them die. To rationalize this policy, the government took an official position of "denialism" on the scientifically undisputed viral cause of HIV infection. To buttress this denialist position, the government then seized upon—and embellished—"traditional" beliefs about HIV's causation and anticolonial ideologies about Western science among rural peoples who had never been exposed to contemporary science.

These embellished myths about "traditional" beliefs and ideologies complicated the efforts of activists to secure universal HIV treatment for several reasons. One was the ambivalence of some activists about imposing their own beliefs to trump rural people's "traditional" medical beliefs and ideologies. As the South Africa chapter shows, a critical, reflective, and historically grounded version of pluralism takes "traditional" beliefs seriously, interpreting those beliefs so as to disrupt the dominant legal order. At the same time, though, these activists' plural sensibility does not consider "traditional" values to be sacrosanct, ahistorical, or authentic.

Yet the analysis that situates traditional practices in their historical context must be subtle, granted that some "traditional" health beliefs and practices were created or embellished by colonial rulers to consolidate their domination of African peoples and legitimate the withholding of medical care to African subjects. At the same time, however, some anticolonial African activists embraced such colonially designed pseudotraditions in order to mock and subvert colonial power. Finally, some traditional practices—even those of colonial design—are in fact rooted in precolonial lifeways and so invite both historical scrutiny and continuing respect. Thus, nuanced historical reflection must engage both activists and community members. In campaigns other than those featured in this volume, such as campaigns around contraceptive practices, ESR advocates are shaping processes for such deliberation in ways that place women, as opinion leaders and community members, in leading roles.

But pluralist reflection on liberal human rights values has still not hit bottom; the process for such activist/community deliberation and the participation norms that guide it must also become the subject of critique. What values guide the design of the deliberative process itself, and who decides that architectural question? Suppose, for example, that a group does not endorse inclusive deliberation as a way to work through challenging problems. Do we defer to that distaste as an expression of an alternative "indigenous" lifeway? Or do we interrogate the colonial history of that supposed rejection, by disenfranchised peoples, of the liberal values of grassroots democracy and equal voice? For while those liberal values are a lynchpin of the dominant world order, how can we tell whether a preference, say, for silent meditation is a politically motivated renunciation of our "logocentric" order or a lingering sign of colonial domination?

The point here is not to trigger vertigo. Rather, it is to suggest that negotiating the pluralist challenge is about subtle, ongoing reflection that takes place in the throes of practice. Perhaps because so many languages, ethnic groups, cultural topographies, and histories mingle in sub-Saharan settings, the African activists in this book are adept at engaging communities in this negotiation in the context of *ongoing* ESR campaigns. Each chapter offers its own account of this interpretive dance. In conclusion, then, the pluralist sensibility of these activists manifests itself in two ways. First, that sensibility shows up through the activists' engagement with counter-legalities that the state's law tends to crowd out. As the Nyamuma case shows, such engagement can give them ideas for alternative legal arrangements in the here and now. And second, as these activists draw inspiration from countervailing normative values and cultural worlds, they reflect on the histories in which those worlds are embedded.[33]

## Human Rights Practice as Redistributive Politics

At every point in their improvisation, the advocates featured in this volume recognize and indeed embrace the politics embedded in their work. They do not pretend that human rights advocacy can be a neutral endeavor, either in how they use its language and tools tactically, or in how they relate its values to their own. Rather, they understand the issues on which they are working as politically contested and having deep roots in colonial histories. They understand "pragmatism" as breaking out of formalist chains. They see performance as a way of embedding human rights in the embodied passion of the people they work with. They view pluralist reflection as the opportunity to delve into brutal colonial histories and their present-day legacies in overtly partisan ways. Finally, as we will explain below, they view tactics that prefigure democratic social welfare institutions as precursors to politically equitable state practice, both within the national state and beyond.

These lawyer-activists view the "Washington Consensus" and "structural adjustment" to be the resurgence of "neocolonial" domination, and have mobilized economic and social rights to challenge them. They expect judges to reflect their own social positions in ways that respond to the redistributive potential of supposedly "neutral" human rights claims. They do not view the lack of "teeth" in human rights laws to be a particular cause for concern because they do not expect courts, on their own, to resolve ideological debates or make distributional decisions that activists would endorse. Finally, they do not expect to build social movement on the basis of formal liberal values. Rather, they seek to draw politically diverse people into human rights campaigns on the basis of converging real-life interests and political commitments.

Because they see their human rights work as political to its core, they have responses to the familiar critiques of ESR-centered social justice advocacy. Consider the skeptics' major arguments and the way that the lawyer-activists' overtly political human rights framework makes those claims irrelevant to their work.

First, skeptics claim, human rights does not deliver what it promises, particularly in the economic and social domains.[34] For to put it simply, no matter how passionate your belief in the power of economic and social rights, ESR advocacy rarely puts bread on the table. The advocates featured here do not have that expectation; rather, they use ESR language and tools to leverage committed engagement and thus mobilize social movement and political power. Through such mobilization, they hope to make greater rich-to-poor redistribution and bolder institutional innovation possible. It is worth noting, however, that the most robust mobilization takes place when human rights activism and preexisting social movements reinforce each other, as they did in the South African Treatment Action Campaign case. In contrast, when there is no preexisting social movement, as was the case in the Nyamuma evictions in Tanzania, it becomes difficult for human rights activists to mobilize political power.

Second, the skeptics fear that by doing economic and social rights, lawyer-activists divert their passion from political organizing. The activists' response is that they are using human rights to *embolden* rather than derail their work.

Third, the skeptics assert that economic and social rights claims raise questions about the allocation of what are inevitably limited national budgets, either among different social welfare sectors or between the social sector and competing priorities. Beyond this, the skeptics claim, economic and social rights issues raise deeper political questions about the development pathway that a nation chooses. Does a nation have to subscribe to a particular theory for how best to promote economic growth in order to meet its people's basic needs? Indeed, does a nation have to subscribe to a growth-based development theory at all in order to best secure for its people a matrix of decent, sustainable ways of life? The ESR lawyer-activists featured here are not daunted by this challenge because they do not use human rights to *evade* such political questions. Rather, in their hands, ESR advocacy becomes a practice in political democracy. Thus, their work seeks to use human rights campaigns to open up *political* debate about where to allocate, when to expand, and how best to renew limited resources in ways that enable all people to live decent lives.

Finally, the skeptics argue that human rights advocacy locks antipoverty activists into a formalist framework that can be deployed to protect the status quo. They claim that such talk deafens those who use it to the political struggles it conceals. For instance, the critics argue that human rights activists claim that all people have a fundamental right to education. Yet in making such a resource-dependent claim, they forget that the rich can call foul if taxes are raised to fund it. "You may claim a right to be schooled," the rich might argue, "but I too have a human right: to keep what I own."

Thus, our ESR activists interpret human rights claims not as formal entitlements founded on natural law or treaty-based rights, but rather as *commitments* to realize the values of dignity, security, and voice, for example, in overtly political but also artfully pluralist ways. Such a politics resonates with the experimentalist intuitions of Roberto Unger[35] and Charles Sabel,[36] as well as Mouffe and Laclau's vision of radical democratic renewal.[37] What these lawyer-activists have done through practical innovation is to translate human rights language and strategies into small steps toward repeatedly disrupted, but continually renewed, political democracy.

Finally, a commitment to redistributive politics signals a normatively informed analytical approach, which searches for nonobvious distributional effects of legal rules and policy frameworks. This kind of analysis guides activists as they mobilize power to change inequitable policies and rules and to reflect on their action. For instance, in the case of the Nyamuma evictions in Tanzania, the lawyer-activists adopted this analytical approach. Through it, they determined that a seemingly neutral government policy of titling traditional lands would be likely to result in land deprivation for pastoral peoples.[38] Similarly, this analytical method enabled them to see how the values and language of ESR could reinforce the political power of the elites who exploit that rhetoric, at the expense of further marginalizing the poor.[39] Scholars have also used this analytical method to determine that seemingly neutral efforts to export the "rule of law" to developing countries have hidden distributional implications.[40]

## Prefiguring Structural Change

Pragmatic and performative strategies of engagement, combined with transformative, pluralist, and redistributive normative commitments: such is the fabric of the human rights practice that emerged from our investigation. Beyond articulating these common features, however, our inquiry aimed to answer two further questions: (1) how can such strategic engagements and normative commitments disrupt inequitable patterns of social and economic development, resource distribution, and institutional design? and (2) how can these interventions generate positive, sustainable change? Our historical institutionalist methodology helped us trace such dynamics.[41] In particular, that methodology enabled us to map how the lawyer-activists' practice could open up generative democratic spaces, in which innovations in the delivery of social goods might sometimes *prefigure* longer-term structural change. In some cases, these prefigurative institutions took an experimentalist form.

The term "experimentalist" refers to democratic experimentalism, a current school of socio-legal thought with multiple dimensions to its project.[42] Its most direct relevance to the Stones of Hope project is that it offers a critique of public bureaucracies that is highly relevant to the realization of social and economic rights. This critique is that such bureaucracies are so rigid, so hierarchical, and so prone to rent seeking that they cannot deliver social goods across wide populations in either effective or "democratic" ways.[43]

In response to this critique, experimentalism proposes novel practices for the democratic delivery of social goods. These innovations typically draw "stakeholders" in a particular delivery system—such as managers, service providers, clients, funders, and wider community members—into a process that addresses specific delivery challenges in deliberative, team-based ways.[44] This problem-solving process is guided by pragmatist values such as learning through experience, cross-learning among different localities, and continual reflection on the quality of the provisional outcomes and the deliberation itself. Experimentalist scholars suggest that both legislatures and courts can and should impose experimentalist reforms on social agencies, like health systems and schools, when such reforms might decrease "structural injustice."[45]

Of particular importance to the Stones of Hope project is the way that experimentalists envision the activist *practices* that can prod legislatures and courts to mandate such deliberative problem-solving frameworks within social welfare institutions. Indeed, one important theme in their work is that a legal system must ensure that a democratic polity can claim "destabilization rights."[46] These are rights to shake up public welfare bureaucracies that have become rigidly hierarchical and immune to citizen accountability. Destabilization rights can be activated by an ESR campaign that launches a lawsuit, such as that in the Zakari case, seeking an experimentalist legal remedy. Such a remedy would mandate a court-supervised framework for long-term deliberation among parties and other stakeholders about how best to "deliver the goods" that the contested right guarantees.[47] Such remedies replace inadequate practices with participatory, accountable, and revisable solutions to the "technical" challenges that obstructed the prior system's capacity to deliver the social good in question, on the ground.

Thus, in appropriate cases, experimentalist lawyers ask courts to hand *back* to administrators, along with other stakeholders, the very problems that they are charged with causing in the first place. Critics have challenged this practice on two grounds. First, critics say that experimentalists overlook the substantial wealth redistribution required to deliver social goods across large and impoverished populations. It is not just that the delivery systems are broken, they insist; it is mainly that the money isn't there. Thus, critics insist that political mobilization around resource distribution must accompany or even dislodge experimentalism entirely as a strategy for progressive social change. Second, critics say that experimentalists are naïve about the huge differences of social and political power between government bureaucrats and the impoverished clients that they serve. Given this power difference, it will be impossible to get even-handed stakeholder representation from all interested groups.

Experimentalists respond to the first criticism by claiming that the resources will be easier to attract when a workable delivery system is emerging. With the second criticism, experimentalists dispute that the power difference is irremediably enormous or that efforts to buttress the power of the "weak" will prove ineffective. Critics in turn respond that this is not an adequate rejoinder to their claim. Notwithstanding this debate, however, experimentalism has inspired a growing body of economic and social rights jurisprudence, some of which comes from the African activists whose work is featured in this volume.[48] Indeed, those advocates design strategies, draft laws, and craft legal remedies that prefigure the practices, institutions, and norms that they hope to put in place over the long term. To explain this dimension, let us turn our attention back to the case of Mohammed Zakari, who was detained in a Ghanaian public hospital because he could not pay his bill.

In that case, the advocates confronted a health finance system in which the law excused certain people from having to pay cash for services and drugs before receiving them. The law required this exemption to extend to "paupers," or indigent people who met a test designed to determine that they were unable to pay. The greatest problem with this scheme was that these formally exempted people were rarely, if ever, actually granted that right, whether they asked for it or not. The blockage took place in the primary care centers, where in spite of the black-letter law, frustrated frontline workers routinely denied impoverished people care. Their reason made sense: they knew that they would never get reimbursed for the free care they provided, no matter what the law guaranteed. And indeed, they were right. At the time of the case, the national government's Ministry of Health had not set up a reliable system for distributing funds from the national budget to reimburse frontline health providers if they provided "paupers" free care.

What was needed to secure Mr. Zakari's "right to health" then was not merely that he be released from the hospital and granted a "pauper" exemption from having to pay the bill for his care. Beyond that, his case exposed the need for the government's entire health finance structure, from the clinic to the national and indeed international levels, to be redesigned—or rather designed—so as to ensure that resources were both secured and distributed in an equitable way. If the range of design options is considered through an economic and social rights lens, then the acceptable options must incorporate human rights values—like dignity, equality, material security, and voice—into the institutional architecture and organizational practices of the exemption system. Furthermore, in keeping with the most capacious human rights aspiration, the resulting system must have the capacity to deliver adequate healthcare to all persons within its range, regardless of their circumstances.

What are the realistic design options for such a system, and what process can be followed that will provide an ongoing preview of that system as it is being designed? The Zakari advocates, through their practice, pointed toward an innovative answer. One part of their idea was inspired by the theories of structural litigation developed in the United States during the 1960s and 1970s.[49] Another part was directly inspired by the democratic experimentalist ideas outlined above. These ideas guided the Zakari advocates to craft a litigation remedy that framed an experimentalist process for delivering exemptions, over the long term.[50]

The goal of this remedy was not to order that the existing system be replaced by another specified model. Rather, the idea of the remedy was to offer a broad, open-textured architectural framework for the ongoing management and redesign of the system—a template that would improve upon the top-down, command-control model. Through this framework, the advocates sought a *process* of ongoing democratic regulatory negotiation. Thus, a council of stakeholders would work together to fill in the details of the exemption system so as to meet specified performance targets. They would repeatedly revise that design as they evaluated how well it was doing and as they came up with ideas for making it better. The system would be decentralized but networked, so that different groups of ground-level stakeholders could learn from one another. Through this process, the system would be challenged to *deliver* the best possible healthcare in the present, as well as over the long term.

Another example of this process in the health sector is in the chapter on the South African Treatment Action Campaign (TAC) for patients living with HIV/AIDS. In this case, the activists did not limit their campaign strategy to an experimentalist litigation remedy. Rather, they saw the litigation as part of a broader, highly politicized social movement that itself offered the potential for health system innovation. Indeed, the long-term strategy of the TAC advocates was to use litigation and grassroots mobilization to pressure the government to work with them to create a new primary health system. Their goal here was a system with the capacity to empower HIV-positive people to comply with complex antiretroviral treatment regimes. Such a system, to work, had to engage health workers, activists, and HIV/AIDS patients in a joint project of innovative healthcare delivery and governance, on the ground. The movement's grassroots Treatment Literacy Campaign was devised in response to this challenge. This campaign focused on primary care clinics, bringing HIV-positive people together with health providers and volunteers to engage in a participatory process of empowering the patients to manage their own healthcare while they advocate for others like themselves. These grassroots treatment centers offered a space for experimentation with an innovative delivery scheme that did not segregate professionals from patients and community members. Thus, this system prefigured the sort of primary healthcare scheme that might have the capacity to realize broad, human rights–based healthcare guarantees.

Eventually, successful litigation and social movement mobilization led the South African government to shift its "denialist" attitude and begin rolling out a massive plan to make HIV/AIDS treatment accessible. Subsequently, TAC has collaborated with the government to devise a national AIDS strategy. This collaboration has relied partly on pilot sites of primary healthcare that reflect innovations originally devised by the Treatment Literacy Campaign. Though this process is still at an early stage, the primary healthcare centers that stakeholders have designed are mobilizing existing resources in new ways, so as to offer higher-quality health access, not just for HIV but for all basic health problems.

In short, prefigurative human rights campaigns build innovative systems of welfare delivery through the networking of microinstitutional experiments. Grassroots mobilization around those experiments in turn opens political space for ongoing critique and contestation around those experiments' human rights dimensions and success on the ground. It is in that political space then that the improvements in people's well-being gained through those institutional innovations might be expanded and sustained.

*creation of a reconfigured political space*

## Chapter 6

# The Long Arc of Pragmatic Economic and Social Rights Advocacy

Peter Houtzager and Lucie E. White

This volume's Introduction, its case studies, and the preceding chapter have pointed out common innovations in the pragmatic economic and social rights (ESR) campaigns of its featured African activists. The volume has documented how these innovative practices can lead to changes in the agencies of government—agencies like Ghana's Ministry of Health—which are charged with securing economic and social rights guarantees. In this chapter we look more closely at the link between those innovative advocacy practices and subsequent changes in the design and delivery of social and other public goods. We examine *how* innovative advocacy links up to institutional change.

Understanding this linkage is critical for ESR practitioners and scholars who hope to use ESR advocacy to challenge structural injustice.[1] Yet this link from advocacy to institutional change has largely escaped close scrutiny from ESR scholars. Scholars have documented the work of leading economic and social rights advocates.[2] They have profiled grassroots organizing efforts in marginalized communities[3] and mapped the dynamics of social justice movements.[4] They have shown how advocates have taken positions that too often have had perverse effects on people's lives.[5] And they have labeled extreme deprivation as structural violence.[6] But they have not yet zeroed in on the actual ways that innovative advocacy, which always includes interaction with social movement, can help to promote and sustain institutional change.

Having an impact on structural injustice[7] requires more than winning lawsuits or sparking social justice mobilization; it requires that such strategic victories achieve innovation in the institutions that provide food, shelter, healthcare, housing, jobs, and the like to impoverished people, on the ground. Thus, ESR advocates must do more than close the gap between the "law on the books" and its implementation.[8] More importantly, they must help reorient key practices of social welfare agencies and other national institutions so that they do a better job of delivering on the promises that ESR entitlements guarantee. Beyond that, ESR advocates must write those innovations back into the law and then embed these legally mandated innovations into the responsible public agencies' practices over the long term.[9]

Thus, in the case of Mohammed Zakari in Ghana, which we set out in Chapter 4, the challenge for the ESR advocates was to translate their advocacy campaign into a reorientation of the government's healthcare delivery system for the poor. Next, they had to write the resulting changes into the law. Then they had to embed these changes into the Ministry of Health's everyday institutional practices, so that its agents changed how they conducted admission and discharge in hospitals and clinics across the nation.

Building on Chapter 5 and the case studies in this volume, this concluding chapter looks at the hard work these advocates faced in helping to make real change. Its goal is to open a conversation about the path between creative ESR advocacy, as it takes place in contemporary Africa, and structural change that can reduce systemic and sustained ESR deprivation. To guide our discussion of this path we present an "arc" that traces how creative African ESR advocates use law and other tactics to produce innovations in the creation and delivery of ESR guaranteed public goods, innovations that they then seek to embed in the practices of public agencies across large classes of people, over the long run. The arc is a heuristic device rather than a theory or a recipe for successful advocacy, and is offered to spark discussion among scholars, activists, claimants, and others rather than to tell them what to do.

As we describe more fully below (in the discussion accompanying Figure 1), the arc traces ESR advocacy as it moves across a series of interconnected temporal fields. Thus, it runs from (1) local "generative spaces" to (2) pressure on national political institutions to change their ESR-relevant practices to (3) actual changes in the practices of government agencies to (4) the spread of those changes into multiple local settings.[10] Social activation within and across those local spaces pushes them toward becoming new generative spaces, which can both sustain the previously implemented institutional changes and promote improved innovation.

We continue by revisiting a few key ideas from Chapter 5. We then set out a conception of "institutions" to orient creative advocates toward a realistic practice of making institutional change. We then take a walk through the arc itself.

## Some Foundations

### Pragmatic Advocacy

The pragmatic nature of the African economic and social rights advocacy featured in this book gives the long arc its distinctive shape. The book's Introduction highlights three features of that advocacy.

First, advocates see the main obstacles to the fuller realization of ESR as residing in sociopolitical institutions, in particular in the routinized institutional practices that support widespread exclusion, discrimination, and poverty. We see this injustice as "structural" rather than the consequence of malicious individuals, dysfunctional agencies, or "corrupt" states.[11] For this reason, any serious ESR advocacy must be concerned with deep institutional change. That is, ESR advocacy must seek the "conversion" of de facto institutional practices to ones more compatible with economic and social rights.[12] Where this requires de jure changes in law, these are pursued. But the arc is long because change in the letter of law is only the beginning of a lengthy process of institutional change. As pragmatists, however, the activists seek to reduce immediate economic and social rights deprivations rather than to topple entire ESR regimes.

The second feature of pragmatic rights activism is the emphasis placed on power relations in every advocacy setting. The commitments of powerful actors, both inside and outside of key institutions, often obstruct the access of vulnerable people to ESR-guaranteed public goods. Such blockage can take place even when those actors neither want to be acting, nor know that they are, in ways that maintain deprivation. The ESR advocates featured in this collection of case studies use human rights language and tools to build the power of economically vulnerable groups, and then use this power to leverage institutional change. They work in multiple arenas, including villages, international bodies like the World Bank, and private conglomerates like pharmaceutical companies, as readily as a national ministry of health or human rights commission. They also work in multiple ways, including, but not limited to, litigation and other conventional lawyering tactics.

Third, African advocates have learned to work both with and against the normative pluralism that orders their social and institutional landscapes. They use the generative tensions inherent in different normativities—the many forms of African religious, positive, customary, human rights, and other order-ings—in an effort to weave ESR values and practices into the hybrid normative fabric of local communities and national institutions. Rather than resist norma-tive pluralism they welcome the generative tension that it brings to their work.

## Why Human Rights?

Though African advocates are skeptical of the universal claims of human rights, they do not let their critique dissuade them from mobilizing the power of those values in the interest of change. Why should they use human rights values as a touchstone for culturally plural and normatively positive institutional change? Before we can answer that question, we should spell out their ESR value com-mitments. Most conservatively, they are the foundational norms that are set out in the Universal Declaration of Human Rights[13] and repeated through the International Covenant on Economic, Social, and Cultural Rights[14] and other official human rights instruments. In the context of ESR, four foundational norms are dominant: *inclusion, equality, participation,* and *security*. Inclusion, equality, and participation figure in the *way* that essential goods are produced and delivered; *security*, in the substantive provision of what it takes to thrive.

With these values as its foundation, human rights can be seen as a shared moral language that cuts across the distinctive commitments of many social and cultural groups. It provides a common tongue through which a wide array of claims can be made. It therefore makes possible social justice mobilization by groups otherwise divided among themselves. Human rights advocacy has been widely critiqued as an "imperial" moral project, one that imposes its own Enlightenment values while "crowding out" other moral orders. Yet it is pre-cisely because of the powerful normative claim of core human rights values across distinctive religions, moralities, ideologies, and customary practices, for example, that rather than crowding out other normative orders, human rights can offer a cross-cutting value field—a legitimate moral force—around which plural discussion and problem solving can be convened.

Finally, human rights practice is distinctive in that it occupies a privileged position from which to contest national and to some extent international re-gimes and public institutions. With few exceptions, human rights treaties point to the nation-state as the bearer of human rights duties and thus the target of human rights claims. Human rights duties are often spelled out in national constitutions. And the agencies, whether "public" or "private," that are typi-cally charged to deliver the goods which ESR guarantee are usually agencies of the national government. Thus, human rights values offer a standard for government performance that is internal to the state itself, and hence both legally protected and legitimate.

## Changing Institutions

### Conversion

Pragmatic ESR advocacy is grounded in a distinctive understanding of institutions. Contrary to the commonplace idea of institutions as government ministries and departments that people encounter as public authority, we have a broader and more disaggregated notion of those entities. We view institutions as specific *public social roles clustered in relatively well-defined political-administrative arenas* such as a national ministry of health, human rights commission, religious order, or customary chieftaincy.[15] These role-clusters express the institution's values and distribute its power. Roles are enacted as people within institutions improvise around loosely scripted public practices. The scripts are loose because people have to interpret their institutional roles and do so through their own predispositions, values, and cross-cutting institutional affiliations.

For example, in the case of the Ghanaian campaign for the right to health, a nurse caring for Mohammed Zakari in one of Accra's public hospitals might belong to a professional association, a religious group, a human rights NGO, and an extended family network, all at the same time. The scope of her improvisation as Zakari's nurse will be restricted by the range of acceptable moves that the hospital, qua institution, will allow. Yet she may nonetheless be able to offer moral and material support to Zakari by improvising in a way that is influenced by her family ties, human rights activism, and professional values at the same time that it is constrained by her bureaucratic role. The normative hybridity and social flux of contemporary African societies provide for a particularly wide repertoire of such improvisations.

ESR activism can create an environment that supports institutions to change in the direction of greater ESR compatibility. Activism can create background legitimacy for the core ESR values of inclusion, equality, security, and voice. At the same time, advocacy can destabilize—or further loosen—institutional scripts. This loosening frees up influential persons and groups inside and outside of the institutions to improvise in new, more "ESR-positive" ways. We see this trend in the case of Ijora-Badia, where community members worked successfully to block a threatened mass eviction. While activists educated both community members and government officials to understand that such mass evictions were human rights violations, advocates gave federal government officials the legal authority to resist the threatened eviction from inside and outside governmental constraints. The widened scope for their improvisation came through the advocacy. The activists' motivation to enact those improvisations in ESR-positive ways came from the overlap of their multiple normative affiliations with core human rights values.

Institutions survive because actors with sufficient power are committed to them. These actors can change over time, however. Furthermore, institutionalist research suggests that as the actors' foundational value commitments shift, institutional practices will vary dramatically.[16] Institutional practices can also vary when new public roles—an internal inspection panel,[17] for instance, or a new tier of supervisory personnel—are layered onto existing ones. We can see several striking examples of these "conversion" processes in the case studies. For instance, in the South African case, the Treatment Action Campaign's social movement and the litigation over drug access for preventing mother-to-child transmission of HIV pushed some denialists out of the nation's health ministry. At the same time, this pressure from without freed other state actors to abandon their own denialist positions. Through these two processes—of exit by some and increased scope for improvisation by others—the institution itself noticeably changed.

In the Nyamuma example, Tanzania's Commission on Human Rights and Good Governance retained its institutional identity over the period covered in the chapter. At the same time, however, the ESR campaign pushed against the agency's foundational norms, legal scaffolding, scripts, and scope for improvisation in a way that eventually enabled some of its staff to bend their improvisations in ESR-favoring ways. Similarly, advocating for new health policies may alter the matrix of formal roles in a ministry of health, the distribution of authority among existing roles, or even the legal architecture or existence of the agency itself. Pushing for health professionals to be trained in community medicine and public health may change the scripts on which officials in a ministry of health draw to improvise how they enact their public roles, without any formal change in these roles.

In an example drawn from farther afield, Latin American political elites early in the twentieth century sponsored official union movements to control and disempower an emerging working class, but under different political circumstances these institutions were subsequently used by the working class to exercise significant power.[18]

Thus, an important lesson from the chapters is that institutional "conversion," or change, can occur as a result of widely different processes and can take many forms.[19] ESR activism can contribute to changes in institutions by shifting their legitimating values or loosening the scripts that guide those institutions' public roles, or indeed by altering the public roles themselves.

## Constraint

Institutionalist research offers a further insight into ways that activists can—and cannot—promote institutional change: institutions change in ways that are path dependent.[20] That is, at the same time that institutional actors have some space for improvisation, institutions are nonetheless constituted around *stabilized* roles, values, and practices. Groups associated with an institution tend to be strongly committed to it; whether situated within or without the institution, those actors tend to experience its practices as natural. Their investment in the institution's continued existence will constrain (though not predetermine) the change that is possible over time. Rarely, if ever, can ESR activism, even when buttressed by robust social movement, simply wipe out existing institutional roles, values, and practices.

Instead, those practices have to be taken into account, modified, and improvised around—converted but not erased—when advocates seek to nudge institutions towards ESR aspirations. Thus, the advocates in the Zakari case were wise to seek fairly minor changes within the Ministry of Health's administration of fee exemptions, rather than pushing for wholesale revamping of the nation's health finance system. Tinkering with the exemption procedures would hardly realize the dream of an ESR-positive health system. But it would push the health ministry's fee collection practices in an ESR-positive direction.

Such path-dependent institutional conversion is rarely the single-handed result of pressure coming at the target institution from the outside. Actors *within* those institutions—from clients to street-level bureaucrats and professionals, to national policy makers—bring multiple societal connections and value commitments to their jobs.[21] In all of the chapters, we see such actors playing direct roles in advocacy or social movement organizing at the same time that they are working to change the agencies from within.

Nevertheless, the activists featured in this volume, all of whom have years of experience working with the most marginalized social groups, have witnessed firsthand the social stigma that attaches to those groups. In order to gain wide sympathy for their campaigns from bureaucratic insiders, advocates must embolden such excluded groups to assert their dignity in effective ways. This work is a major theme in the Ijora-Badia case, where sympathetic actors inside the bureaucracy began to work for the threatened communities only *after* Badia residents publicly proclaimed their right to a home. Or consider the South African case, where TAC-leaning bureaucratic insiders could not act forthrightly from within the national government until TAC's social movement had begun to heat up on the streets.

In addition to path-dependent conversion, redistribution of wealth is a critical feature of ESR-positive social change. Rich-to-poor redistribution, especially in zero-sum situations, may require overt contestation as well as benign deliberation among interested groups. Yet even in such cases, constructing a sharp dichotomy between ESR advocates and agency "insiders" is as unhelpful as it is inaccurate. Indeed, in most of the cases in this volume key public officials and professional groups located in civil society facilitate, support, or generate advocacy in distinct fields of the arc.[22]

Thus, our concept of institutions and their change envisions change agents interacting inside and outside national state institutions through activism in local, national, and international fields. Given that picture, it should be clear that we emphatically do *not* understand action in the local field to arise from private citizens and local communities acting in civil society on their own. Such "spontaneous" action can certainly set in motion some of the processes discussed here. But from the case studies we have no evidence that such episodes can trigger ESR-enhancing innovations on a scale beyond that of the community in which they arise.

## The Long Arc: A Picture

As we discussed at the beginning of this chapter, the arc in Figure 1 shows a series of discrete but interrelated fields of pragmatic advocacy. We set out the local sociopolitical field, the field of state power, and the political administrative arena as reference points that can help guide our understanding of ESR advocacy, rather than as the foundations for a theory of rights advocacy or a road map to successful campaigns. Few of the cases in this volume run the entire arc, and some start midway and appear to move in the opposite direction.

Furthermore, the metaphors can be taken too far; by suggesting a relatively linear sequence of stages of institutional change, the figure oversimplifies the complex process it seeks to convey. Indeed, while severely constrained by resources, ESR advocates often work simultaneously in several fields through

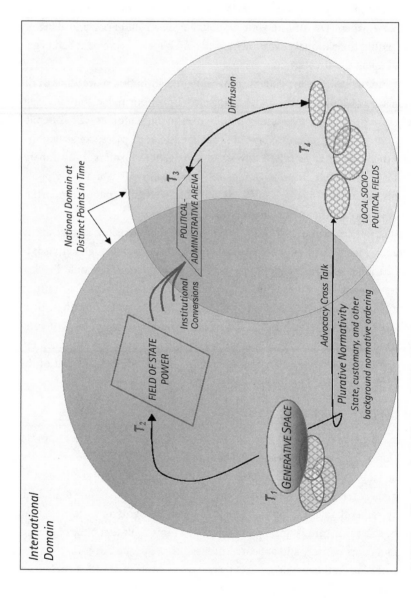

FIGURE 1  The Long Arc of Pragmatic ESR Advocacy

their extended networks. They shift their energy back and forth across fields depending on where activity is heating up. In addition, there are multiple feedback loops across the sites. Developments in the national political arena in response to grassroots social justice mobilization will reverberate in the original local sites. As a broad array of actors enters public debate in the political arena, experimental solutions that have been "carried up" are reinterpreted, re-signified, and brought back to generative space.

The linked sites in Figure 1 constitute the arc, but there is an important prehistory in which the conditions for a generative space form. We start our walk through the arc with this prehistory.

## First Steps

### "Heating Up" the Local Sociopolitical Field

A part of the prehistory of the arc is found in the local sociopolitical field. In this site a rich array of social groupings is active. Some of these groups may organize to address the routine deprivations in their everyday lives. Thus, in Nima, long before advocates framed Mohammed Zakari's detention as a violation of his right to health, youth groups regularly joined together to pick up garbage. Mothers' clubs regularly shared childcare. In both cases, groups used mutual self-help rather than claims on the state: they did not perceive their deprivation as a sociopolitical problem.[23] In addition to such self-help community improvement groups, a number of other groups are typically active in the sociopolitical field in their distinctive ways: religious groups are preaching; a human rights NGO may be delivering legal aid; a group of traders is discussing market conditions or infrastructure needs with public authorities. A few groups will be more self-consciously political and seek to contest local political power, though not necessarily to remedy specific forms of deprivation and rarely through an ESR frame.

The local sociopolitical field is a hybrid fabric of values, norms, and legalities that guide the activities of these different groupings, weaving together their variable commitments. This fabric is made up of a complex of partially overlapping and intersecting normativities—including "hard" civil laws, customary legal systems, international norms, and the like.[24] Hence, the mothers' clubs act in the spirit of solidarity; the legal aid NGO, in the spirit of human rights; and the traders, on the basis of their economic interests.

In some circumstances such activities "heat up," becoming more intense, numerous, and contentious. Particular types of events are likely to help trigger this heating up. An event such as the eviction of community members in Nya-muma, Tanzania, or the detention of an elderly man for hospital charges in Nima, or villagers wasting away from AIDS in South African townships may put in stark relief the inadequacy of particular institutions to prevent patent injustice and provide essential goods. Groups already active on the socio-political field may then *notice* the event, experiencing it to challenge their val-ues and call into question the implicated institution's legitimacy. The denser the networks of locally active groups, the more likely that *someone* will no-tice the event and understand it to be problematic. Political contestation over the definition of and responsibility for the experienced deprivation comes into play.[25] Contending groups, some with clear preexisting normative commit-ments and others newly created and with open commitments, develop differ-ent definitions, naming and framing the event in distinctive ways. As such contestation heats up, the institutional roles and normative commitments of relevant groupings come into question and are loosened.

As this broader ferment builds, seasoned ESR advocates use well-timed, pragmatic action to concentrate diffuse social and political energy around clearly framed manifestations of injustice. They frame the "root causes" of the event as inadequacies of state action. They link it to larger clusters of ongoing injustice that are incompatible with multiple, overlapping normative commit-ments at play on the local field. While the hybrid normative fabric of the field can resist change and thus poses a significant challenge to advocates, it also provides rich materials with which to loosen up existing institutional roles and normative commitments.

In order to mobilize the field, advocates weave ESR values into their nam-ing of the event and through the existing normative fabric, working pragmati-cally with legal and normative forces that are at play. In this process there is much creative ESR-positive resignification of symbols and practices that have historically reinforced and reproduced injustices. Through community orga-nizing, public events, and other activities, vulnerable groups coalesce and see their capacity for contestation, and hence their social and political power, grow. When the advocacy "takes hold," the resulting mobilization disrupts the par-ticular institutional arrangement that locks into place the structural inequality in question.

In the local contestation that ensues, it is possible that one set of values wins out. Sometimes the event comes to signify widespread ESR deprivation. On other occasions, other interpretive frameworks, such as religion or individual moral culpability, win out. We see such an outcome when people in Nima interpreted the piles of garbage in their community to reflect their own laziness rather than the government's failure at waste disposal. In sociopolitical fields such as those in contemporary sub-Saharan Africa, where hybrid normative tapestries have been woven, a single value system seldom "wins" this war over words. Rather, what comes out of this struggle to name the event is a hybrid interpretation, framing multiple forms of responsive political action. We see this outcome in the context of the South African AIDS pandemic, when the devastation, though widely perceived as horrendous, evoked different interpretations for groups who endorsed different normative frames. Thus, some responded by repudiating "Western" medicine; others saw the pandemic as a legacy of colonial governance, a violation of human rights, or the government's failure to treat HIV as a viral infection.

### Generating Institutional Innovation

Pragmatic ESR advocates try to convert heated local fields into "generative" spaces from which innovative and ESR-positive institutional change can emerge. Generally, they are most likely to do so if they can interpret the underlying structural injustice to call for both redistribution of power and path-dependent institutional conversion. Blaming individual actors seldom helps in this effort. At the same time, however, the importance of *integrating* redistribution with institutional innovation must be underscored. Thus, part of the challenge for Ghana's Mohammed Zakari campaign was to extract more and fairer healthcare funding from domestic and international sources,[26] while a second part was to convert existing health-sector institutions so that they had the capacity to "absorb" and distribute that funding in ways that would strengthen, rather than undermine, the political capacities and health status of beneficiary communities. Often ESR lawyer-activists confront the frustration of a heated local field cooling down as the immediacy of the triggering event passes and people's energy dissipates without any noticeable change. Worse, it is not uncommon for a group that is decidedly not ESR-friendly to coalesce and impose a moral or ideological framing that undercuts ESR values altogether. This risk was certainly present in the Zakari case, where many groups with "traditional" values, fundamentalist ideologies, or links to the ruling political party viewed the healthcare that the government already provided as a very good deal.

"Generative spaces" can arise when groups place the triggering "event" in a "justice" frame[27] and then enter into redistributive contestation, deliberative engagement, and institutional experimentation so as to imagine and even try out previously unimaginable win-win ESR delivery strategies. As key parties continue to gain leverage, they may be willing to engage in dialogue that generates new institutional options. The results can be small shifts in the scripts that local public officials follow, or even the creation of entirely new social roles and scripts.

An example of the latter comes from South Africa's TAC case study. There TAC succeeded in framing South Africa's AIDS pandemic as a result of the government's "denialist" stance toward the infection's viral cause. Once this frame was in place, TAC's ESR campaign fought to get antiretroviral drugs from the South African state and international sources. At the same time, TAC experimented with a treatment literacy campaign (TLC) in the local clinics where those drugs would be distributed. Contestation with groups framing the pandemic in other ways did not cease at this point. Yet TAC had gained enough legitimacy to lead multiparty institutional experimentation on the ground.

Sociopolitical agitation can morph into experimentation in many ways. One of the recurrent mechanisms, however, is the emergence of a person or group with "convening authority." Such a party is viewed as a legitimate leader across the community and thus can bring contesting groups together into a focused ESR campaign. These campaigns typically include both targeted social movement and locally anchored institutional experimentation. The convening authority can vary considerably; in our cases, the role was played by a range of different actors. The advocates and community residents, in turn, responded to those authorities in differing ways. In the Ijora-Badia case, the convening authority was community elders who were urged by a charismatic lawyer to play the role. In the Treatment Action Campaign in South Africa, the Constitutional Court provided one focus for activist energy, motivating local improvisation and consolidating mobilization around ESR norms. In Ghana, law students from the United States carried with them the legitimacy of Western legal expertise, while the son of a revered politician, by endorsing those students, gave them the added legitimacy of his own status.

The convening authority helps delimit and bound the generative space by providing some stability to the cast of persons and groups relevant to focused contestation and institutional experimentation. At best, this authority does not impose a strategic plan or institutional reform from "above" or "without." Rather, it brings local power holders and interested groups into a deliberative dialogue that can produce inventive campaign strategies integrated with non–zero sum institutional innovation. At best, this convening authority can inspire those groups to envision institutional strategies that can shake up and reimagine institutions and effectively break through structural injustice.

The normative hybridity of local social fields makes the convening of contesting parties quite challenging. This is because each of the relevant normative orders has its own authoritative figures, such as religious leaders, traditional chiefs, lawyers, and hospital or health clinic directors, all of whom have convening power among their respective constituencies. It is when one or more of these authorities can convene groups from across a plurality of normative fields that a generative space is most likely to form. The convening power may have a strong coercive element, such as when a court orders stakeholders to negotiate their own solution to an institutional blockage,[28] or a priest threatens damnation if relevant parties do not reform their behavior.[29]

In contrast to localized activities such as community clean-up days, which are limited to the sociopolitical field, the generative space engages local actors with those from other spheres. Often, nonlocal actors are representatives of state power. Such state agents may be present in the socio-legal field, doing what they can to heat it up. They may enter—or be recruited—as convening authorities, as when activists go to court to seek structural orders requiring stakeholders to sit down and talk. They may take part in deliberative activity or themselves become targets of political pressure. In all of our cases, public authority was brought into the generative space in some way: in Lagos the World Bank's inspection panel was invited to tour the at-risk community; in Tanzania, the Commission on Human Rights and Good Governance was invoked; in South Africa, the social movement group went to court; and in Ghana, a public hearing brought Zakari's case to the Ministry of Health's attention. Such engagement with the state does not guarantee that local experimentation will eventually diffuse across wide swaths of territory and large numbers of people; yet, in order for such spread to take place, state power almost inevitably becomes involved.

At the same time that ESR advocates bring the state into generative spaces, they also appeal to international nongovernmental organizations, networks, and similar groups. In our cases, such networks include the law schools that sent students into Nima, and an international housing rights NGO in the case of the Lagos evictions. Such linkages to external groups matter both because of the international legitimacy of the framings that such groups can bring to the underlying problems and because ESR campaigns require funding and other resources, such as information and skills, that these organizations can provide.

When ESR advocacy, convening authority, and state power are all present—as they are in our cases—localized advocacy and experimentation can inspire broad reframing, ferment, organizing, and experimentation in other locales.[30] We see this process clearly in the case of Nyamuma, where a local landgrab and murders became the basis of a national challenge to profit-oriented ecotourist development; an individualized program of land tenure; and a commodified regime of land use and housing exchange. In spite of the deeply ideological roots of these policies, the Nyamuma resistance is starting to generate local alternatives to this system that might find their way into changes in national property law.

So far, we have used a temporal frame to describe the arc linking sociopolitical fields, localized generative spaces, and broad state power. Yet this time frame is not fact but heuristic. The South African case shows how a generative space need not be merely local. Nor must it precede the emergence of agitation for institutional change on the national scale. In the TAC case, the most interesting local institutional experimentation took place in "treatment literacy" programs, which were championed by the TAC but endorsed by the state and sited at preexisting local government primary care clinics. The treatment literacy programs were then implemented through collaboration among national public health officials, local clinic personnel, TAC members, and HIV patients. Some of the members of each of these groups were also TAC activists.[31] Thus, these local spaces had both public and private, local and national, dimensions. Cross talk among these local sites was made possible through the national public health bureaucracy, the national TAC social movement, and informal networks. Thus, the state, national social movement, and local experimentation were brought together at these local sites. A generative space had emerged through state intervention and national social movement.[32]

## Beyond Local Boundaries

Contemporary social justice advocacy heavily values local or decentralized actions, in the belief that close proximity to the "people" ensures the relevance, efficacy, and "authenticity" of the advocacy. This belief is part of a larger zeitgeist that is powerfully distrustful of large and bureaucratic organizations, in government, in the market, and in civil society.[33] Pragmatic African advocates, however, see firsthand how today's unprecedented concentrations of wealth and power in the hands of elites are deeply implicated in the extreme deprivation that we call structural injustice. Thus, the lawyer-advocates in this book struggle against efforts of national governments, foreign investors, and international organizations to create ecotourism sites on land used by pastoralist groups, or shopping centers on the sites of impoverished people's homes. Such affronts are clearly driven by forces beyond local boundaries. Combating deprivation over the medium to long term therefore requires advocacy on a national and international scale.

In several cases in this volume African advocacy arising from generative space has pushed for change in national and international fields. This does not occur through the routinization of innovation into "best practices" that the nation-state can project across wide areas. Rather, advocates specifically target national institutions where the new ESR-positive practices are especially likely to "take" and flourish. This work requires the mapping of each relevant national ESR-delivery framework, such as the health delivery system, looking for sites where a problem would be resolved by the innovation on offer. In the TAC case, for example, the treatment literacy innovation responds to the health system's problem of educating impoverished people to comply with HIV drug regimes. The Zakari case's stakeholder strategy for realizing the "pauper" fee exemption would provide the exemption to all of Ghana's impoverished people, not just those in Nima. Neither new legislation nor a court order is the goal of such work, yet such tactics may create the legitimating force that drives the innovation.

Pragmatic advocates recognize that embedding innovation in national-level institutions is a path-dependent process: the political and institutional histories of the nation-state constrain what is possible.[34] Loosening the commitment of significant actors to existing institutional practices is also context-specific. Insiders' stakes in particular institutional practices vary across national states, issue areas, and time. For these reasons, off-the-shelf campaign models or innovations will not work. Rather, advocates must constantly test strategies in different arenas, seek out unexpected allies, and engage in deliberations with what appear to be immovable parties.

The ovals in Figure 1 delimit national territorial space and institutions in which advocacy that attempts to shift the practice of those institutions takes place. For heuristic purposes, one might think of those moments as two distinct points in time. However, those moments are not necessarily sequential. Nor are they always exclusively national: they sometimes have a porous relationship with the international domain.

At **T2** in the figure, advocacy seeks to loosen the commitments of influential policy actors; that is, it targets those who shape government policy, such as elected officials in legislatures (where functioning), powerful international organizations such as the World Bank, national religious leaders, and so forth. At **T3** advocacy directly targets the public bureaucracy and related implementation networks, pressuring these to convert to ESR-positive practices. This second moment is distinct from **T2**, yet it can occur simultaneously, as in the Ijora-Badia, Zakari, and TAC cases, in which public hearings enabled government officials to testify in both their personal and representative capacities at the same time.[35] The two ovals in the figure are distinct from the international space. Each oval thus represents a field of national action that is not analytically distinct from the other.

The sort of political agitation that takes place in the generative space, at **T1**, is the vital force that loosens the commitments of national and international parties at **T2**. In order to get the campaign noticed and "taken up" at **T2**, activists must work across numerous arenas—international, cross-national, regional, local, "public," "private," and "hybrid." They must also use unconventional spaces such as South Africa's Council for Competition or the World Bank's inspection panel to build energy for institutional change on a national scale.[36] They must combine rights talk, public hearings, shaming, legislative advocacy, legal argument, media work, formal litigation, and other tools to convince, cajole, and pressure influential actors. They must entice different groups, including contending parties, to coalesce into broad coalitions with sufficient power to move those opposed or indifferent to change. Coalitions that bring parties into the public sector, reformist professionals for example, and that cut across class have historically played a particularly significant role in major institutional change. The human rights framing of pragmatic advocacy facilitates the formation of such alliances because of its powerful normative content and the focus on structural problems and solutions.

In the cases examined here, however, advocacy does not end with the creation of a new program, an agreement to take action, or the passage of legislation. It goes further: it influences the ongoing institutional practices of agencies charged with the delivery of targeted ESR entitlements. This institutionalization of ESR-positive changes into such sustained shifts in organizational practice is represented as **T3** on the long arc. To bring about such shifts, the activists must focus on the values and behaviors of the actors responsible for the institution's activities, actors such as middle-level managers, professionals, and street-level bureaucrats. At the same time, they must not overlook the commitments of those in formal positions of power.

Within every public bureaucracy are reformers, often members of professional groups that seek both greater control over their work and the power to conduct their work in a way that is consistent with their professional training. For example, doctors in the public health sector have been a major force for institutional change in a wide range of countries. Similarly, in the Ghana right to health campaign, professional nurses appeared at a community-wide public hearing to claim that their own right to practice their profession was obstructed by the lack of drugs, supplies, and other resources for the patients they treated in public clinics. And in the case of Ijora-Badia's threatened eviction, there is some evidence that officials within state housing agencies sympathized with residents' plight and gave them support when SERAC's litigation shifted their own work roles to allow this.

When advocacy triggers ESR-positive institutional conversion, that change can often be what we have called "prefigurative" of more substantial innovation (see Chapter 5). Two examples are especially striking. First, in the Zakari case, the right-to-health campaign on behalf of Mohammed Zakari pushed the Ministry of Health toward more participatory administrative practices. Among the campaign's many tactics was to seek a structural injunction that would have required the ministry to use stakeholder deliberation to define and implement the pauper exemption regarding the payment of required hospital fees. Impoverished people themselves would be included in the deliberative process. This innovation would have moved the ministry qua institution in a human rights–positive direction because the reformed institution would have included the lowest-income people in a participatory governance process on an equal basis with others, even governmental, professional, and civic elites.

Another example comes from the TAC case. As the campaign gained momentum, a successful lawsuit prompted the government to make antiretroviral drugs available to prevent mother-to-child transmission of HIV. Through movement pressure, the drugs were eventually made available in the most impoverished rural areas as well as in urban centers, thus pushing the government toward a more inclusionary HIV distribution policy. Furthermore, because of the historic—and continuing—discrimination against impoverished rural areas in South Africa, this pressure to provide AIDS drugs inclusively also nudged the government toward a health system that was less discriminatory—and more egalitarian—with respect to poverty and geography. Finally, the TAC movement pressured the government to change the primary health system and the front-line health clinics to be more accessible to impoverished rural peoples, who are often unschooled. To accomplish this, TAC activists worked outside and inside government to set up treatment literacy programs in those clinics. The programs used highly participatory popular education techniques to educate patients about HIV infection and its treatment, while connecting them with activist clinic workers and the broader movement for economic and social rights. This effort was highly successful, not just in teaching patients how to comply with HIV treatment but also in changing primary care clinics into more egalitarian, inclusive, participatory, and thus effective health delivery institutions.

While the cases show several examples of such embedding of institutional innovation in the national field, it is important to recognize that such shifts in institutional practice generally happen in the context of powerful forces that can press for institutional reversal. Indeed, as we have seen, actors situated within institutions have multiple allegiances besides the workplace, allegiances such as family, religion, and ethnic and civic organizations. As we have seen among the ESR-promoting Ghanaian nurses, such values can motivate institutional actors to play an active role in ESR-positive change. At the same time, however, family values, for instance, can cut both ways. And work-affiliated organizations such as unions or professional associations can offer institutional insiders values that support institutional change. Yet as the Latin American example cited above demonstrates, the values promoted by unions, for instance, sometimes shift between ESR erosion and ESR promotion (or vice-versa) in historically contingent ways. Thus, ESR-positive local innovations do not always lead to deep and sustained institutional change at the national level. But while it is important to acknowledge this risk, the cases emphatically show that creative ESR advocacy *can* indeed promote significant and durable institutional change.

## Diffusion of Institutional Innovation

The long arc runs back down to local sociopolitical fields at **T4**. This descent represents the diffusion of institutional innovations across relevant communities. Diffusion is a surprisingly complex and uneven process. It is driven forward by the ongoing negotiation of policies, resources, and practices between local actors and national authorities and across localities as they contest among themselves for what the national government has on offer.[37] The ability to draw down national practices and accompanying resources varies depending on legacies of past efforts,[38] the skills and entrepreneurship of local officials and elites,[39] the connection between local groups and power holders at the national level,[40] and the strength of religious, ethnic, and similar local-national networks.[41]

Scholarly research bears out this account. Both socio-legal studies and political sociology show that the same policies and institutions land very differently across communities, depending on the capacity of local government, opinion leaders, and community members to actively demand implementation in their respective regions.[42] The most deprived communities and regions tend to have weaker government presence, a more impoverished civil society, less robust local-national networks, and thus less capacity to draw down institutional innovations that help to realize ESR guarantees.[43] The result can be a downward spiral of structural injustice, for the diffusion of effective ESR innovation is not only uneven but also unequal in ways that discriminate against the people who are already most in need.

Social justice mobilization can help to change this result. It can counter regional inequalities at the national level, and level the power of local elites that might seek to block the projection of innovative, ESR-friendly, practices. Mobilization can also help to establish links between local communities and national-level government agencies. It can activate communities to demand nationally mandated ESR-positive policies and secure an increased flow of ESR-guaranteed social goods. The treatment literacy experiments in the TAC case study offer a compelling example of this dynamic.

Outside of Africa, but increasingly within Africa as well, participatory budgeting innovations offer a well-documented instance of an ESR-infused institution diffusing to the grassroots. These experiments vividly show how sustained advocacy and iterative negotiation can drive diffusion of innovations that have moved through the long arc from generative space through government uptake and back down to local diffusion.In the heated context of neighborhood activism in the Brazilian port city of Porto Alegre, the Union of Neighborhood Associations of Porto Alegre (UAMPA, for its Portuguese acronym), an alliance of neighborhood associations, demanded that citizens have a greater role in setting municipal budget priorities.[44] Through this process, they sought to break through longstanding clientelism and underprovision of basic services in poor regions of the city. It was 1985, during the national democratic transition. The city was in a heightened state of ferment as diverse strands of pro-democracy activists mobilized. When the Workers' Party was elected to the city government in 1989, UAMPA coalesced behind the idea of a participatory budget (PB).[45] The new administration's Planning Secretariat was instructed to develop and implement participatory budgeting.

During the first couple of years, the secretariat limited participation, sometimes inadvertently, in various ways. First, it divided the city of 1.3 million into five large districts. Discussions were led by city officials who relied on specialized language and sought to impose their own proposals.[46] Negotiations with UAMPA led to a division of the city into sixteen districts. UAMPA's effort to restrict participation to members of neighborhood associations lost to the open public assemblies in each district that had been proposed by urban movements and other actors. Subsequently, community activists insisted that the budgeting process have a public works plan listing the investment priorities of the districts, which Goldfrank observes "became the centerpiece of the PB, with thousands of copies printed each year so that citizens could check on the projects the administration promised to carry out."[47] When city officials wanted to concentrate PB expenditures within a small number of districts to produce high-visibility improvements, community leaders fought for a more equitable distribution and greater respect for priorities set by the districts themselves. After significant protest over the government's poor organization and failure to implement PB priorities, participatory budgeting was moved from the Secretariat for Planning to a new city planning and budget office, under the direct supervision of the mayor. The equity and inclusiveness of the budgetary process, not to mention the extent of citizens' real influence over budgetary decisions, was determined by such iterative negotiations over the ensuing decade.

Even in a city with reasonable physical infrastructure, diffusion was highly uneven and discriminated against some of the poorer regions. In the first two years, participation in the budgeting process was not only low but also concentrated in districts that had deep and ongoing traditions of political activism. Participation expanded through cross talk between community leaders. This process helped less advantaged neighborhoods in other parts of the city see improvements in the sewerage, healthcare facilities, schools, and so forth. In the poorest parts of the city or where particularly strong clientelist networks prevailed, the city itself hired community organizers to increase PB's community uptake and counter its unequal diffusion. Organizers sought out new community leaders, disseminating information, "politicizing the pothole" in community discussions, and providing guidance to emerging activists.[48] In 2000 the budgeting process had fourteen thousand participants, drawn primarily from the city's lower-income districts, and distributed relatively equally across these districts.[49]

Diffusion therefore is a contingent and contested process rather than a foregone conclusion. ESR advocacy has a long arc because it is difficult for the most deprived areas to learn about and draw down national innovation and resources. To accomplish this sort of "radical inclusion," ESR activists must exert pressure at the national as well as city levels at the same time that they promote cross talk and advocacy within and across locales. All of this work can amount to an unpredictable catalyst for diffusion to the most-deprived areas, where the ability to learn about and draw down national innovation and resources is lowest.

## Conclusion

The pragmatic ESR activism in this volume focuses on addressing specific problems rather than changing regimes as a whole. It highlights redistribution achieved hand in hand with ESR-infused institutional change. This kind of change shifts the values, scripts, and improvised practices of state agents in ways that afford claimants greater inclusion, equality, security, and enhanced capacity to deal with the target agencies. At its best, this kind of activism can help people get what they need to survive. It can also help them get those goods in ways that promote their capacities as economically empowered and politically engaged citizens. The case studies demonstrate that such hopes for ESR activism, though never achieved in full measure, are more than a dream.

# Epilogue

Jeremy Perelman and Lucie E. White

The arc of the moral universe is long but it bends toward justice.

*Martin Luther King Jr.*[1]

The campaigns featured in this book have an important common theme. Each responds to an injustice that manifests itself in the lives of individuals or communities. Yet rather than repairing discrete injuries, the advocates understand that such suffering is enmeshed with that of others in a web we have called structural injustice. These advocates share a talent for perceiving, translating, and responding to injustice in such systemic terms. This does not mean that they have shifted their focus away from the crying needs of real people and toward the cool world of policy change. Rather, they have undermined structures of injustice in ways that build political power for the disenfranchised. They have worked in a way that prefigures institutions infused with equality, inclusion, security, and voice for the delivery of social goods. Whether it be protecting destitute South Africans from full-blown AIDS, or resisting forced eviction at the hands of the Lagos State government, or freeing a sick man from the hospital where he went for care, or responding to the mass eviction and random assassination of Tanzanian pastoralists who sought to use their ancestral land—in all of these cases the advocates have reclaimed human rights to respond to structural violence.

At the end of his life, Martin Luther King Jr. noted that the long arc of the moral universe ultimately bends toward justice. Perhaps the most important lesson of this book is that this path does not come about because of fate. Rather, it comes from the insight, creativity, and courage of people like those featured in this book.

REFERENCE MATTER

# Notes

## Foreword

1. Paul Hunt, "Using All the Tools at Our Disposal: Poverty Reduction and the Right to the Highest Attainable Standard of Health" (2006), available at: http://www2.essex.ac.uk/human_rights_centre/rth/docs/Hunt_proof%5B1%5D.pdf

2. Committee on Economic, Social and Cultural Rights, *General Comment 3: The Nature of States Parties Obligations* (Art. 2, para. 1), Committee on Economic, Social and Cultural Rights, 5th Sess. (1990), reprinted in Compilation of General Comments and General Recommendations Adopted by Human Rights Treaty Bodies at 18, U.N. Doc. HRI/GEN/1/Rev.5 (2001), at para. 14.

3. A/RES/55/2, para 2.

## Introduction

The authors wish to thank all participants in the Stones of Hope project, notably Willy Forbath and Duncan Kennedy as well as John Nockleby, for their insightful comments on earlier drafts of this introduction. Our thanks also go to Moira Harding for her extraordinary assistance throughout this project. We also thank Ellen Keng for her help in preparing the manuscript. Finally, we wish to acknowledge the remarkable men and women whose work have inspired us to take on this project.

1. Excerpt from Affidavit of Abdullah Abdul Muman, taken by Harvard Law School students in January 2003 and read by Mr. Muman at a public hearing in Nima, Accra, Ghana, in January 2003. A copy is on file with Professor Lucie White at Harvard Law School.

2. On radical poverty, see Thomas Pogge, "Why Inequality Matters," in *Global Inequality*, ed. David Held and Ayse Kaya (Cambridge, UK: Polity, 2007), at 223.

3. See Iris Marion Young, "Responsibility and Global Justice: A Social Connection Model," *Social Philosophy and Policy* 23 (2006): 102–30. Reprinted in *Global Challenges: War, Self-Determination and Responsibility for Justice* (New York: Polity, 2006). According to Young, structural injustice exists "when social processes put large categories of persons under a systematic threat of domination or deprivation of the means to develop and exercise their capacities, at the same time as these processes enable others to dominate

or have a wide range of opportunities for developing and exercising their capacities" (at 114). Structural injustice is a "moral wrong," but not like a wrongful individual action or a willful action like state repression. Rather it "occurs as a consequence of many individuals and institutions" pursuing their interests "within given institutional rules and accepted norms." Under this conception, "all the persons who participate . . . in the ongoing schemes of cooperation that constitute these structures are responsible for them"; not in the sense of having directly caused or intended the process and its outcomes but "in the sense that they are part of the process that causes them" (114). Young contrasts standard models of responsibility in moral and legal theory that "require that we trace a direct relationship between the action of an identifiable person or group and a harm" (115) with a "social connection model" in which "individuals bear responsibility for structural injustice because they contribute by their actions to the processes that produce unjust outcomes." Responsibility comes not from the nature and effects of our particular actions but "from belonging together with others in a system of interdependent processes of cooperation and competition through which we seek benefits and aim to realize projects" (119). For a critical comment on Young's conception of structural justice and responsibility, see Jacob Schiff, "Confronting Political Responsibility: The Problem of Acknowledgment," *Hypatia* 23 (2008): 99–117. On human rights and the unequal structures of the global economy, see Thomas Pogge, ed., *Freedom from Poverty as a Human Right: Who Owes What to the Very Poor?* (New York: Oxford University Press and UNESCO, 2007).

4. See Judith Shklar, *The Faces of Injustice* (New Haven: Yale University Press, 1992).

5. See Balakrishnan Rajagopal, *International Law from Below: Development, Social Movements and Third World Resistance* (New York: Cambridge University Press, 2003), analyzing the political determinants of development policies that have violent effects.

6. There is much theoretical discussion about the meanings of human rights. However, in this volume, we use *human rights* and *economic and social rights* in the ways that activists themselves understand these expressions; see the discussion of our dialogic methodology for eliciting activists' human rights consciousness infra in the section "Our Method."

7. *Stones of Hope* touches upon a variety of recent debates, situated at the intersection of socio-legal, political science, and development literatures, which address poverty, development, or economic and social rights concerns. This literature can be grouped into three clusters. The first cluster of works offers theoretical interpretations of human rights activism. Works representative of this approach include Mark Goodale and Sally Engle Merry, eds., *The Practice of Human Rights: Tracking Law Between the Global and the Local* (New York: Cambridge University Press, 2007), examining from a primarily anthropological perspective how human rights discourse is mobilized, utilized, and transformed by groups and organizations around the world against various forms of violence, and mapping out a broad field of practices that mediate between the universal discourse of human rights and its local appropriations; Boaventura de Sousa Santos and César A. Rodríguez-Garavito, eds., *Law and Globalization from Below: Towards a Cosmopolitan Legality* (New York: Cambridge University Press, 2005), exploring how "subaltern" actors resist and subvert global legal institutions to promote grassroots social justice but dismissing the potential of human rights to promote progressive change; Daphne Barak-

Erez and Aeyal M. Gross, eds., *Exploring Social Rights: Between Theory and Practice* (Portland, OR: Hart, 2007), analyzing from a theoretical perspective the limited place of social and economic rights in globalized legal orders, without however focusing on global poverty as a human rights challenge or offering a robust account of human rights strategies that go beyond litigation; and Peter Newell and Joanna Wheeler, eds., *Rights, Resources, and the Politics of Accountability* (New York: Zed Books, 2006), exploring social and economic rights struggles around the world through a case study method, without focusing specifically on human rights innovations emerging from African practices. For an analysis of the structural factors shaping the global trajectory of public interest law, see Scott Cummings and Louise Trubek, "Globalizing Public Interest Law," *UCLA Journal of International Law and Foreign Affairs* 13 (2009): 1. A second cluster of works focuses on intersections between human rights, poverty, and development. It includes works such as *Freedom from Poverty as a Human Right: Who Owes What to the Very Poor?* (supra n. 3); *International Law from Below: Development, Social Movements and Third World Resistance* (supra n. 5); and Upendra Baxi, *The Future of Human Rights* (New York: Oxford University Press, 2002), the second and third sources are written from a critical postcolonial perspective, exploring how Third World social movements challenge Western, market-based notions of development and human rights. A third cluster of works argues that mainstream human rights institutions and practices can successfully challenge poverty. Works within this cluster include Philip Alston and Mary Robinson, eds., *Human Rights and Development: Towards Mutual Enforcement* (New York: Oxford University Press, 2005), and Mashood Baderin and Robert McCorquodale, eds., *Economic, Social, and Cultural Rights in Action* (New York: Oxford University Press, 2007), both exploring the intersection between human rights and development at the level of formal human rights treaties and institutions; David Bilchitz, *Poverty and Fundamental Rights: The Justification and Enforcement of Socio-Economic Rights* (New York: Oxford University Press, 2007), offering philosophical and doctrinal arguments supporting the enforceability of social and economic rights, without exploring the broader range of strategies used by human rights advocates; and Malcolm Langford, ed., *Socio-Economic Rights Jurisprudence: Emerging Trends in Comparative and International Law* (New York: Cambridge University Press, forthcoming), offering a rich survey of comparative and international case law on socioeconomic rights, limited to the study of jurisprudence.

8. See Makau Mutua, "Savages, Victims and Saviors: the Metaphor of Human Rights," *Harvard International Law Journal* 42 (2001): 201. See also Makau Mutua, "The Ideology of Human Rights," *Virginia Journal of International Law* 36 (1996): 589, and *Human Rights: A Political and Cultural Critique* (Philadelphia: Pennsylvania Studies in Human Rights, 2008). For a different African postcolonial perspective on the broader debate around the cross-cultural legitimation of human rights universalism, see Abdullahi Ahmed An-Na'im, *Cultural Transformation and Human Rights in Africa* (New York: Zed Books, 2002).

9. See, e.g., Duncan Kennedy, "The Structure of Blackstone's Commentaries," *Buffalo Law Review* 28 (1979): 205, and "The Critique of Rights in Critical Legal Studies," in *Left Legalism/Left Critique* (Durham: Duke University Press, 2002).

10. See David Kennedy, *The Dark Sides of Virtue: Reassessing International Humanitarianism* (Princeton: Princeton University Press, 2004).

11. See Goodale and Merry, supra n. 7. See also Sally Engle Merry, *Human Rights and Gender Violence: Translating International Law into Local Justice* (Chicago: University of Chicago Press, 2005), and "Transnational Human Rights and Local Activism: Mapping the Middle," *American Anthropologist* 108 (2006): 38–51, both offering a theoretical framework that captures the various ways transnational human rights discourse is translated and becomes meaningful in local context.

12. See all sources in n. 11. See also Mark Goodale, "Locating Rights, Envisioning Law Between the Global and the Local," in Goodale and Merry, supra n. 7. Seeking to move beyond global/local dichotomies and transnational network analysis to capture the encounter between transnational human rights discourse and local actors, Goodale and Merry articulate a concept of "betweenness" to

> both emphasize the nonuniversality of human rights practice, and create an intentionally open conceptual space which can account for the way actors encounter the idea of human rights through the projection of the legal and moral imagination [ . . . ] betweenness is meant to express the ways in which human rights discourse unfolds ambiguously, without a clear special referent, in part through transnational networks, but also, equally important, through the projection of the moral and legal imagination by social actors whose precise location within these networks are (for them) practically irrelevant. (at 22)

*Stones of Hope* does refer to the translation and mediation role of human rights activists. Furthermore, it builds on the concept of "betweenness." However, the focus of *Stones of Hope* is less about "*locating* the practice of human rights" (emphasis added, at 22) than it is about the normative commitments of critical liberalism and legal pluralism that motivate the human rights advocates featured in this volume, as well as the several strategies of engagement that those advocates embrace. See discussion on "critical legal liberalism" and legal pluralism in Chapter 5 of this volume.

13. See Goodale, supra n. 12. "The study of human rights suggests that the 'practice' that is being documented and analyzed has the potential to transform the framework through which the idea of human rights itself is understood" (at 4).

> The practice of human rights describes all the many ways in which social actors across the range talk about, advocate for, criticize, study, legally enact, vernacularize, and so on, the idea of human rights in its different forms. By social actors we mean all of the different individuals, institutions, states, international agencies, and so on, who practice human rights within any number of different social contexts, without privileging any one type of human rights actor [ . . . ] In defining the practice of human rights in this way we draw attention to both the diversity of ways and places in which the idea of human rights—again, in its legal, conceptual and discursive forms—emerges in practice, and the fact that the practice of human rights is always embedded in preexisting relations of meaning and production." (at 24)

14. Martin Luther King Jr., speech at the Lincoln Memorial, Washington, DC, August 28, 1963, available at: http://www.americanrhetoric.com/speeches/Ihaveadream.htm. See also David L. Chappell, *A Stone of Hope: Prophetic Religion and the Death of Jim Crow* (Chapel Hill: University of North Carolina Press, 2003).

15. Binyavanga Wainaina, *Vanity Fair*, June 2007, p. 94.

16. The reader will note that although coming from a variety of countries in West, East, and Southern Africa, the activists featured in this volume all pertain to former British colonies and hence, with the partial exception of South Africa, to a common law culture.

17. On transnational activist networks generally, see Margaret Keck and Kathryn Sikkink, *Activists Beyond Borders: Advocacy Networks in International Politics* (Ithaca: Cornell University Press, 1998).

18. On the hegemony and circulation of dominant forms of knowledge, see Julieta Lemaitre, *Legal Fetishism: Law, Violence and Social Movements in Colombia* (S.J.D. dissertation, Harvard Law School, 2007).

19. Three features of the African context can be highlighted: (1) radical poverty, (2) "weak" institutions, and (3) lingering postcolonial political turmoil. First (1), the context in which Stones of Hope activists operate is most often one in which radical poverty mocks the power of human rights tools. Sub-Saharan poverty affects a wide swath of the world's most disenfranchised populations in an unremitting way (for a comparative outlook on African poverty and inequality, see Pogge, supra n. 2): according to the World Health Organization, about fifteen thousand Africans die each and every day of diseases—HIV/AIDS, malaria, tuberculosis—that are preventable and treatable. Widespread inequality and extreme poverty are widely acknowledged to rank highest among the immediate causes of these dramatic figures. While extreme poverty has diminished both in absolute numbers and as a share of the population in East and South Asia since 1981, it has doubled in sub-Saharan Africa over the same time: more than three hundred million Africans currently survive on less than one dollar a day, a figure that represents about half of Africa's total population. Furthermore, these statistics are embedded in disturbing and accelerating patterns of global inequality: as the twentieth century witnessed "unequaled" levels of income growth globally, Africa's share of world GDP has sharply declined compared to the beginning of that century. See "World Health Report 2008: Primary Health Care—Now More Than Ever" (World Health Organization, 2008), at 3–5, pointing to the fact that twenty of the twenty-five countries where mortality under the age of five is still two-thirds or more of the 1975 level are in sub-Saharan Africa, and comparing sets of countries according to their combined rate of GDP growth and life expectancy: about 66 percent of the population in the "fragile" and "low-income countries under stress" group, which has seen this combined rate stagnate, live in Africa. Thus, the Stones of Hope activists are among the relatively small group that works against the most pervasive, extreme poverty on the globe. Unlike some, they do not turn away from its mind-numbing scope or heart-numbing costs. They do not use the typical cause lawyer's moves to evade the human feel of such structural injustice (see Austin Sarat and Stuart Scheingold, eds., *Cause Lawyering and the State in a Global Era* [New York: Oxford University Press, 2001], and *The Worlds Cause Lawyers Make: Structure and Agency in Legal Practice* [Stanford: Stanford Law and Politics, 2005], exploring through case studies the way human rights advocates in the global South are simultaneously adapting to and attempting to shape the legal, political, and economic

features of globalization, mostly through legalist strategies). They do not plot out incremental test-case strategies based on achieving small but feasible legal victories at the outer boundaries of the core injustice, as it is experienced by the great mass of people (see, e.g., *Georgina Ahamefule vs Dr Alex Molokwu & anor* [Nigeria, Federal High Court *ID/1627/2000*, 2000], a case brought up by advocates at the Social and Economic Rights Action Center, one of the organizations featured in this volume, which boldly articulates a claim of discrimination and violation of the right to health in the case of an auxiliary nurse who was dismissed by her employer based on her HIV-positive status, which she contracted by pricking her finger on a needle, and who was also denied medical treatment and access to court on the same grounds). Rather, without exception, they confront the core injustice head on. Second (2), so-called weak institutions undermine the efforts of many African activist lawyers to make conventional liberal claims for human rights violations. These activists tend to have few formal legal forums in which to bring human rights claims. Their nations' colonial histories have typically stripped precolonial state-formations of their political and legal foundations, thus leaving postcolonial states devoid of indigenous sites for raising broad moral claims (for a discussion on essentialist notions of indigeneity and legitimacy, see Mahmood Mamdani, *Citizen and Subject* [Princeton: Princeton University Press, 1996]). At the same time, postcolonial legal institutions such as courts, legislatures, executive agencies, enforcement bodies, local governments, and the like are often politically illegitimate and lacking in the material resources and management structures to grant the remedies offered by law. Thus it is hard for lawyers to gain much leverage from "legal" tactics in their human rights campaigns. Third (3), the boundaries of African nations reflect the colonial partitioning rather than precolonial ethnic groups. Partly as a result of this, political turmoil has repeatedly weakened nonstate social formations and undermined broad political participation in many African nations. In other words, the legacies of colonial occupation, including political instability, repressive leadership, and long-term economic deprivation, have ripped the fabric of many African societies. Yet in spite of these obstacles, the Stones of Hope activists have defiantly reclaimed the power of human rights values and visions. They have withstood scorn from fellow Africans for allying with those Northern human rights zealots who invoke *their* version of human rights to save them (see Mutua, supra n. 8), an argument which cuts particularly deeply in sub-Saharan Africa because of the continent's particularly moralistic colonial history, in which self-righteous missionaries were the advance guard of military occupation.

20. These were the Rockefeller Foundation's Villa and Conference Center, in Bellagio, Italy; the (U.S.) Law and Society Association's annual meeting, in Berlin (2007) and Accra, Ghana (2008); the Harvard University Africa Initiative and Harvard Law School Roundtable on African Human Rights Lawyers' Practice Innovations, in Cambridge, MA (May 2008); and a working session at the Institute for Development Studies, University of Sussex, in Brighton, United Kingdom (June 2009).

21. The methodology that informs the collaborative production of this volume is based on interpretive or hermeneutic methods of qualitative research, which involve active engagement by the interpreter with the subject of interpretation. These include

theories of reflexive dialogue (see Donald Schön, *The Reflective Practitioner* [New York: Basic Books, 1983]) and popular education (see Paulo Freire, *Pedagogy of the Oppressed* [New York: Seabury Press, 1970]) as well as grounded theory methodology (see Anselm Leonard Strauss and Juliet Corbin, eds., *Grounded Theory in Practice* [Thousand Oaks: Sage, 1997]).

22. These theoretical approaches were selected, not through some systematic evaluation of the contenders but rather through a quest for practice theories that illuminated the case studies, while also reflecting the interests and expertise of the activists and scholars on the team. For an analysis based on these theoretical approaches, see Chapter 5 of this volume.

23. Boaventura de Sousa Santos and César A. Rodríguez-Garavito, "Law, Politics, and the Subaltern in Counter-hegemonic Globalization," in *Law and Globalization from Below: Towards a Cosmopolitan Legality*, ed. Boaventura de Sousa Santos and César A. Rodríguez-Garavito (New York: Cambridge University Press, 2005).

24. See Chapter 6 for a more extensive discussion of this concept.

25. For historical institutionalist and path dependency analysis in the political science field, see James Mahoney, *The Legacies of Liberalism: Path Dependence and Political Regimes in Central America* (Baltimore: Johns Hopkins University Press, 2001); James Mahoney and Dietrich Rueschemeyer, eds., *Comparative Historical Analysis in the Social Sciences* (New York: Cambridge University Press, 2003); James Mahoney and Kathleen Thelen, eds., *Explaining Institutional Change: Ambiguity, Agency, and Power in Historical Institutionalism* (forthcoming); Paul Pierson, *Politics in Time: History, Institutions and Social Analysis* (Princeton: Princeton University Press, 2004); Paul Pierson and Theda Skocpol, "Historical Institutionalism in Contemporary Political Science," in *Political Science: State of the Discipline*, ed. Ira Katznelson and Helen V. Milner (New York: Norton, 2002), 693–721.

26. Peter Houtzager, "From Polycentrism to the Polity," in *Changing Paths: International Development and the New Politics of Inclusion*, ed. Peter Houtzager and Mick Moore (Ann Arbor: University of Michigan Press, 2003). For another institutionalist approach to the global politics of development, see Sanjeev Khagram, "Restructuring the Global Politics of Development: The Case of India's Narmada Valley Dams," in *Restructuring World Politics: Transnational Social Movements, Networks and Norms*, ed. Sanjeev Khagram, James Riker, and Kathryn Sikkink (Minneapolis: University of Minnesota Press, 2002), using social movement and international relations theories to analyze the success of transnational civil society campaigns against the Narmada Valley Dam Project in India, and suggesting that a dialectical interaction between new transnational coalitions of local social movements and international NGOs, on the one hand, and the spread of international norms on the protection of indigenous peoples, human rights, and environmental preservation, on the other hand, explains the success of these campaigns; also suggesting that the institutionalization of these norms at the national and international levels, as well as the existence of a sustained grassroots social movement in the context of India's open democratic regime, offered key "political opportunities" and avenues of contestation for these transnational coalitions to leverage their campaigns,

and that, at the same time, the transnational coalitions, legitimated by sustained domestic social mobilization, contributed to the spread of international norms.

27. On the notion of framing, see William A. Gamson, *Talking Politics* (New York: Cambridge University Press, 1992).

28. See John Gaventa's three-faceted, Rubik's cube-like model to aid advocates in the pragmatic analysis of power in "Reflections of the Uses of the 'Power Cube' Approach for Analyzing the Spaces, Places and Dynamics of Civil Society Participation and Engagement," CFP Evaluation Series No. 4 (2005).

29. Though we did not see every feature in every case, there was enough commonality to make them a useful heuristic.

30. Such as litigation, the collection of affidavits, hearings before official bodies, and civil society organizations.

31. Id. See Duncan Kennedy, "The Stakes of Law, or Hale and Foucault!" *Legal Studies Forum* 15 (1991): 327.

32. See supra n. 25.

33. See Houtzager, supra n. 26.

34. For further elaboration on the pluralist theme, see Chapter 5 in this volume.

## Chapter 1

1. Hereinafter referred to as Badia. Located within Apapa Local Government Area, Badia lies at latitude 3° 23' N. and longitude 4° 22' E.

2. See *World Urbanization Prospects: The 2003 Revision*, United Nations, 2003.

3. Prior to the discovery of crude oil, agriculture was the backbone of the Nigerian economy. The country was a major exporter of cocoa, cotton, rubber, and groundnuts and was self-sufficient in staple food production.

4. In 1970 oil accounted for 32.9% of Nigeria's trade stock compared to non-oil trade stock of 67.1%. In 2002 oil represented 94.95% of the country's export earnings as against 5.05% of non-oil export earnings. See Central Bank of Nigeria, Changing Structure of the Nigerian Economy (2000); Central Bank of Nigeria, Annual Report and Statement of Accounts (2002).

5. Report of the Presidential Task Force on Lagos Mega City, 2006, p. 13.

6. Francisco Abosede, "Housing in Lagos Mega City—Improving Livability, Inclusion and Governance" (Paper presented at the Social and Economic Rights Action Center's [SERAC] International Conference on Building Nigeria's Capacity to Implement Economic, Social and Cultural Rights: Lessons Learned, Challenges and the Way Forward, Abuja, September 27–28, 2006) (on file with the author).

7. See Project Appraisal Document for the *Lagos Metropolitan Development and Governance Project* (World Bank, June 7, 2006), at 2 (on file with the author).

8. There are many different regimes of land ownership, use, and tenure simultaneously at play in Nigeria; a detailed mapping of these regimes is beyond the scope of this chapter.

9. Land Use Act, 1978 (Section 1).

10. Id., Section 2(1)(a).

11. Id., Section 2(1)(b).

12. Id., Section 15(a).

13. Id., Section 15(b).

14. Id., Section 22.

15. See Federal Republic of Nigeria, *National Housing Policy Document* (August 1990), at 2. About 50,000 of the 202,000 housing units were earmarked to be built in Lagos.

16. See Federal Republic of Nigeria, *National Housing Policy Document* (2002), at 14.

17. See, for example, the work of the Slum Dwellers International, an international federation of slum communities that helps its 5.6 million members across 14 countries to build savings, secure land, and build housing, in *The New Global City: Bigger, Richer, Poorer* (Ford Foundation Report, Spring/Summer 2005) (see also http://www.sdinet.co.za/).

18. Credit of $63 million for the LDSP was approved by the executive directors of the International Development Agency (IDA) on June 17, 1993. Agreements between the IDA, the federal government of Nigeria, and the Lagos State government were entered into on July 30, 1993, and the agreements became effective on April 21, 1994. According to the LDSP financing plan, $63 million was provided by the IDA, $20 million by the Lagos State government, and $2.0 million by the Japan International Cooperation Agency (JICA). The IDA's $63 million credit was scheduled to be disbursed during the project's expected completion period of five years and allocated as follows: (1) Civil works except drain maintenance (a) Apapa drainage, $10.3m (b) Surulere channel, $10.0m (c) Lagos Island drainage, $5.7m (d) mainland drainage, $9.6m (e) transfer station and land fill, $1.3m (f) urban renewal demonstration, $1.8m; (2) Drain maintenance, $5.3m; (3) Supply of goods and equipment, $4.0m; (4) Training, technical assistance, and construction supervision, $9.0m; (5) Unallocated, $6.0m.

19. According to the Staff Appraisal Report, Lagos Drainage and Sanitation Project, Report No. 11307–UNI (May 10, 1993), at 1, the LDSP was designed to improve health standards and living conditions in areas of Lagos subject to regular flooding and to improve the economic functioning of the city by improving storm water drainage in priority areas of the city and improving drain maintenance procedures. It would also support initial steps in upgrading other urban services by preparing plans, feasibility studies, and designs for urban upgrading and by improving human wastewater disposal, and would continue support to the Lagos State Waste Management Authority for organizational and system development. Physical components of the project would include the rehabilitation, regrading, clearing, and aligning of existing storm water drains in three areas of the city.

20. "All Slums in Lagos to Go: Makoko, Ijora, Badiya, Ilubirin & 11 Others Affected," *PM News*, July 15, 1996, pp. 1, 5.

21. Established in May 1995, the Social and Economic Rights Action Center (SERAC) is a nongovernmental, nonpartisan, and nonprofit organization concerned with the promotion and protection of economic, social, and cultural rights in Nigeria (http://www.serac.org/).

22. Yaw Ansu, country director for Nigeria, letter to SERAC, dated July 15, 1997.

23. See the socioeconomic survey carried out by SERAC between February and March 2007 (Social and Economic Rights Action Center [SERAC], Baseline Socio-Economic Survey of Badia-East, Apapa Local Government Area, Lagos State, March 2007), which found that 88.3% of the population was extremely dissatisfied with the overall living conditions in the community. About 86.1% expressed a strong commitment to improving and remaining in the community, while 88.7% expressed a strong commitment to contribute financially to the improvement of the living conditions in the community. Over 42% are unemployed, and of those that are employed, more than 49% earn below $100 monthly. Remarkably, over 80% save a part of whatever income they may receive. Of the population of 207 surveyed, 60% were male and 47% were between the ages of 21 and 30 years.

24. See Max Weber, "The Economy and the Arena of Normative and De Facto Powers" (1914), in *Economy and Society*, ed. Guenther Roth and Claus Wittich (New York: Bedminster Press, 1968).

25. See generally Hannah Arendt, *The Human Condition* (New York: Anchor Books, 1959).

26. John Scott, *Power (Key Concepts)* (New York: Polity, 2001), at 10.

27. Established in 1987, the Civil Liberties Organization (CLO) is Nigeria's premier human rights group concerned with the defense and protection of civil and political rights.

28. Following their eviction, hundreds of residents moved into and occupied unfinished and abandoned government housing estates located at Ilasan (about 20 km from their former home). An attempt by the government to further evict them from the occupied location was stopped by a court injunction obtained on their behalf by the CLO and collaborating solicitors. Following public outrage over the evictions, the government subsequently allocated the apartments to the occupants in lieu of resettlement.

29. A few months later, when the state and the Oniru family began to parcel out Maroko land to high-ranking government officials and affluent developers, Justice Ayorinde had a street named after him, perhaps in recognition of his conspiratorial role in the dispossession of the poor from the land.

30. *Alhaji Mudashiru Kokorowo and Others v. Lagos State Government and 4 Others* (Suit No. M/394/90).

31. I was a young lawyer at the CLO involved in developing and implementing the organization's legal strategy; the case left indelible impressions on my mind. It raised profound questions about law, rights, and their application to poverty and social justice struggles. The case was a major inspiration for the establishment of SERAC and its community-based strategies for the protection of social and economic rights.

32. This was not unexpected. Under the vicious military dictatorship of General Sani Abacha, it was difficult to trust anyone or any institution. State spies and agents at large all too often posed as workers for legitimate institutions gathering information that was then used to identify and penalize dissent or acts capable of being interpreted as "acts against state security."

33. SERAC's operational methodology is founded upon its mutually reinforcing programs: the Monitoring and Advocacy Program (MAP), the Community Action Program (CAP), the Legal Action Program (LAP), and the Policy Action Program (PAP).

Under the banner of its Forced Eviction Prevention Program (FEPP), the organization, in collaboration with the community, designed and implemented various initiatives and activities, including person-to-person contact, outreach and sensitization meetings, focused group discussions, on-site legal clinics, training workshops, creative use of local and international media, dramas, and role plays. In addition, the organization widely distributed posters and handbills in the English and Yoruba languages within and beyond the target communities. It also promoted solidarity visits by more experienced leaders and organizers from similar communities, such as Maroko (which was demolished in July 1990) to share their organizing and mobilizing knowledge and experience, and to inspire the leaders and people of Badia.

34. Further complicating matters, the human rights education process discussed below gave the Oluwole group a language through which to express their distrust and resentment of the Ojoras' possible claims on the land and support of the demolition plan.

35. The program of education was generally delivered by means of formal and informal education, personal and group contact, information dissemination, leaflets, posters, handbills, workshops, seminars, conferences, dramas, village and town meetings, peer group learning techniques, and role plays.

36. Forced eviction constitutes a gross violation of human rights. According to the United Nations Committee on Economic, Social and Cultural Rights, forced eviction denotes "the permanent or temporary removal against their will of individuals, families and/or communities from the homes and/or land which they occupy, without the provision of, and access to, appropriate forms of legal or other protection" (U.N. Committee on Economic, Social and Cultural Rights [CESCR], *General Comment No. 7: The Right to Adequate Housing: Forced Evictions [Art. 11(1) of the Covenant]*, May 20, 1997, E/1998/22, par. 3). In addition to being a major violation of the right to adequate housing, and the prohibition of forced evictions recognized by the International Covenant on Economic, Social and Cultural Rights (ratified by Nigeria in 1993), forced eviction is a brazen violation of the right to life, right to a fair hearing, right to the dignity of the human person, and the right to a private and family life guaranteed by the Constitution of the Federal Republic of Nigeria and the African Charter on Human and Peoples' Rights.

37. See supra, n. 18.

38. The independent inspection panel was established by the World Bank Resolution No. 93-10/Resolution IDA 93-6 with authority to investigate complaints from project-affected persons regarding violations of the bank's policies, procedures, and loan agreements in the context of implementation of the bank's funded project.

39. The request stated that the LDSP's implementation was in violation of OD 4.30 on Involuntary Resettlement (June 1990), which required participation of host communities during project planning and implementation stages; OD 4.15 on Poverty Reduction (December 1991), which provided for the active involvement of project beneficiaries beginning from the early stages of a poverty reduction project; OD 4.20 on Gender Dimensions of Development (April 1994), which aimed to reduce gender disparities and enhance women's participation in the economic development of their countries by requiring that gender considerations be integrated into assistance programs; OD 10.70

on Project Monitoring and Evaluation (September 1989), which provides for continuous assessment of project implementation in relation to project beneficiaries for the permanent improvement of overall management practice within borrower agencies; Operational Policy/Bank Procedure 10.04 on Economic Evaluation of Investment Operations (April 1994), which specifies that projects should integrate financial, institutional, technical, sociological, and environmental considerations; Articles of Agreement of the International Development Association, Article V, Section 1(g), which conditions project financing; and the project's Credit Agreement, Credit Number 2517–0, which identifies the project's purpose to improve health standards and living conditions in areas of Lagos subject to regular flooding.

Paragraph 1 of the Request for Inspection states that [T]he International Development Agency of the World Bank is financing the Lagos Drainage and Sanitation Project (hereinafter "the Project") and is conducting a pilot project in association with the Lagos Urban Renewal Board in Ijora Badia and Ijora Oloye, both slum communities in Lagos. Under this project, over 2,000 persons have been forcibly evicted from their homes and businesses. The evictions were carried out by officials of the Lagos State Ministry of Environment and Physical Planning (an agency that announced that in July 1995 it would clear fifteen slum communities thereby rendering approximately 1.2 million people homeless under the above referenced World Bank-assisted project), the Lagos Urban Renewal Board and heavily armed police and other security forces who harassed and beat residents who tried to salvage their personal properties from their homes as bulldozers reduced their dwellings to mere rubble. The project officials extorted huge sums of money from desperate victims with unkept promises to save their homes and properties from destruction.

In flagrant violation of the Bank's Operational Directive, the Constitution of the Federal Republic of Nigeria, the International Covenant on Economic, Social and Cultural Rights (ICESCR) and other relevant international Human Rights Instruments, the World Bank and its partner the Federal Military Government of Nigeria neglected, failed or refused to consult with the host communities in the development, planning, and implementation of the project. The residents of the host communities were not provided adequate notice prior to the commencement of the demolitions. At the time of filing this Request, the victims have neither been resettled nor compensated for their losses.

The Request for Inspection stated further as follows:

Paragraph 3:

Our interests have been, and continue to be, directly and adversely affected by the failure of the Bank to comply with its policies, procedures, and the credit agreement in the implementation of the project. The demolition of the homes and destruction of properties of the victims without compensation, resettlement or rehabilitation constitutes a massive violation of the rights of the victims to adequate housing recognized by Article 11 of ICESCR as well as their right to the dignity of the human person under Section 31 of the Constitution of the Federal Republic of Nigeria 1979. SERAC is concerned with the promotion and protection of social and economic rights in Nigeria. SERAC is mandated to broaden the access of individuals and communities to information and to strengthen their participation in the design and implementation of social and economic policies and programs which affect them. The stakeholders' rights to adequate housing, education, adequate standards of living, security of the person, a healthy environment, food, health, work, respect of dignity inherent in a human being, freedom of movement, family life, water, privacy, information, the right to chose one's own residence, and the right to adequate compensation when forcibly evicted have been violated under the design and implementation of the Project.

Paragraph 4:
The Bank has violated its policies, procedures, and the Credit Agreement because the host communities were not consulted during the Project's planning stage. Where brief discussions were held, the consultation was nullified by insufficient follow-up efforts to ensure that the Community Development Associations understood their roles and rights as stakeholders in the Project. Further, the host communities have not been able to effectively express their opposition during the Implementation Phase of the Project based on their well-founded fears of government-sponsored persecution as solidified by the presence of heavily armed agents during the demolitions. When presented with a partial itemized list of the names of displaced persons (attached), the Bank and the borrower failed to ensure that the identified evictees were resettled or compensated for their losses.

Paragraph 5:
We believe our interests and the stakeholders' rights have already been, and will likely continue to be, materially and adversely affected as a direct result of the Bank's policy violations. This has caused, and is likely to continue to cause, the Project stakeholders to suffer destruction of their livelihoods, culture, communities, and homes. Commuting times to employment opportunities, health care and day care sites have been, and will likely continue to be, extended. Stakeholders have been terrorized by heavily armed forces during the demolitions. Stable access to utilities have, and will likely continue to be, dismantled. The host communities have experienced, and will likely continue to experience severe declines in their already fragile living conditions. Further, women, children, undocumented landholders, and the disabled are especially vulnerable under the Project as they suffer disproportionately whenever forcibly evicted from their homes and businesses.

Paragraph 6:
We believe the action is the responsibility of the Bank because it is a specialized agency of the United Nations and is therefore bound by the U.N. Charter which provides for the promotion and protection of human rights. In contravention of those rights, the Bank has failed in its role to monitor the military government of Nigeria's repressive implementation of the Project and to respond promptly and seriously with credible evidence of human rights violations under the Project. Moreover, the Bank has an obligation to suspend the membership of the Federal Government of Nigeria pursuant to article VII, sec. 2, of the Articles of Agreement of the International Development Agency (IDA) for its failure to fulfill its obligations to the IDA, and is obligated under international law not to provide aid to the military government because it has shown a clear and consistent pattern of gross and systematic human rights violations.

A full text of SERAC's Request for Inspection and the Inspection Panel's Decision is on file with SERAC.

40. World Bank Inspection Panel Report (INSP/R98–5) November 10, 1998 (Request for Inspection—Nigeria: Lagos Drainage and Sanitation Project (Credit No. 2517–UNI).

41. Id.

42. Id.

43. *Chief Ogunyemi Adewale vs. The Governor of Lagos State & 4 Others* (Suit No. M/419/2003).

44. SERAC's executive director, Felix Morka, was named a member of the project's steering committee, the highest policy- and decision-making organ of the project.

45. This section of the chapter was written by Duncan Kennedy, who offers the following: My thanks to Lama Abu-Odeh, Alice Amsden, Willie Forbath, Jerry Frug, Jeremy Perelman, Kerry Rittich, and Lucie White for helpful comments. Errors are mine alone. I found Felix Morka's chapter valuable and very interesting. I want in this comment to suggest, in a tentative and, I am afraid, quite schematic way, a direction for the design of anti-eviction campaigns. I need to say at the outset that I am not an expert (for a discussion of social justice lawyering and power in South Africa, see Lucie White, "To Learn and Teach: Lessons from Driefontein on Lawyering and Power," *Wisconsin Law Review* [1988]: 699). These are the remarks of a sympathetic bystander who has done some work on low-income housing policy in the U.S. context (see Duncan Kennedy, "Legal Economics of U.S. Low Income Housing Markets in Light of 'Informality' Analysis," *Journal of Law in Society* 4 [2002]: 71, and "The Limited Equity Coop as a Vehicle for Affordable Housing in a Race and Class Divided Society," *Howard Law Journal* 46 [2002]: 1).

46. The discussion of neighborhood change that follows is derived from the housing economics literature. The pieces that have influenced me the most are Matthew Edel, "Filtering in a Private Housing Market," in *Readings in Urban Economics*, ed. Matthew Edel and Jerome Rothenberg (New York: MacMillan, 1972); Charles L. Leven, James T. Little, Hugh O. Nourse, and Robert Read, "Neighborhood Change," in *Neighborhood Change: Lessons in the Dynamics of Urban Decay*, ed. Charles Leven et al. (New York: Praeger, 1976); Rolf Goetze, *Understanding Neighborhood Change* (Cambridge, MA: Ballinger, 1979); and Peter Marcuse, "Gentrification and Abandonment," *Journal of Urban and Contemporary Law* 28 (1985): 195, and "Neutralizing Homelessness," *Socialist Review* 18 (1988): 1.

47. See Edesio Fernandes and Ann Varley, eds., *Illegal Cities: Law and Urban Change in Developing Countries* (New York: Zed Press, 1998). See also Balakrishnan Rajagopal, *International Law from Below: Development, Social Movements and Third World Resistance* (New York: Cambridge University Press, 2003).

48. See Raymond Atuguba and Mwambi Mwasaru, "'I Refuse to Let Go of the Land': Malindi Citizens, Salt Farmers, and the Land Question in Kenya" (presentation at Stones of Hope workshops; manuscript on file with the editors of this volume).

49. See Duncan Kennedy, "The Critique of Rights in Critical Legal Studies," in *Left Legalism/Left Critique*, ed. Wendy Brown and Janet Halley (Durham: Duke University Press, 2002).

50. Duncan Kennedy, "Three Globalizations of Law and Legal Thought: 1850–2000," in *The New Law and Economic Development: A Critical Appraisal*, ed. David Trubek and Alvaro Santos (New York: Cambridge University Press, 2006).

51. See William Simon, *The Community Economic Development Movement: Law, Business and the New Social Policy* (Durham: Duke University Press, 2002); David Barron, "The Community Economic Development Movement's Double Standard," *Stanford Law Review* 56 (2003): 701.

52. See generally Gerald Frug, "The City as a Legal Concept," *Harvard Law Review* 93 (1980): 1057; Gerald Frug and David Barron, "International Local Government Law," *The Urban Lawyer* 38 (2006): 1; Gerald Frug and David Barron, *City Bound: How States Stifle Urban Innovation* (Ithaca: Cornell University Press, 2008), 144–64.

53. Kennedy, "The Limited Equity Coop," supra n. 45; Duncan Kennedy and Leopold Specht, "Limited Equity Housing Cooperatives as a Mode of Privatization," in *A Fourth Way? Privatization, Property, and the Emergence of New Market Economies*, ed. Gregory Alexander and Grazyna Skapska (New York: Routledge, 1994); Duncan Kennedy, "Neither the Market nor the State: Housing Privatization Issues," in id.

54. See Hernando de Soto, *The Mystery of Capital: Why Capitalism Triumphs in the West and Fails Everywhere Else* (New York: Basic Books, 2000). For a critical perspective on de Soto's approach, see Chapter 3 in this volume. See also Kerry Rittich, "The Properties of Gender Equality," in *Human Rights and Development: Toward Mutual Reinforcement*, ed. Philip Alston and Mary Robinson (New York: Oxford University Press, 2005).

55. For the critique of neoliberal property rights development strategy, see Joel Ngugi, "The World Bank and the Ideology of Reform in International Development Discourse," *Cardozo Journal of International and Comparative Law* 14 (2006): 313; *Indonesian Journal of International Law* 3 (2006): 316; Joel Ngugi, "Policing Neo-liberal Reforms: The Rule of Law as a Constraining and Enabling Discourse," *University of Pennsylvania Journal of International and Economic Law* 26 (2006): 513; Joel Ngugi, "Re-examining the Role of Private Property in Market Democracies: Problematic Ideological Issues Raised by Land Registration," *Michigan Journal of International Law* 25 (2004): 467.

56. See Thomas Grey, "The Disintegration of Property," in *Liberty, Property and the Law*, ed. Richard Epstein (New York: Gardland, 2000), and Charles Donahue, "The Future of Property Predicted from Its Past" (id.); Duncan Kennedy and Frank Michelman, "Are Property and Contract Efficient?" *Hofstra Law Review* 8 (1980): 711.

57. Celestine Nyamu-Musembi, "How Should Human Rights and Development Respond to Cultural Legitimization of Gender Hierarchy in Developing Countries?" *Harvard International Law Journal* 41 (2000): 381; Sylvia Kang'ara, "Rethinking Property: Language, Meaning and Institutions," *Hague Yearbook of International Law* 13 (2000): 35–42. See generally David Kennedy, "The 'Rule of Law,' Development Choices and Political Common Sense," Trubek and Santos, supra n. 50.

58. See generally Alexander and Skapska, supra n. 53.

59. See generally David Kennedy, "Laws and Developments," in *Law and Development: Facing Complexity in the 21st Century*, ed. John Hatchard and Amanda Perry-Kasaris (Portland, OR: Cavendish, 2003).

60. See Michael Porter, "What Is Strategy?" *Harvard Business Review*, November–December (1996): 61–78; Raphael Kaplinsky, *Globalization, Poverty and Inequality: Between a Rock and a Hard Place* (Malden: Polity, 2005).

61. See Alice Amsden, *Escape from Empire: The Developing World's Journey Through Heaven and Hell* (Cambridge, MA: MIT Press, 2007); Alice Amsden and Wan Wen Chu, *Beyond Late Development: Taiwan's Upgrading Policies* (Cambridge, MA: MIT Press, 2003); Alice Amsden, *The Rise of "The Rest": Challenges to the West from Late-Industrializing Economies* (New York: Oxford University Press, 2001).

62. See Saskia Sassen, *The Global City: New York, London, Tokyo*, 2nd ed. (Princeton: Princeton University Press, 2001).

63. See generally Kennedy, "Legal Economics of U.S. Low Income Housing Markets in Light of 'Informality,'" supra n. 45. For discussion of a similar argument in the U.S. context, see Duncan Kennedy, "The Effect of the Warranty of Habitability on Low Income Housing: 'Milking' and Class Violence," *Florida State Law Review* 15 (1987): 485, 517–18.

64. See Edesio Fernandes and Raquel Rolnik, "Law and Urban Change in Brazil," in Fernandes and Varley, supra n. 47.

65. Thomas Shannon, *An Introduction to the World System Perspective*, 2nd ed. (Boulder: Westview, 1996).

## Chapter 2

1. The 2008 National HIV Survey indicates that 10.9% of all South Africans over 2 years old were living with HIV in 2008 (against 10.8% in 2005). Among those between 15 and 49 years old, the estimated HIV prevalence was 16.9% (against 16.2% in 2005). HIV prevalence peaked to 32.7% for females aged 25–29 years old (2008 South African National HIV Prevalence, Incidence, Behaviour and Communication Survey, available at: *http://www.hsrc.ac.za/Document-3238.phtml*).

2. The African National Congress was South Africa's leading anti-apartheid political movement, and since May 1994 it has been the nation's governing party.

3. Mark Heywood, "Shaping, Making and Breaking the Law in the Campaign for a National HIV/AIDS Treatment Plan," in *Democratising Development: The Politics of Socio-Economic Rights in South Africa*, ed. Peris Jones and Kristian Stokke (Boston: Martinus Nijhoff, 2005), 181, 183.

4. Id., at 184.

5. Anonymous, "Castro Hlongwane, Caravans, Cats, Geese, Foot & Mouth and Statistics: HIV/AIDS and the Struggle for the Humanisation of the African," March 2002, available at: http://www.virusmyth.com/aids/hiv/ancdoc.htm. The authors of this article are likely Mokaba and other ANC officials; see Ulrike Kistner, *Commissioning and Contesting Post-Apartheid's Human Rights: HIV/AIDS, Racism, Truth and Reconciliation* (Piscataway: Transaction, 2003), 161, crediting the ANC and Mokaba with authorship; Mark Heywood, "Current Developments: Preventing Mother-to-Child HIV Transmission in South Africa: Background, Strategies and Outcomes of the Treatment Action Campaign Case Against the Minister of Health," *South African Journal of Human Rights* 19 (2003): 278, 284, reporting that Mokaba admitted the document was jointly penned by the ANC.

6. Thabo Mbeki, "Z. K. Matthews Memorial Lecture." Delivered at the University of Fort Hare, October 12, 2001, available at: http://www.anc.org.za/ancdocs/history/mbeki/2001/tm1012.html

7. Heywood, supra n. 3, at 285.

8. Id., at 286.

9. Id.

10. Id., at 299–300.

11. Id.

12. Interview with Zackie Achmat, Bellagio, Italy, December 2006 (on file with editors).

13. *News Hour*, interview with President Thabo Mbeki, Washington, DC, February 10, 2002.

14. Justice Yvonne Mokgoro, "Constitutional Claims for Gender Equality in South Africa: A Judicial Response," *Albany Law Review* 67 (2003): 565, 566.

15. South Africa's Constitutional Court's reasonableness review doctrine has been crafted in a way that calls for sociohistorical, contextual, and structural analysis, much as U.S. left legal academics imagine in anticaste countermodels of "substantive" equal protection. Thus, the Court's doctrine calls for examining the social vulnerability of complainants; their position in social structures of advantage and disadvantage; the long- and short-term historical contexts of property or resource allocations; and the extent and severity of needs, disadvantage, and deprivation in the instant case. All of these factors are weighed against the demands on public resources, which addressing the deprivations entails. Much weight is given to the needs of the most deprived or disadvantaged.

16. Achmat interview, supra n. 13.

17. Heywood, supra n. 3, at 186–88.

18. Id., at 189–90.

19. Id., at 190–92.

20. Id., at 193.

21. Id., at 194.

22. Id., at 194.

23. Id., at 195–97.

24. Id., at 199.

25. Id., at 197.

26. Id., at 199–200.

27. Id., at 202–4.

28. Id., at 205–6.

29. Id., at 206, n. 49.

30. TAC newsletter, *Equal Treatment*, March 2004, p. 4, available at: http://www.tac.org.za/community/news_2004

31. *Treatment Action Campaign v. Minister of Health*, 2005 (6) SA 363 (T), available at: www.tac.org.za/community/news_2004

32. The HIV and AIDS and STI Strategic Plan for South Africa, 2007–2011, can be found at: http://www.doh.gov.za/docs/misc/stratplan/2007–2011/index.html

33. Jonny Steinberg, *Sizwe's Test: A Young Man's Journey Through Africa's AIDS Epidemic* (New York: Simon and Schuster, 2008), 204.

## Chapter 3

The authors would like to thank Lucie White and Jeremy Perelman for their work in initiating the larger project of which this chapter is a part, and all of the participants in the Stones of Hope project for their comments on earlier versions of the chapter.

1. The village was known as "Remaining Nyamuma" because most of the village of Nyamuma had already been relocated in 1994 as a result of an extension of the borders of the neighboring Ikorongo Game Reserve at that time.

2. Many of the villagers had migrated to Remaining Nyamuma from elsewhere, some as a consequence of land shortages in their traditional villages, others following an earlier eviction from yet another village, Nyanguge, in January 2000. See LHRC, "Protection of Wildlife and Human Rights on a Balance Sheet: A Case of Killings in the Serengeti National Parks" (2002), available at: alpha.web2–netshine-hosting.co.uk/lhrc/index.php?option=com_docman&task=cat_view&gid=44&Itenud=56 (accessed August 1, 2008).

3. Multiple actors were involved in the evictions at Nyamuma. Some, such as the district commissioner and the district police commander, exercised authority grounded in formal Tanzanian law; others, the "Ritongo," derived their power from the customary authority of the traditional village security system. The relation between these actors and the different roles they played—in the events leading up to Nyamuma, during the evictions themselves, and in the aftermath—are complex. Jurisdiction between the formal and the informal systems of rule overlapped; the boundaries between them were uncertain; and how the groups exercised authority "in fact" often diverged from the official account of their actual power. While our account doesn't investigate these relations in detail, we do note that the issues highlight the limits of analyzing a legal dispute with reference to state actors and institutions and through the lens of formal legal entitlements alone.

4. We are mindful in the account that follows of the "politics of reporting": the questions of what gets told and to whom, what is suppressed, why, and at what cost and benefit. Both the violations at Nyamuma and the solutions to them implicate the choices and decisions of a number of actors. At the same time, Nyamuma is only one incident among many that will engage these players, some of whom encounter one another on a repeated basis. Because the players do not stand on a level playing field—they have different options, resources, concerns, and relations to one another—it is worth bearing in mind that there can be no "complete" account of what has happened.

5. Issa G. Shivji, "Constructing a New Rights Regime: Promises, Problems and Prospects," *Social and Legal Studies* 8 (1999): 253–76. At 259: "On the global terrain of social and political discourse, the developmental and the human rights discourses were locked in battle. They were polarized and became mutually exclusive. This meant that the developmental discourse and the human rights discourse ran parallel." Or at 260: "the liberal theory (of rights) ruled out of court any link between individual rights and eco-

nomic justice, while developmental theory was prepared to sacrifice individual rights in the pursuit of socio-economic justice."

6. For a collection of papers that probe this relationship, see Philip Alston and Mary Robinson, eds., *Human Rights and Development: Toward Mutual Reinforcement* (New York: Oxford University Press, 2005).

7. Celestine Nyamu-Musembi and Andrea Cornwall, "Putting the 'Rights-Based Approach to Development' into Perspective," *Third World Quarterly* 25 (2004): 1415.

8. Gobind Nankani, John Page, and Lindsay Judge, "Human Rights and Poverty Reduction Strategies: Moving Toward Convergence," in *Human Rights and Development: Toward Mutual Reinforcement*, ed. Philip Alston and Mary Robinson (New York: Oxford University Press, 2005), 475; Roberto Danino, "Legal Aspects of the World Bank's Work on Human Rights: Some Preliminary Thoughts," in *Human Rights and Development: Toward Mutual Reinforcement*, ed. Philip Alston and Mary Robinson (New York: Oxford University Press, 2005), 509.

9. David Kennedy, "The International Human Rights Movement: Part of the Problem?" *Harvard Human Rights Journal* 15 (2002): 101–25.

10. Gayle Rubin, "The Traffic in Women: Notes on the Political Economy of Sex," in *Toward an Anthropology of Women*, ed. Rayna Reiter (New York: Monthly Review Press, 1975).

11. Kituo cha Sheria na Haki za Binadamu, K. L. Gamaya, Clement J. Mashamba, and Lupa Ramadhani, *The Human Calamity of the Evictions at Nyamuma-Serengeti: Legal and Human Rights Implications* (Dar es Salaam: Legal and Human Rights Centre, 2005).

12. The Commission came into being in 2000 in amendments to Tanzania's Constitution Act, Art. 129, and the *Commission for Human Rights and Good Governance Act, 2001*, Act No. 7 (2001), in operation March 2002. Commissioners are appointed by the president on the recommendation of an appointments committee. It is a hybrid institution, having jurisdiction as ombudsman as well as for the protection of human rights and good governance. More details on the Commission's mandate and function are provided in Section 4.1 of the LHRC Report, supra, and the Commission's website, www.chragg.org. See also Mambo, Jilde Alois, "The Paris Principles on Establishment of National Human Rights Institutions and Realization of Fundamental Rights and Freedoms: A Case Study of the Commission for Human Rights and Good Governance in Tanzania (May 15, 2008)" (Commission for Human Rights and Good Governance, forthcoming), available at: http://ssrn.com/abstract=1154642

13. In January 2002, the LHRC sent out two investigators to Nyamuma. While they were taking photographs and videos of the site, they were arrested and their film and equipment were confiscated by the police.

14. These killings are documented in another LHRC publication, "Protection of Wildlife and Human Rights on the Balance Sheet" (2003).

15. LHRC, supra n. 14, at 43.

16. That case was commenced in 2005 in the Tanzanian High Court, Land Division. At trial, it was determined that the Commission's decisions were not enforceable by the High Court, but that finding has now been appealed. The appeal was finally heard by a

three-judge panel of the Court of Appeal on April 22, 2008, and a decision, dated October 11, 2008, was released on January 22, 2009. The decision allowed the appeal, finding that the High Court had erred in law in its determination that the decisions of the Commission were not enforceable by the courts and in its refusal to consider the case on its merits. The case has now been referred back to the High Court on the merits. See Court of Appeal of Tanzania, Civil Appeal No. 88 of 2006, *Legal and Human Rights Center v. Thomas Ole Sabaya and Four Others* (dated October 11, 2008, read January 22, 2009). As of June 2009, the case has not yet been heard by the High Court and the complainants remain displaced.

17. Issa G. Shivji, *Let the People Speak: Tanzania Down the Road to Neoliberalism* (Dakar, Sénégal: Codesria, 2006), 181. While the context for Shivji's remark was somewhat different—the legal struggles over customary land rights following villagization, in the mid-1980s—its point is well taken here. Since many of those legal cases emanated from the Arusha region, they also played a role in creating the historical context of displacements and struggles over land that underlie the Nyamuma evictions.

18. The wider problem of forced evictions in Africa is documented by Paul Ocheje in "In the Public Interest: Forced Evictions, Land Rights and Human Development in Africa," *Journal of African Law* 51 (2007): 173–214.

19. See the move to *ujamaa* land described in LHRC, supra n. 14, at 9. A further discussion of the history of land conflicts in the Arusha region is to be found in Shivji (2006), supra n. 17, at 178.

20. The enduring legacy of colonial rule often includes problems with democratic legitimacy arising from institutions and rules that are preserved even while rulers change. Some of this is evident in the Tanzanian case, particularly in relation to the regulation of hunting. See generally Mahmood Mamdani, *Citizen and Subject: Contemporary Africa and the Legacy of Late Colonialism* (Princeton: Princeton University Press, 1996).

21. LHRC, supra n. 14, at 8.

22. Patrick McAuslan, *Bringing the Law Back In: Essays on Land, Law and Development* (Aldershot: Ashgate, 2003), 249.

23. The opposition focused around the liberalization of land tenure that would enable land to be owned individually rather than communally, with the aim of promoting foreign investment. Critics were concerned that this would also have the effect of displacing and marginalizing pastoralists and poor farmers. See Issa G. Shivji, *Not Yet Democracy: Reforming Land Tenure in Tanzania* (London: International Institute of Environment and Development, 1998), 105.

24. Nordic Consulting Group, "Review of the First Phase of the Property and Business Formalisation Program (PBFP) in Tanzania" (October 16, 2005), available at: http:www.npaid.org/filestore/NCGReviewPBFPTanzania-FinalReport.pdf (accessed August 1, 2008).

25. Hernando de Soto, *The Mystery of Capital: Why Capitalism Triumphs in the West and Fails Everywhere Else* (New York: Basic Books, 2000).

26. A summary of the expected commercial benefits of formalization, based on a study done by de Soto's organization, the Institute for Liberty and Democracy, on Tan-

zanian informal economic practices from 2003 to 2005, is contained in de Soto, "The Challenge of Connecting Informal and Formal Property Systems: Some Reflections Based on the Case of Tanzania," in *Realizing Property Rights*, ed. Hernando de Soto and Francis Cheneval (Zurich: Frank/Wynkin de Worde, 2006).

27. Klaus Deininger, *Land Policies for Growth and Poverty Reduction*, World Bank Policy Research Report Series (Washington, DC: World Bank; Oxford and New York: Oxford University Press, 2003); Kerry Rittich, "The Future of Law and Development: Second Generation Reforms and the Incorporation of the Social," in *The New Law and Economic Development: A Critical Appraisal*, ed. David M. Trubek and Alvaro Santos (Cambridge, UK: Cambridge University Press, 2006), 203. It is worth noting that these land reforms bear no relation to earlier development strategies that focused not on reforms to land law but rather on the redistribution of land itself. Indeed, it is significant that even though they almost invariably involve alterations to existing entitlements, projects to promote land titling are almost entirely disconnected from questions of land distribution.

28. See Celestine Nyamu-Musembi, "Breathing Life into Dead Theories About Property Rights: de Soto and Land Relations in Rural Africa," Working Paper 272, Institute of Development Studies, University of Sussex, United Kingdom, October 2006.

29. The bias in favor of commercial activities flows in part from the fact that where value is determined by price on the market, wealth generated in noncommodified economies tends to be systematically undervalued or simply is not valued at all. See Lourdes Beneria, *Gender, Development and Globalization: Economics as If People Mattered* (New York: Routledge, 2003).

30. Deininger, supra n. 27.

31. See the trend toward acquisition of large tracts of land in the developing world to ensure food security for those in the wealthier and more industrialized states. "Buying Farmland Abroad: Outsourcing's Third Wave," *The Economist*, May 21, 2009, available at: http://www.economist.com/world/international/displaystory.cfm?story_id=13692889

32. See Kerry Rittich, "The Properties of Gender Equality," in *Human Rights and Development: Toward Mutual Reinforcement*, ed. Philip Alston and Mary Robinson (New York: Oxford University Press, 2005).

33. While "tradition" in the usual sense of entitlements based on uses "since time immemorial" is not at issue here, it is clear that the ongoing conflicts over land implicate multiple "traditions" of varying historicities on the part of different social groups.

34. The process works as follows: "The TIC writes to regional commissioners, who in turn write to District Authorities, who in turn order village executive officers to identify suitable lands in their villages and report back within eleven days." Shivji, supra n. 17, at 176.

35. As Professor Shivji notes, "In practice, these lands are usually prime lands already used by peasants, which means when they are alienated the inevitable evictions take place, giving rise to perpetual land disputes." Id., at 177.

36. Both the tourism policy and the plan can be accessed at: www.tourismtanzania.go.tz

37. "Integrated Tourism Master Plan for Tanzania Strategy and Action Plan Update," at 35. The report goes on to identify two acts of particular relevance, the Wildlife Act of 1974 and the Village Act of 1982, and notes:

These acts were designed to ensure that villages benefit from wildlife utilizations and encourage local communities to support tourism/recreational activities outside national park boundaries. However, lack of clarification in the act as to who actually has the right to authorize or even enter into contracts with regard to the non-consumptive use of an area (i.e. whether the local community or the game department) is inhibiting the full realization of the expected benefits from these initiatives.

38. LHRC (2003), supra n. 14, at 8.

39. See generally LHRC (2003), supra n. 14.

40. LHRC Report (2002), supra n. 2.

41. Baldus and Cauldwell, "Tourist Hunting and Its Role in Development of Wildlife Management Areas in Tanzania" (2004), available at: http://www.cic-wildlife.org/index .php?id=209 (accessed August 7, 2008).

42. The Grumeti Reserves properties are now being managed by Singita, a high-end wildlife tourism company in Africa. See http://www.singita.com/index.php/game-reserves /lodges-and-camps-in-tanzania/singita-sasakwa-lodge/

43. www.leat.or.tz

44. "Barrick's Dirty Secrets: Communities Worldwide Respond to Gold Mining's Impacts" (Oakland, CA: Corpwatch, 2007).

45. For a description of LEAT actions regarding the Bulyanhulu Mine and related links, see www.leat.or.tz/activities/buly

46. www.leat.or.tz/about/pr/2003.11.24.hrc.tarime.injunction.php (We have not yet been able to ascertain whether the injunction was respected by the government, or if adequate compensation has now been paid.)

47. LHRC, supra n. 14, at 25.

48. The original funding for the complaint came from the Washington, DC–based World Resource Institute. However, as an organization focused on environmental accountability, it was not in a position to provide funds to enable the Commission to actually hear directly from all of the complainants. These funds were eventually provided to the LHRC by the Swedish embassy.

49. In this instance, the largest funders were the development agencies of national governments, mostly European.

50. Shivji notes this contradiction precisely in a discussion of human rights abuses relating to the Maasai in the Ngorongoro Conservation Area: "In fact, those who sponsor umpteen human rights seminars on the one hand, also with the other supply the equipment and wherewithal to MNR (Management of Natural Resources)," who are accused of harassing the Maasai in the Ngorongoro Conservation Area (supra n. 17, at 182).

51. The shooting described took place on September 20, 1997. See LHRC Report, supra n. 2. The Tanzanian tourism policy is available at: www.tourismtanzania.go.tz

52. Locals who were interviewed by the media had connected the killings with the presence of some officials from the Frankfurt Zoological Society (which has a long-

standing relationship with the Serengeti National Park) in the park and a perceived corresponding step-up of antipoaching enforcement activities. While the LHRC had also been concurrently investigating the incident, no LHRC representatives had made such claims to the media.

53. Sherene Hertel, "New Moves in Transnational Advocacy: Getting Labour and Economic Rights on the Agenda in Unexpected Ways," *Global Governance* 12 (2006): 263–81.

54. For example, Human Rights Watch, one of the largest and best-known international human rights NGOs, only began its forays into economic and social rights less than ten years ago, and they remain a small part of its mandate to this day.

55. See Duncan Kennedy's comment, in Chapter 1 of this volume, on the possible ways of configuring land and land tenure entitlements in the wake of the disintegration of property, and the extent to which they may effect compensation to those who are evicted.

56. For example, the LHRC Report (2003) documents that the 1998 wildlife policy incorporates an emphasis on community-based conservation, which permits local people to have access to wildlife resources through the creation of wildlife management areas. At Section 6.6., the report observes that "the concept and practice of community based conservation has not yet been fully adopted and practiced in many parts of the country," notably, the western corridor of the Serengeti National Park.

57. For a consideration of community consultation requirements in the context of the squatter movement in Johannesburg, see William Forbath et al., Chapter 2 of this volume.

58. Contemporary examples of effective anti-eviction struggles may lie close at hand. See, for example, the successful resistance against evictions and foreclosures organized by low-income tenants in Boston and by advocates and students from the Harvard Legal Aid Bureau in the wake of the subprime mortgage and financial crisis. See Harvard University Committee on Human Rights Studies, Harvard Law School, and the Swiss Ministry of Foreign Affairs, *Property Rights for the Poor: Conceptual Challenges, Pragmatic Responses*, Harvard Law School, April 26–27, 2009.

59. See Duncan Kennedy's comment in Chapter 1 of this volume.

60. For an argument to this effect, see Dani Rodrik, *One Economics, Many Recipes: Globalization, Institutions, and Economic Growth* (Princeton: Princeton University Press, 2007).

## Chapter 4

Jeremy Perelman and Katharine Young would like to thank the staff at the Legal Resources Center, Professor Lucie White, and the people of Nima and Mamobi for their various powerful insights that led to the completion of this chapter. In addition, they would like to thank the participants of the Stones of Hope project, particularly William Forbath, Peter Houtzager, and Kerry Rittich for valuable comments on a previous draft.

1. International Covenant on Economic, Social and Cultural Rights, December 16, 1966, 993 U.N.T.S., Art. 12. Ghana ratified the ICESCR, without reservations, on September 7, 2000.

2. Ghana's 1992 Constitution, Art. 34(2), establishing the right to good healthcare as a directive principle of state policy.

3. See Michael McCann, *Rights at Work: Pay Equity Reform and the Politics of Legal Mobilization* (Chicago: University of Chicago Press, 1994), 288, adopting a "dynamic longitudinal perspective" in evaluating the work of rights; see also Bryant G. Garth, "Power and Legal Artifice: The Federal Class Action," *Law and Society Review* 26 (1992): 237, showing an enduring effect of class action lawsuits.

4. Legal consciousness literature has flourished since the mid-1980s, particularly in the area of poverty and welfare rights studies. See, e.g., Austin Sarat, "'The Law Is All Over . . . ': Power, Resistance and the Legal Consciousness of the Welfare Poor," *Yale Journal of Law and Humanities* 2 (1990): 343, exploring how the welfare poor's identity and consciousness is partly constructed through their interaction with the welfare system, and emerges as a legal consciousness of power and domination, as well as one of resistance.

5. Useful studies of this program include Delali Margaret Badasu, "Implementation of Ghana's Health User Fee Policy and the Exemption of the Poor: Problems and Prospect," in *African Population Studies Supplement A to vol. 19 (2004)* (Institute of African Studies), available at: https://tspace.library.utoronto.ca/bitstream/1807/5822/1/ep04031 .pdf (accessed July 26, 2009), at 290, describing the progressive introduction of user fees in the Ghanaian healthcare system, and pointing to the introduction of a system of exemptions in 1992, with input from international donors. For a discussion of the 1987 pan-African Bamako Initiative, which set out the principles of entrenched user fees for public facilities across Africa, see Gay Hutton, "Charting the Path to the World Bank's 'No Blanket Policy on User Fees'" (IDFID Health Systems Resource Centre, 2004).

6. Hospital Fees Act, 1971, Sections 2, 4. Section 2, setting out "general exemptions from hospital fees," establishes that

No fees shall be paid in respect of services rendered in a hospital to—

(a) any person certified in writing by a medical officer to be unable to pay those fees on the ground of poverty

7. Mahama Ayariga, one of the Legal Resources Center's founders and its original executive director, was pursuing a Masters of Law at Harvard Law School at that time. Thus, he was technically an intern like all of us, but in practice acted as the Legal Resources Center's leader.

8. The right-to-health campaign in Nima had also previously involved a public hearing featuring community members, healthcare providers, and local officials, as well as a correspondence with the local World Bank office around the issue of exemptions. See "Right to Health Campaign, 2002 Internship Report" (Legal Resources Center, January 2002) (on file with authors).

9. "White people," in Twi (most prevalent African language spoken in Ghana).

10. For a description of the colonial origins of this facility and its current segregation along socioeconomic lines and with a bias towards civil servants, see Randolph Quaye, *Underdevelopment and Health Care in Africa: The Ghanaian Experience* (Lewiston: Mellen University Press, 1996), 112.

11. See "Voices of the Poor" (World Bank, 1999), available at: http://web.world-bank.org/WBSITE/EXTERNAL/TOPICS/EXTPOVERTY/0,,contentMDK:20622514 menuPK:336998pagePK:148956piPK:216618theSitePK:336992,00.html (accessed July 26, 2009), a widely publicized World Bank study undertaken at the turn of the century to collect the voices of "60,000 poor women and men from 60 countries, in an unprecedented effort to understand poverty from the perspective of the poor themselves." Compare with the effort to collect narratives in Pierre Bourdieu (trans. Priscilla Parkhurst Ferguson et al.), *The Weight of the World: Social Suffering in Contemporary Society* (Oxford: Polity, 1999).

12.

1. An order for mandamus compelling the Ministry of Health to

(a) make regulations that establish criteria and procedures for defining at the time of initial registration whether a prospective patient is "unable to pay . . . fees on the ground of poverty" and, as such, entitled to the exemption under ss 2(a) and 4(2) of the Hospital Fees Act 1971, after consulting with Members of the Parliament, the Ministry of Health, the Ministry of Finance, health system and finance experts, health care providers and low income health consumer groups;

(b) implement the exemption scheme in Ridge Hospital and all other public health facilities covered under the Hospital Fees Act 1971.

2. A mandatory injunction compelling the authorities of the Ridge Hospital to exempt Mohammed Zakari from payment of his medical costs on the grounds of poverty under ss 2(a) and 4(2) of the Hospital Fees Act 1971.

3. A declaration that the refusal of the authorities of Ridge Hospital to release Mohammed Zakari, [ . . . ] on the sole ground that he could not pay his medical bill, even though he qualifies for an exemption under the Hospital Fees Act 1971, was unlawful and constituted a violation of his right to be free from unlawful detention and restriction under articles 14 and 33 of the Constitution.

4. A declaration that the failure of the Ministry of Health to have established criteria and procedures for realizing the entitlement under ss 2(a) and 4(2) of the Hospital Fees Act 1971, and the refusal or neglect of the authorities of the Ridge Hospital to exempt Mohammed Zakari from the cost of his medical services, when he qualifies as an exempt patient under the Hospital Fees Act 1971, constitute a simple and egregious violation of his right to health under articles 33 and 34 of the Constitution, a violation of the principle of non-discrimination on the grounds of social and economic status under article 17(2) of the Constitution and a violation of his right to administrative justice under article 23 of the Constitution.

13. E.g., Jody Freeman and Laura Langbein, "Regulatory Negotiation and the Legitimacy Benefit," *NYU Environmental Law Journal* 9 (2001): 60, reporting evidence that agency negotiation of rules generates more learning and better-quality rules compared to conventional rule making for environmental protection.

14. Ghana's common law system, its adversarial court processes, and independent judiciary make this process of "borrowing" broadly feasible, with the knowledge that local institutions would take up these ideas in new—and sometimes unpredictable—ways.

15. Interview with Raymond Atuguba, cofounder of the Legal Resources Center, in Berlin, Germany (July 2007).

16. "Government Sued over Hospital Fees Act," *Ghanaian Times*, January 23, 2003, front page.

17. "3 Billion Cedis Voted for Medical Bills," *Daily Graphic*, January 29, 2003.

18. Interview by Jeremy Perelman with Nihad Swallah, community organizer, Legal Resources Center, in Accra, Ghana (January 13, 2005).

19. Id.

20. For an early articulation of rights-claiming as meaning-making beyond formal legal institutions, see William Felstiner, R. L. Abel, and Austin Sarat, "The Emergence and Transformation of Disputes: Naming, Blaming, Claiming," *Law and Society Review* 15 (1980–81): 631.

21. Important commentary tracks the developments that have taken place as a result of constitutional litigation around economic and social rights in South Africa, India, and Colombia, among others; see, e.g., comparative commentary in Roberto Gargarella, Pilar Domingo, and Theunis Roux, eds., *Courts and Social Transformation in New Democracies: An Institutional Voice for the Poor?* (Burlington: Ashgate, 2006).

22. The emphasis being *may*: for a legal pluralist challenge to the mirror thesis, see Brian Z. Tamanaha, *A General Jurisprudence of Law and Society* (New York: Oxford University Press, 2001).

23. E.g., Sanford Levinson, "The Rhetoric of the Judicial Opinion," in *Law's Stories: Narrative and Rhetoric in the Law*, ed. Peter Brooks and Paul Gewirtz (New Haven: Yale University Press, 1996), 187.

24. This moment can be interpreted as a break from the subtle ordering and distribution of roles embedded in "progressive" programs framed in public law terms, such as human rights education. For an ethnographic study of a public law-engineered program in the United States, in which law can at the same time seek to "create social spaces within which communities take shape" while ordering voices and constraining social life in subtle and dynamic ways, see Lucie E. White, "Ordering Voice: Rhetoric and Democracy in Project Head Start," in *The Rhetoric of Law*, ed. Austin Sarat and Thomas R. Kearns (Ann Arbor: University of Michigan Press, 1994), 186.

25. For the distinction between the politics of justice and the politics of pity, see Luc Boltanski (trans. Graham Burchell, 1993), *Distant Suffering: Morality, Media, and Politics* (New York: Cambridge University Press, 1999), suggesting that the international humanitarian movement is mobilized by the latter rather than the former. The notions of justice and injustice that accompanied our experience suggest that the politics of justice can play an important role in the response to suffering—responses established from positions of closeness and distance.

26. On the importance of individual life trajectories in the formation of identity, legal consciousness, and the "activation" or inactivation of rights, see David Engel and Frank Munger, *Rights of Inclusion: Law and Identity in the Life Stories of Americans with Disabilities* (Chicago: University of Chicago Press, 2003).

27. The research memo developed for the brief reproduced commentary on the

ICESCR, as well as Indian and South African case law. This memo (dated January 10–11, 2003) included a discussion of the Indian constitution's right to life, interpreted by the Indian Supreme Court with respect to its directive principles of state policy to include a duty to provide emergency medical treatment (*Samity v. State of W.B.* [1996], 4 S.C.C. 37 [Sup. Ct. India]), and the South African constitution's right to access healthcare, and the South African Constitutional Court's assessment of this duty as requiring the government to make reasonable efforts to provide healthcare (*Soobramoney v. Minister of Health, Kwazulu-Natal* 1998 [1] SA 765 [CC] [S. Afr.]; and *Minister of Health v. Treatment Action Campaign* 2002 [5] SA 721 [CC]).

28. An example of this type of international human rights activism is the recent work around the emergence of the 2006 United Nations Convention on the Rights of Persons with Disabilities; see Michael Stein, "Disability Human Rights," *California Law Review* 95 (2007): 75; see also Harvard Law School project on disability, available at: http://www.hpod.org/ (accessed July 26, 2009).

29. See Roland Robertson, "Glocalization: Time-Space and Homogeneity-Heterogeneity," in *Global Modernities*, ed. Mike Featherstone, Scott Lash, and Roland Roberston (Thousand Oaks: Sage, 1995), 25–44, suggesting glocalization as an approach to "transcend" the debate about global "homogenization" versus "heterogenization." For a political analysis of glocalization as embracing neoliberal and left-wing features, see William Forbath et al., Chapter 2 in this volume.

30. E.g., Paul Gewirtz, "Narrative and Rhetoric in the Law," in *Law's Stories: Narrative and Rhetoric in the Law*, ed. Peter Brooks and Paul Gewirtz (New Haven: Yale University Press, 1996), 2, 5–6, raising the question as to whether "telling stories [ . . . ] has a distinctive power to challenge and unsettle the legal status quo, because stories give uniquely vivid representation to particular voices, perspectives and experiences of victimization traditionally let out of legal scholarship and ignored when shaping legal rules." The early writing on legal storytelling focused on the trial or on judgment production—and not the wider cultural processes that we document in Nima.

31. Interview with Jennifer Pendelton, former Harvard Law School intern, in Cambridge, MA (January 22, 2008).

32. Cf. Spencie Love, *One Blood: The Death and Resurrection of Charles R. Drew* (Chapel Hill: University of North Carolina Press, 1996), exploring a story of trauma in African-American folklore, which channeled black anger, outrage, and despair.

33. E.g., William Forbath, *Law and the Shaping of the American Labor Movement* (Cambridge: Harvard University Press, 1991); Hendrik Hartog, "Pigs and Positivism," *Wisconsin Law Review* 1985 (1985): 899.

34. We use "truths" advisedly. As Spencie Love puts it, "a group's shared memories, frequently expressed in the form of historical legends, may often be inaccurate as to surface details, but within them are important truths about that group's historical experiences" (Love, supra n. 32, at 5).

35. Paul R. Thompson, *The Voice of the Past: Oral History*, 3d ed. (New York: Oxford University Press, 2000), 30; see also 166, noting the special dependence on oral sources for anthropologists and historians of Africa.

36.  See, e.g., Gary Bellow and Martha Minow, eds., *Law Stories* (Ann Arbor: University of Michigan Press, 1996), challenging the "war stories" notion in legal commentary.

37.  In this sense, the effect resembles the "opportunity spirals" described by McAdam et al. for the changing actions in contentious politics; see Doug McAdam, Sidney Tarrow, and Charles Tilly, *Dynamics of Contention* (New York: Cambridge University Press, 2001), 243.

38.  Gordon W. Allport and Leo Postman, *The Psychology of Rumor* (New York: Holt, 1947), 75, 100, applying this to changes in both individual and social memory.

39.  Id., at 86.

40.  Id., at 86. Indeed, Love explains the multiple versions of the legend of Charles Drew with an account of this psychology; see Love, supra n. 32.

41.  Id., at 140. The availability of a verbal label provides an anchorage effect on the form of the retention and report. The implications are analogous to the availability heuristic, which has been adapted to current behavioral law and economics literature; see Richard H. Thaler and Cass R. Sunstein, *Nudge: Improving Decisions about Health, Wealth and Happiness* (New York: Penguin Books, 2009).

42.  See A. J. van der Walt, "Modernity, Normality, and Meaning: The Struggle Between Progress and Stability and the Politics of Interpretation: Part 2," *Stellenbosch Law Review* 11 (2000): 226, 227–30.

43.  Preparatory written notes for a recruitment talk for "Making Rights Real: The Ghana Project" to law school students, Stanford, CA, 2005. Ellipses indicate pause or silence; emphasis indicates voice.

44.  The blueprint is a longstanding planning idea in the field of development; see, e.g., Emory M. Roe, "Development Narratives, Or Making the Best of Blueprint Development," *World Development* 19 (1991): 287, seeking to address the criticisms of what is "stenciled whole-cloth from pre-made plans and blueprints."

45.  "The World Bank Participation Sourcebook" (World Bank, 1996); see also "Poverty Reduction Strategy Papers: A Factsheet" (International Monetary Fund), available at: http://www.imf.org/external/np/exr/facts/prsp.htm (accessed April 8, 2010).

46.  UN Economic and Social Council (ECOSOC), Committee on Economic, Social, and Cultural Rights, *Report on the Fifth Session, Supp. No. 3*, Annex III ¶ 10, U.N. Doc. E/1991/23 (1991) (*General Comment No. 3*). For commentary on the different legal and monitoring approaches to which this concept has been put, see Katharine G. Young, "The Minimum Core of Economic and Social Rights: A Concept in Search of Content," *Yale Journal of International Law* 33 (2008): 113.

47.  We liken this to the "chastened neoliberalism" of the post-Washington Consensus. For an expression of the now-mediated relationship between blueprints and local knowledge, see Dani Rodrik, *One Economics, Many Recipes: Globalization, Institutions, and Economic Growth* (Princeton: Princeton University Press, 2007), 155, 164–65.

48.  Frances Stewart and Michael Wang, "Poverty Reduction Strategy Papers Within the Human Rights Perspective," in *Human Rights and Development: Towards Mutual Reinforcement*, ed. Philip Alston and Mary Robinson (New York: Oxford University Press, 2005), 447, 456–57, 466.

49. The Highly-Indebted Poor Country Initiative (HIPC) makes the production of PRSPs conditional on relief. Ghana is an HIPC member.

50. Tony Killick and Charles Abugre, "Institutionalizing the PRSP Approach in Ghana," in *Report Submitted to the Strategic Partnership with Africa* (2000), ch. 3; cited in Stewart and Wang, supra n. 48, at 464–65.

51. Charles F. Sabel and William H. Simon, "Destabilization Rights: How Public Law Litigation Succeeds," *Harvard Law Review* 117 (2004): 1016.

52. Indeed, the Legal Resources Center has pursued and expanded its right-to-health campaign around the lack of access to healthcare for the poor and the continuing practice of hospital detentions in the context of Ghana's subsequent health financing system (see Epilogue, below).

53. National Health Insurance Act (Act 650), 2003; National Health Insurance Regulations (L.I. 1809), 2004.

54. Hutton, IDFID, supra n. 5, at 1.1, predicting that user fees would cease as a viable national financing instrument, "not so much through further presentations of the negative impact of user fees (which are mainly circulated amongst academicians and donor agencies), but instead through dialogue at the highest political level with players the government can trust."

55. See "Report on Healthcare Access in the Bongo and West Mamprusi Districts of Ghana," Legal Resources Center, January 18, 2008 (on file with authors).

## Chapter 5

1. See Makau Mutua, "Savages, Victims and Saviors: The Metaphor of Human Rights," *Harvard International Law Journal* 42 (2001): 201. See also Makau Mutua, "The Ideology of Human Rights," *Virginia Journal of International Law* 36 (1996): 589, and *Human Rights: A Political and Cultural Critique* (Philadelphia: Pennsylvania Studies in Human Rights, 2008). On how human rights activists should reconceptualize what human rights can be, see Upendra Baxi, *The Future of Human Rights* (New York: Oxford University Press, 2002), and "Failed Decolonisation and the Future of Social Rights: Some Preliminary Reflections," in *Exploring Social Rights: Between Theory and Practice*, ed. Aeyal Gross and Daphne Barak-Erez (Portland, OR: Hart, 2007).

2. It is certainly the case that mainstream human rights lawyers often rely on remedial strategies other than litigation—reporting, lobbying, media "shaming" work, for instance. Furthermore, the formal practice of stating a claim requires a good deal of improvisation, as the positive law of human rights is usually vague and the remedies usually soft.

3. For a general comment on the justiciability of economic and social rights, pointing to the oft-articulated difficulty to implement these rights through "traditional legal remedies such as court actions" (at 275) and the availability of other "soft" remedies such as administrative remedies, monitoring, and benchmarking, see Henry Steiner and Philip Alston, "Justiciability and the Role of Courts in Developing Economic and Social Rights," in *International Human Rights in Context: Law, Politics, Morals* (New York: Oxford University Press, 2000), 275–300; see for instance 275–77, referring to the U.N.

Committee on Economic, Social and Cultural Rights, *General Comment No. 9* (1998) on "legal or judicial remedies."

4. On the use of structural remedies in public interest litigation in the United States, see Owen Fiss, "The Supreme Court 1978 Term: Foreword: The Forms of Justice," *Harvard Law Review* 93 (1979): 1; Abraham Chayes, "The Role of the Judge in Public Law Litigation," *Harvard Law* Review 89 (1976): 1281.

5. See Chapters 2 and 6 in this volume.

6. See Chapters 1 and 3 in this volume.

7. On nonstate actors and human rights activism, see Philip Alston, *Non-State Actors and Human Rights* (New York: Oxford University Press, 2005), pointing to a nonstate locus of accountability, such as corporate actors, but mostly using a victim/remedy adversarial approach.

8. See Introduction in this volume.

9. See Richard H. McAdams, "A Focal Point Theory of *Expressive Law*," *Virginia Law Review* 86 (2000): 1649–1729.

10. See Steven Lukes, *Power: A Radical View,* 2nd ed. (New York: Palgrave Macmillan, 2005); Antonio Gramsci, *Selections from the Prison Notebooks* (New York: International Publishers, 1971).

11. See Chapter 4 in this volume.

12. See Raymond A. Atuguba and Mwambi Mwasaru, "'I Refuse to Let Go of the Land': Malindi Citizens, Salt Farmers, and the Land Question in Kenya" (manuscript on file with authors).

13. The articulation of a "critical legal liberalism" lens was drawn from the following references: Jeremy Waldron, "Rights and Needs: The Myth of Disjunction," in *Legal Rights*, ed. Austin Sarat and Thomas R. Kearns (Ann Arbor: University of Michigan Press, 1996), 87–109, showing how strategies of rights articulation can both complement and go further than strategies of needs articulation, by carrying with them an idea of respect for persons and self-respect, as well as an invitation to explore the networks of duties and responsibilities in the claims of needs satisfaction; Nancy Fraser, "Social Justice in the Age of Identity Politics," in *Redistribution or Recognition? A Political-Philosophical Exchange* (New York: Verso, 2003), 7–27, 71–99, 106–9, contrasting, in her effort to link up politics of equality and identity, "transformative" struggles with affirmative strategies—the former pointing to root causes and structures, the latter to short-term and particularist interests—and recommending that transformative politics engage more with universalist ideals; Thomas Pogge, *World Poverty and Human Rights* (Cambridge, UK: Polity, 2002), 1–26, seeking to emphasize the deep moral salience of human rights and to provide a conceptual foundation to global distributive justice, and advocating for global institutional reforms that would alter the present inequality of bargaining power between nation-states and allow for disenfranchised populations to have a say in the shaping of the global economic order; Amartya K. Sen, "Elements of a Theory of Human Rights," *Philosophy and Public Affairs* 32 (2004): 315, demonstrating the rational foundation of social and economic rights within a theory of human rights, but warning against fitting social and economic rights into the "juridical cage" of legal rights, preferring in-

stead to focus on agitation, monitoring, and other strategies to foster political support for rights; Alan Hunt, "Rights and Social Movements: Counter-Hegemonic Strategies," *Journal of Law and Society* 17 (1990): 309, responding to the "myth of rights" idea—that rights tend to co-opt and disassemble the political energy and demands of social movements—with "rights without illusion," a Gramscian analysis showing how each demand is raised in a preexisting field of debate; and suggesting that rights can be counter-hegemonic as they introduce elements that transcend the discourse, and frame particularist interests, as universal; Michael W. McCann, *Rights at Work: Pay Equity Reform and the Politics of Legal Mobilization* (Chicago: University of Chicago Press, 1994), ch. 8, also responding to the "myth of rights" idea and legal realist critiques of rights by drawing on social movement theory to show how rights tactics and discourse actually "work" as cultural conventions in the practice of social change; and articulating a "legal mobilization thesis" that points to the effect of rights mobilization on law conceived broadly as a "complex repertoire of discursive strategies and symbolic frameworks that structure ongoing social intercourse and meaning-making activity among citizens."

14. This transformative interpretation of liberal rights thus draws into activist politics the power of the liberal philosophical arguments of thinkers like John Rawls (see *A Theory of Justice*, 2nd ed. [Cambridge: Belknap Press of Harvard University Press, 1999]); Henry Shue (see *Basic Rights Subsistence, Affluence, and U.S. Foreign Policy*, 2nd ed. [Princeton: Princeton University Press, 1996]); and Amartya Sen, Jeremy Waldron, and Thomas Pogge (supra n. 13).

15. In concrete terms, this may mean using housing rights to challenge evictions or trespass laws upholding property rights, health rights to challenge interpretations of intellectual property rights, or women's rights to security to challenge immunity in tort. Examples from South Africa include: *Minister for Public Works v. Kyalami Ridge Association* 2001 (3) SA 1151 (CC), the right to emergency housing altered the rule-of-law demand for positive legal authorization to affect property interests; *President of the Republic of South Africa v. Modderklip Boerdery (Pty) Ltd* CCT 20/04 (CC), at first instance, the right to private property was infringed when the government failed to provide emergency housing, which led to squatting on private land; the Constitutional Court instead held against the government on the basis that both the property owner and squatters were not provided adequate legal redress in the eviction dispute; *Pharmaceutical Manufacturers Association (PMA)* Case No. 4183/98, the South African Medicines Act, amended to allow cheap patented drugs, was challenged by the PMA on the basis of being a WTO violation; TAC intervened to assert that the legislation was valid because it was part of the duty to fulfill the right to healthcare access; the case settled before court; *Carmichele v. Minister for Safety & Security* CCT 48/00 (CC), women's right to protection from violence challenged police immunity in tort law, so that police were held liable for complainant's assault after releasing a violent repeat offender on bail without considering the safety of women in the community.

16. See the critical legal studies literature, e.g., Duncan Kennedy, "The Stakes of Law, or Hale and Foucault!" *Legal Studies Forum* 15 (1991): 327, articulating the general idea that because rights rely on contestable, malleable, and morally laden concepts, they

invite counterclaims, especially by dominant groups. Transformative rights strategies therefore ought to take into account how, for instance, neoliberal "rule-of-law" programs and international trade and investment regimes and related claims coexist with international human rights law and constitutional protections.

17. Critical liberal or "transformative" rights claims seek to move beyond small gains and ameliorative paradigms of the liberal welfare state. Such incremental strategies may co-opt or compromise transformative claims; see Nancy Fraser, supra, n. 13, suggesting that small gains in strategies may result in political backlash against rights claimants.

On the idea of confronting structural injustice head-on rather than through incrementalist steps, see Introduction, n. 19.

18. International Covenant on Civil and Political Rights (U.N. 1966), Art. 11: "No one shall be imprisoned merely on the ground of inability to fulfill a contractual obligation."

19. On legal pluralism and human rights, see Sally Engle Merry, "Legal Pluralism and Transnational Culture," in *Human Rights, Culture and Context*, ed. Richard Wilson (London: Pluto Press, 1997), 28–48.

20. See Chapter 6 for discussion of normative hybridity.

21. Boaventura de Sousa Santos and César A. Rodríguez-Garavito, "Law, Politics, and the Subaltern in Counter-hegemonic Globalization," in *Law and Globalization from Below: Towards a Cosmopolitan Legality*, ed. de Sousa Santos and Rodríguez-Garavito (New York: Cambridge University Press, 2005).

22. Partha Chatterjee, "Populations and Political Society," in *The Politics of the Governed: Reflections on Popular Politics in Most of the World* (New York: Columbia University Press, 2004).

23. Chatterjee elaborates on a space of "governmentality" in which marginal population groups are able to compel the postcolonial state to negotiate their entitlements, often in illegal ways. He explores various forms of the "politics of the governed," which operate *outside* of the traditionally defined arena of civil society and the formal legal institutions of the state. Political society, for Chatterjee, is the democratic political space in which non-elite populations and government agencies have a necessarily *political* relation, as governmental agencies must "descend" to confront and engage with politically and often illegally or informally mobilized demands. These mobilizations within political society can have, Chatterjee argues, transformative effects among subaltern populations.

24. See postcolonial literature challenging indigenous culture on anti-essentialist and ahistorical grounds; e.g., Renato Rosaldo, *Culture and Truth: The Remaking of Social Analysis* (Boston: Beacon Press, 1993).

25. On alternative legalities, see Boaventura de Sousa Santos and César A. Rodríguez-Garavito, supra n. 21.

26. Some theorists equate human rights with natural law. However, the activists featured in this volume understand human rights and the Enlightenment values that undergird it as but one of many alternative legalities, which does not have normative priority over others.

27. See Hernando de Soto, *The Mystery of Capital: Why Capitalism Triumphs in the*

*West and Fails Everywhere Else* (New York: Basic Books, 2000), and the discussion in Ruth Buchanan, Helen Kijo-Bisimba, and Kerry Rittich, Chapter 3 of this volume.

28. On alternative possibilities to configure land rights, housing rights, and markets, see Duncan Kennedy, Chapter 1 of this volume, and "The Limited Equity Coop as a Vehicle for Affordable Housing in a Race and Class Divided Society," *Howard Law Journal* 46 (2002): 85–125, and "Legal Economics of U.S. Low Income Housing Markets in Light of 'Informality' Analysis," *Journal of Law in Society* 4 (2002): 71–98; see also Ruth Buchanan, Helen Kijo-Bisimba and Kerry Rittich, Chapter 3 of this volume.

29. See Rosaldo, supra n. 24.

30. See Mary Louise Pratt, *Imperial Eyes: Studies in Travel Writing and Transculturation* (New York: Routledge, 1992).

31. On the legacy of British indirect colonial rule and its use of authoritarian possibilities in culture, on subjectivity and citizenship in Africa, see Mahmood Mamdani, *Contemporary Africa and the Legacy of Late Colonialism* (Princeton: Princeton University Press, 1996).

32. See generally Stephen Addae, *The History of Western Medicine in Ghana 1880–1960* (Durham, UK: Durham Academic Press, 1997).

33. Robert Cover, "*N-omos* and Narrative," in *Narrative, Violence and the Law*, ed. Cover et al. (Ann Arbor: University of Michigan Press, 1993), 95–172.

34. For a summary of some of the "skeptics'" arguments, see David Kennedy, *The Dark Sides of Virtue: Reassessing International Humanitarianism* (Princeton: Princeton University Press, 2004).

35. See, e.g., Roberto Unger, *Democracy Realized: The Progressive Alternative* (New York: Verso, 1998).

36. See, e.g., Charles Sabel and Joshua Cohen, "Directly Deliberative Polyarchy," *European Law Journal* 3 (1997): 313–40.

37. See Laclau and Mouffe, *The Radical Democratic Imaginary* (New York: Routledge, 1998).

38. More generally, distributive analysis has opened up an academic debate in development economics about whether development policies that were aimed to help the poor through "trickle down" policies have in fact increased their income in absolute terms or decreased income inequality. Similarly, distributive analysis opens the question of how effective "pro-poor" development policies can be. For an increasingly assertive position within this debate, see Giovanni Andrea Cornia, "Inequality, Growth and Poverty: An Overview of Changes over the Last Two Decades," in *Inequality, Growth and Poverty in an Era of Liberalization and Globalization*, ed. Giovanni Andrea Cornia (New York: Oxford University Press, 2004), pointing to data showing that contrary to assumptions that "inequality is good for growth and poverty reduction," high initial levels or rising levels of inequality impact negatively the rate of poverty reduction through economic growth, and the GDP growth rate itself. Cornia shows that the overall distributive impact of some of the liberalization policies of the Washington Consensus—particularly capital flows liberalization—is often shown to increase income inequality, thus affecting poverty reduction. The solution to this problem, in his view, is a set of pro-poor or

redistribution-friendly development policies. See also Ravi Kanbur, "Growth, Inequality and Poverty: Some Hard Questions," *Journal of International Affairs* 58 (2005): 223–32, framing the debate as a structured opposition between professional groups and views favoring either long-term or short-term gains in poverty and inequality reduction. On the debate about the relationship between absolute poverty, relative inequality, and economic growth, as well as the effectiveness and nature of pro-poor development policies, see also Nancy Birdsall, "Why Inequality Matters," *Boston Review of Books*, April 2007; David Held and Ayse Kaya, eds., *Global Inequality* (Malden: Polity, 2007); and Anthony Shorrocks and Rolph van der Hoeven, eds., *Growth, Inequality, and Poverty: Prospects for Pro-Poor Economic Development* (New York: Oxford University Press, 2004).

39. On the distributional and political features of the current human rights discourse, see Upendra Baxi, *The Future of Human Rights* (New York: Oxford University Press, 2002), calling for a politics *for* human rights that places injustice and the concerns of the "rightless people in struggle and communities of resistance" at center stage, and thereby departs from the contemporary politics of human rights. Such politics are marked by the appropriation of human rights language and logics by global capital, and by the emergence of a "trade-related, market-friendly human rights paradigm" for globalization, which is about to erase all gains of the universalist human rights era. Importantly for the purpose of this project, Baxi also offers an analysis of "human rights markets" to depict current funding patterns, advocacy techniques, and institutional structures of the human rights movement in terms of "investment," "consumption," and competitive "entrepreneurship," thereby alerting its main actors to the dangers of the co-optation, mainstreaming, and "commoditization of human suffering" within global governance.

40. See David Trubek and Alvaro Santos, "The Third Moment in Law and Development Theory and the Emergence of a New Critical Practice," in *The New Law and Economic Development: A Critical Appraisal*, ed. Trubek and Santos (New York: Cambridge University Press, 2006), offering a postrealist legal analysis of the current "law and development" moment that highlights the obvious and more subtle ways in which development policies that rely on seemingly neutral legal and judicial reforms may have distributive consequences by favoring market-friendly private law regimes. Although such reforms offer a set of supposedly "neutral" background rules of property and contract for a level playing field on which market transactions can take place, these rules systematically benefit those who already have wealth, and thus further impoverish the poor. Furthermore, although these rules are constructed by "private law" judicial decisions, they are no less coercive and interventionist than public regulatory law. These rules therefore play a key role in the distribution of economic resources and political power in society.

41. See discussion of historical institutionalism, Introduction of this volume.

42. See Roberto Unger, supra n. 35, outlining the original background vision of "democratic experimentalism," which describes a project of institutional imagination and innovation applied to current economic, social, and political structures, seeking to overcome the old dichotomies of public versus private, and command versus market, and instead to bring together a "progressive alternative" that links up technological and economic growth with individual emancipation and a certain understanding of agency,

structure, and change; see also the works of Charles Sabel, William Simon, Susan Sturm, and Joshua Cohen (all cited below).

43. See Joshua Cohen and Charles Sabel, supra n. 36, proposing a radical new institutional vision of democracy, where a form of "directly-deliberative polyarchy" manages to promote collective decision making in public arenas for citizens who use public services, thereby decentralizing power and solving problems locally.

44. Stakeholders are the public institutions, private institutions, and community representatives and groups that are all affected by a decision, beyond the litigation model of claimant and government. Benchmarking basically requires a process of setting feasible standards, with ongoing peer review, where "laggards" are required to report back and are given technical assistance to improve things; see Michael Dorf and Charles Sabel, "A Constitution of Democratic Experimentalism," *Columbia Law Review* 98 (1998): 267. In the experimentalist view: legislatures are to declare areas of policy, like education, community safety, and environmental health, as open to local deliberation by stakeholders, facilitated by processes of benchmarking; administrative agencies in turn provide the infrastructure for information exchange between and among these stakeholders, seeking to reduce the costs of information for different problem solvers; and constitutional courts do not set out to review arrangements on the basis of substantive constitutional rights but promote decision making elsewhere that occurs in directly deliberative ways, for example, by using the remedy to hand the decision back to stakeholders.

45. See Cohen and Sabel, supra n. 36, suggesting that legislatures, courts, executives, and administrative agencies continue to operate in the experimentalist mode but that their operations change markedly—particularly as they are able to bring social movements into their ongoing deliberation and decision making. See Charles F. Sabel and William H. Simon, "Destabilization Rights: How Public Law Litigation Succeeds," *Harvard Law Review* 117 (2004): 1015, exploring a series of legal challenges that have held public institutions to account in the provision of schools, mental health services, prisons, police services, and housing and finding that a renewed practice of public law litigation is emerging and can be most successful when conceived as a process of "destabilization rights enforcement."

46. Id.

47. Case studies and examples of public policy "experiments" include areas such as schools (see James Liebman and Charles Sabel, "A Public Laboratory Dewey Barely Imagined: The Emerging Model of School Governance and Legal Reform," *New York University Review of Law and Social Change* 28 [2003]: 183) and community policing (see Dorf and Sabel, supra n. 44).

48. An example of innovative, experimentalist-type remedies crafted in African courts by participants in this project include *Minister of Health v. Treatment Action Campaign*, 2002 (5) SA 721 (CC), July 5, 2002 (access to healthcare, government restriction of the provision of antiretroviral drugs to prevent mother-to-child transmission, failure of government to provide a comprehensive policy for combating mother-to-child HIV transmission), in South Africa. See also the complaint in *Mohammed Zakari v. Ministry of Health and others* (on file with the authors), filed in the High Court of Accra,

Ghana, in January 2003. The experimentalist features of the remedies in *Treatment Action Campaign* and *Mohammed Zakari* are discussed in detail in Chapters 2 and 4 of this volume.

49. See Abraham Chayes, supra n. 4.

50. They might have produced a similar framework through a statute.

## Chapter 6

1. Here we again draw on Young (see Introduction, n. 3), whose notion of structural injustice is of a moral wrong that "occurs as a consequence of many individuals and institutions" pursuing their interests "within given institutional rules and accepted norms" (114). She observes that "when social processes put large categories of persons under a systematic threat of domination or deprivation of the means to develop and exercise their capacities, at the same time as these processes enable others to dominate or have a wide range of opportunities for developing and exercising their capacities," then we have structural injustice.

2. See, e.g., Tamara Jezic and Chris Jochnick, "Human Rights Dialogue 2, Introduction," available at: http://www.cceia.org/resources/publications/dialogue/2_02/ in http://unjobs.org/authors/chris-jochnick

3. See, e.g., Scott Cummings, "Law in the Labor Movement's Challenge to Wal-Mart: A Case Study of the Inglewood Site Fight," *California Law Review* 95 (2007): 1927.

4. See, e.g., Doug McAdam, "Recruitment to High-Risk Activism: The Case of Freedom Summer," *American Journal of Sociology* 92 (1986): 64–90; Sidney Tarrow, *Power in Movement: Social Movements, Collective Action and Politics* (New York: Cambridge University Press, 1998).

5. See, e.g., Derrick Bell, "Serving Two Masters: Integration Ideals and Client Interests in School Desegregation Litigation," *Yale Law Journal* 85 (1976): 470.

6. See, e.g., Thomas Pogge, *World Poverty and Human Rights* (Cambridge, UK: Polity, 2002).

7. See Young, supra n. 1.

8. For an overview of legal realism, see, e.g., Brian Leiter, "American Legal Realism," University of Texas Law Public Law Research Paper No. 42 (2002).

9. In this chapter we use "social rights institutions" to denote the practices of government that produce and deliver social goods such as healthcare, housing, food, jobs, and education to all people in ways that are consistent with the directives of human rights law.

10. Sometimes the uptake of these practices might stimulate renewed grassroots activism that pushes those local spaces toward becoming new generative spaces. These spaces might then promote a new round of innovation. Although some of the case studies point toward this potential, they do not show this potential realized in any detail.

11. See supra n. 1 and discussion in Introduction and Chapter 5 of this volume.

12. The idea that *institutions* can deviate from human rights values is not foreign to the law. Owen Fiss described how structural litigation in the United States in the 1970s was motivated by a conviction that entire public institutions, like prisons, mental

hospitals, school systems, and the like, could be shaped around values that defied due process ideals, such as basic procedural fairness, in the ways that those institutions were designed and functioned; see Owen Fiss, "The Supreme Court 1978 Term: Foreword: The Forms of Justice," *Harvard Law Review* 93 (1979): 1. Similarly, the practices that institutions such as health ministries enact can deviate from human rights values.

13. United Nations Universal Declaration of Human Rights, available at: http://www.un.org/en/documents/udhr/

14. United Nations International Covenant on Economic, Social, and Cultural Rights, available at: http://www2.ohchr.org/english/law/cescr.htm

15. Analysts of institutions tend to adopt one of two broad definitions: (1) institutions as the "rules of the game" designed to facilitate cooperation among parties (property rights and congressional rules are often used as examples), for instance, in the new institutional economics and rational choice institutionalism (see Barry Weingast, "Rational-Choice Institutionalism," in *Political Science: State of the Discipline*, ed. Ira Katznelson and Helen Milner [New York: Norton, 2002]); or (2) institutions as social relations and practices that have over extended periods of time acquired a degree of solidity and as a consequence shape people's behavior; for example in the work of historical institutionalists (see Theda Skocpol, *Protecting Soldiers and Mothers: The Political Origins of Social Policy in the United States* [Cambridge, MA: Belknap Press/Harvard University Press, 1992]); James Mahoney, "Path Dependence in Historical Sociology," *Theory and Society* 29 (2000): 507–48; Paul Pierson, "Increasing Returns, Path Dependence, and the Study of Politics," *American Political Science Review* 94 (2000): 251–68; and Kathleen Ann Thelen, *How Institutions Evolve: The Political Economy of Skills in Germany, Britain, the United States, and Japan* (New York: Cambridge University Press, 2004). Our view is closer to the latter. Historical institutionalists, however, normally use a highly aggregated notion of institutions, collapsing a number of distinct dimensions that have their own (sometimes contradictory) causal effects into a single one. The resulting understanding of how institutions function and how they change is therefore "thinner" than the one we adopt.

16. Cf. Margaret Somers, "Citizenship and the Place of the Public Sphere: Law, Community, and Political Culture in the Transition to Democracy," *American Sociological Review* 58 (1993): 587–620; Ruth Berins Collier and David Collier, *Shaping the Political Arena: Critical Junctures, the Labor Movement and Regime Dynamics in Latin America* (Princeton: Princeton University Press, 1991); Peter Houtzager, "Collective Action and Political Authority: Rural Workers, Church, and State in Brazil," *Theory and Society* 30 (2001): 1–45; and see Thelen, supra n. 15.

17. Such an internal review board became one of the forums in which advocates in the Ijora-Badia case challenged the community's forced eviction. See Chapter 1 in this volume.

18. Cf. Thelen, supra n. 15, who provides a similar example from Germany, where in the late nineteenth century Bismark created a vocational training system as part of a larger institutional project intended to undermine organizations of industrial workers, but in the twentieth century it became a pillar of the country's social-democratic arrangement and is even today fiercely defended by industrial unions.

19. Here we draw on Thelen, supra n. 15, who defines a number of ways in which institutional change can occur, for example through conversion of existing structures to new goals or values or by layering of new institutional structures on top of existing ones. We use "institutional conversion" to cover all forms of substantial institutional change, and then mention specific forms of conversion, including layering. See also Margaret Weir, "When Does Politics Create Policy? The Organizational Politics of Change," in *Rethinking Political Institutions: The Art of the State*, ed. Ian Shapiro, Stephen Skowronek, and Daniel Galvin (New York: New York University Press, 2006).

20. Cf. Arthur L. Stinchcombe, *Constructing Social Theories* (New York: Harcourt, Brace & World, 1968); Pierson, supra n. 15; Mahoney, supra n. 15; and Thelen, supra n. 15.

21. For a particularly illuminating example, see Judith Tendler, *Good Government in the Tropics* (Baltimore: Johns Hopkins University Press, 1997, ch. 2); as well as Jonathan Fox, "The Difficult Transition from Clientelism to Citizenship: Lessons from Mexico," *World Politics* 46 (1994): 151–84.

22. This argument is well developed in Tendler, supra n. 21. Further, there are many prominent examples from other regions, including the universalization of healthcare in Brazil, in which the movement of public health workers (*sanitaristas*) located at various levels of the state (local, state, and federal) played a determinant role in producing what is one of the most significant ESR advances in that country since the early 1970s (see Monika Dowbor, "Origins of Successful Health Sector Reform: Public Health Professionals and Institutional Opportunities in Brazil," *IDS Bulletin* 38 [2008]: 74–81).

23. See Committee on Economic, Social and Cultural Rights, *General Comment No. 14* on "the right to the highest attainable standard of health," ICESCR Art. 12. See also the preamble of the World Health Organization's constitution: "The enjoyment of the highest attainable standard of health is one of the fundamental rights of every human being without distinction of race, religion, political belief, economic or social condition."

24. A long tradition of socio-legal and legal anthropological literature explores intersecting normativities in Africa. See, e.g., Sally Falk Moore, *Social Facts and Fabrications: "Customary" Law on Kilimanjaro, 1880–1980* (Lewis Henry Morgan Lectures) (New York: Cambridge University Press, 1986).

25. See William Felstiner, R. L. Abel, and Austin Sarat, "The Emergence and Transformation of Disputes: Naming, Blaming, Claiming," *Law and Society Review* 15 (1980–81): 631.

26. The funding for Ghana's health system has typically been distributed in "silos" designated for different purposes. Many development theorists would claim that the sources of Ghana's health funding are insufficient to meet its needs, and that additional funds must be raised through progressive domestic taxation, of the mining sector, for instance, and greater international aid. See Jeffrey Sachs, *The End of Poverty* (New York: Penguin Press, 2005); and Jim Kim et al., eds., *Dying for Growth: Global Inequality and the Health of the Poor* (Monroe: Common Courage Press, 2000), both presenting arguments for this position.

27. See William A. Gamson, *Talking Politics* (New York: Cambridge University Press, 1992).

28. Consider, in the U.S. context, *Willie M. v. Hunt*, U.S. Court of Appeals, Fourth Circuit, 681 F.2nd 818 (1982).

29. The generative space shares some characteristics with the deliberative spaces democratic experimentalists have identified and explored, but there are substantial differences. In both cases, a convening force is critical to pushing contesting parties and other stakeholders together in order to find novel non–zero sum institutional reforms. For hard democratic experimentalists, national legislatures and judiciaries should play this role. In the case of pragmatic advocacy, convening authorities can take varied forms and in different fields. Pragmatic advocacy differs also in its approach to plural normativities and its emphasis on contestation as a way to build the power of economically vulnerable groups.

30. Generative spaces often emerge in response to violence or some catastrophic event.

31. See Chapter 2.

32. Cf. Tendler, supra n. 21, chs. 2 and 6.

33. See Peter Houtzager, "Introduction: From Polycentrism to the Polity," in *Changing Paths: International Development and the Politics of Inclusion in International Development*, ed. Peter P. Houtzager and Mick P. Moore (Ann Arbor: University of Michigan Press, 2003), at 2.

34. Cf. Thelen, supra n. 15; Skocpol, supra n. 15; Pierson supra n. 15; Tendler, supra n. 21; and Merille S. Grindle, *Going Local: Decentralization, Democratization, and the Promise of Good Governance* (Princeton: Princeton University Press, 2007).

35. Though we have no clear examples from the case studies, the effort to effect bureaucratic change—**T3**—can occur apart from or prior to the appeal to individual state actors that takes place at **T2**.

36. For accounts of such advocacy see Chapter 1 (on TAC campaign against "big pharma") and Chapter 2 (on South Africa's Council for Competition).

37. This negotiation takes place in iterative cycles.

38. See Albert O. Hirschman, *Getting Ahead Collectively: Grassroots Experiences in Latin America* (Elmsford: Pergamon Press, 1984), at 42–43; and Laurence Whitehead and George Gray-Molina, "Political Capabilities over the Long Run," in *Changing Paths: International Development and the Politics of Inclusion in International Development*, ed. Peter P. Houtzager and Mick P. Moore (Ann Arbor: University of Michigan Press, 2003).

39. Grindle, supra n. 34.

40. See Richard C. Crook and James Manor, *Democracy and Decentralisation in South Asia and West Africa: Participation, Accountability and Performance* (New York: Cambridge University Press, 1998).

41. See Richard C. Crook and Alan Sturla Sverrisson, "Decentralisation and Poverty-Alleviation in Developing Countries: A Comparative Analysis or, Is West Bengal Unique?" IDS Working Paper No. 130 (Brighton: Institute of Development Studies, 2001).

42. See, in legal sociology, Richard L. Abel, "Law in Context, the Sociology of Legal Institutions, Litigation in Society," in *Law and Social Enquiry*, ed. Robin Luckham (New

York: International Center for Law and Development, 1981); Boaventura de Sousa Santos, "Law: A Map of Misreading: Towards a Postmodern Conception of Law," *Law and Society* 14 (1987): 279–302; Boaventura de Sousa Santos, *Toward a New Common Sense: Law, Science and Politics in the Paradigmatic Transition* (New York: Routledge, 1995); and Alan Hunt, *Explorations in Law and Society: Toward a Constitutive Theory of Law* (New York: Routledge, 1993), among many others. Similar findings come from comparative historical sociology; see Guillermo O'Donnell, "On the State, Democratization, and Some Conceptual Problems: A Latin American View with Glances at Some Postcommunist Countries," *World Development* 21 (1993): 1355–69; Somers, supra n. 16; Patrick Heller, K. N. Harilal, and Shubham Chaudhuri, "Building Local Democracy: Evaluating the Impact of Decentralization in Kerala, India," *World Development* 35 (2007): 626–48; and Whitehead and Gray-Molina, supra n. 38.

43. See O'Donnell, supra n. 42; Jeffrey Herbst, *States and Power in Africa* (Princeton: Princeton University Press, 2000); Grindle, supra n. 34. This disparity in government capacity across regions reflects disparities in political power and civil society's capacity at the national and local levels.

44. For an introduction to Porto Alegre's participatory budgeting, see Rebecca Abers, "From Clientelism to Cooperation: Participatory Policy and Civic Organizing in Porto Alegre, Brazil," *Politics and Society* 26 (1998): 511–37; Boaventura de Sousa Santos, "Participatory Budgeting in Porto Alegre: Toward a Redistributive Democracy," *Politics and Society* 26 (1998): 461–510; and Leonardo Avritzer, *Democracy and the Public Space in Latin America* (Princeton: Princeton University Press, 2002).

45. The Workers' Party had a political commitment to participatory governance and political incentives: traditionalist (clientelist) politicians and a more-or-less programmatic opposition controlled the city assembly, responsible for passing the city budget. The party worked with mobilized groups to create a city participatory budget as an extralegal public institution that would circumvent the city assembly (de Sousa Santos, supra n. 44).

46. Here we draw heavily on Benjamin Goldfrank, "Making Participation Work in Porto Alegre," in *Radicals in Power: The Workers' Party (PT) and Experiments in Urban Democracy in Brazil*, ed. Gianpaolo Baiocchi (New York: Zed Books, 2003).

47. Id., at 35.

48. Abers, supra n. 44, at 532.

49. Gianpaolo Baiocchi, *Militants and Citizens: The Politics of Participatory Democracy in Porto Alegre* (Stanford: Stanford University Press, 2005), at 14.

## Epilogue

1. Tenth Anniversary Convention of the S.C.L.C., Atlanta, August 16, 1967.

# Index

Abel, Richard L., 224n20, 236n25, 237n42

Abers, Rebecca, 238nn44,48

Abosede, Francisco Bolaji, 20

Abugre, Charles, 227n50

Achmat, Zackie, 51, 57, 59, 60–61, 72, 76; on *Minister of Health v. Treatment Action Campaign*, 69; on TAC and anti-apartheid struggle, 61; and Treatment Literacy Campaign, 79–80, 86

Addae, Stephen: *The History of Western Medicine in Ghana*, 231n32

*Adewale v. The Governor of Lagos State*, 38

Africa Mashariki Gold Mine, 105–6

African Charter on Human and Peoples' Rights, 209n36

African Commission on Human and Peoples' Rights, 35

African Festival of Arts and Culture (1973), 18

Alexander, Gregory: *A Fourth Way?*, 213nn53,58

*Alhaji Mudashiru Kokorowo and Others v. Lagos State Government and 4 Others*, 29, 208nn30,31

Allport, Gordon W., 140; *The Psychology of Rumor*, 226n38

Alston, Philip, 227n3; *Human Rights and Development*, 201n7, 217n6; *Non-State Actors and Human Rights*, 228n7

Amsden, Alice, 48

An-Na'im, Abdulahi Ahmed: *Cultural Transformation and Human Rights in Africa*, 201n8

Ansu, Yaw, 27

Arendt, Hannah, 29

*ARVs in Our Lives*, 79–80

Ashafa, Oladipo, 26

Atuguba, Raymond, 125–26, 144, 212n48, 228n12

Avritzer, Leonardo: *Democracy and the Public Space in Latin America*, 238n44

Ayariga, Mahama, 125–26, 133–34, 139, 144, 222n7

Ayensu, Edward, 36

Ayorinde, Ligali, 208n29

AZT, 60, 78

Badasu, Dalali Margaret, 222n5

Baderin, Mashood: *Economic, Social, and Cultural Rights in Action*, 201n7

Baiocchi, Gianpaolo: *Militants and Citizens*, 238n49

Baldus, Rolf, 220n41

Bamako Initiative, 222n5

Barak-Erez, Daphne: *Exploring Social Rights*, 200n7

Barrick Gold, 98, 105–6

Barron, David, 213nn51,52

Baxi, Upendra: *The Future of Human Rights*, 201n7, 227n1, 232n39

Bell, Derrick, 234n5

Bellow, Gary: *Law Stories*, 226n36

Beneria, Lourdes: *Gender, Development and Globalization*, 219n29

Bilchitz, David: *Poverty and Fundamental Rights*, 201n7

triggering events, 181–84, 195, 237n30
Trubek, David, 232n40
Trubek, Louise, 201n7
Tshabalala-Msimang, Manto, 64, 68, 69, 70, 74–76, 77, 82, 88

Unger, Roberto, 166, 232n42
United Nations: Committee on Economic, Social and Cultural Rights, 66, 209n36, 236n23; Convention on the Rights of Persons with Disabilities, 225n28; Covenant on Economic, Social, and Cultural Rights, 175; Development Programme (UNDP), 20; Human Settlements Programme (UN-Habitat): slums defined by, 21; Universal Declaration of Human Rights, 106, 175, 235n13
United States: ACT-Up, 79; Agency for International Development (USAID), 77–78; civil rights movement in, 55, 69, 86–87; Gay Men's Health Crisis (GMHC), 79; HIV/AIDS treatment in, 84; NAACP/*Brown v. Board of Education*, 55–56, 69; Project Head Start, 224n24; structural litigation in, 169, 228n4, 234n12; *Willie M. v. Hunt*, 237n28
urbanization, 19–21, 41–42

Van der Hoeven, Rolph: *Growth, Inequality, and Poverty*, 232n38
Van der Walt, A. J., 226n42
Varley, Ann: *Illegal Cities*, 212n47
Vienna Declaration, 110
VIP Hunting Safaris/Grumeti Reserves, Ltd., 104
voice. *See* participation

Wainaina, Binyavanga, 3, 203n15
Waldron, Jeremy, 228n13, 229n14
Wang, Michael, 226n48
Washington Consensus, 165, 231n38
Weber, Max, 28
Weingast, Barry, 235n15

Weir, Margaret, 236n19
Wheeler, Joanna: *Rights, Resources, and the Politics of Accountability*, 201n7
White, Lucie E., 212n45, 224n24
Whitehead, Laurence, 237n38, 238n42
women: discrimination against, 140, 209n39; rights of, 163, 229n15
World Bank, 17, 150, 174; International Development Agency (IDA), 207n18, 210n, 211n; Lagos Drainage and Sanitation Project (LDSP), 26–27, 28, 34–37, 152, 185, 207nn18,19, 209n39; Lagos Metropolitan Development and Governance Project (LMDGP), 39–40, 212n44; PRSP blueprint on reducing poverty, 142–43; relations with SERAC, 8, 9, 10, 27, 34–37, 152, 209n39; and Tanzanian land reform, 99, 100, 219n27; "Voices of the Poor," 223n11
World Bank Inspection Panel, 35–37, 157, 185, 188, 209nn38,39, 237n36
World Health Organization, 90, 203n19, 236n23
World Resource Institute, 220n48
World Trade Organization: Trade-Related Aspects of Intellectual Property Rights agreement (TRIPS), 57

Young, Iris Marion: on structural injustice, 199n3, 234n1
Young, Katharine G., 226n46

Zakari, Mohammed: and Legal Resources Center (LRC), 124–27, 129–33, 143, 144; litigation regarding, 129–31, 136–38, 150–51, 157, 159–60, 168, 169–70, 178, 189, 223n12, 233n48; postdischarge detention of, 127–29, 150–51, 157, 181, 185, 195; press conference of, 12, 133–35, 143, 150, 154; significance of, 122–23, 135–43, 150–51, 159–60, 169–70, 173, 176, 178, 183, 187, 188, 189
Zuma, Jacob, 71, 72
Zwedala, Nontsikelelo, 77–78